Educating a Diverse Nation

Educating a Diverse Nation

Lessons from Minority-Serving Institutions

CLIFTON CONRAD & MARYBETH GASMAN

Harvard University Press

CAMBRIDGE, MASSACHUSETTS, & LONDON, ENGLAND

2015

Library of Congress Cataloging-in-Publication data is available from
the Library of Congress.

ISBN 978-0-674-73680-1

To the students, staff, faculty, and administrators
at Minority-Serving Institutions throughout the nation

Contents

Acknowledgments

We want to give special acknowledgment to the following individuals for their work on this book. Each of them assisted in myriad ways, including interviews, data analysis, literature searches, project organization, and project management. We are grateful for their intellect, passion, and commitment.

Thai-Huy Nguyen
Todd Lundberg
Felecia Commodore
Andrés Castro Samayoa
Yvonne Hyde Carter
Michael Armijo
Ufuoma Abiola
Heather Huskey Collins

Writing this book was pure joy and a consummate learning experience for each of us. While we both went into the project with some knowledge of Minority-Serving Institutions, low-income and first-generation students, and students of color, we could not have imagined all we would learn over the course of the past four years. We are most grateful to the students, staff, faculty, and administrators at the twelve Minority-Serving Institutions who participated in this study for their generosity, enthusiasm, and valuable contributions. We hope that we have elevated their voices as leaders in our nation's efforts to empower students.

Thai-Huy Nguyen and Todd Lundberg served as the lead research assistants on this project and helped us with every aspect of the research and implementation of the project. They are both first-rate scholars who care deeply about the future of our colleges and universities and the students they serve. We are also both thankful to the University of Wisconsin–Madison and the University of Pennsylvania for their support as well as the support of our colleagues at these institutions.

We benefited greatly from the help of our editors. Elizabeth Knoll at Harvard University Press pushed us to think differently and in new ways about presenting the stories of these institutions. This book is immeasurably better because of her careful eye, imaginative spirit, and thoughtful suggestions. We are also thankful to Jennifer Moore, who helped us to think about wider audiences during the earlier stages of the book by providing feedback on our proposal and early chapters.

Lastly, we are indebted to the three funders that made it possible for us to conduct this study—the Kresge Foundation, Lumina Foundation for Education, and USA Funds—and the program officers who worked with us: Tina Gridiron, Caroline Altman Smith, and Pat Roe. Without this support, this project would never have happened. All three of these funders and all three program officers are deeply committed to supporting student success.

I, Clif Conrad, would like to express my deep appreciation to three people in particular: Marybeth Gasman, Todd Lundberg, and Julia Conrad. Marybeth brought not only a deep commitment to this project, but a cheerful willingness to contribute in countless ways to a partnership filled with endless back-and-forth, candor, laughter, and joy throughout this entire adventure. I would also like to acknowledge and express my deep gratitude to Todd Lundberg, one of the most passionate, ethical, thoughtful, and kind collaborators I have ever had the pleasure to work with. He has earned my deepest respect and admiration. My beloved Julia honored my commitment to this project and contributed to our study in numerous ways. And, not least, I am grateful to the five grandchildren—Sofia, Perrin, Eleanor, Nora, and Langston—for taking time to play with their grandpa. Without all of these people, none of this would have been possible.

I, Marybeth Gasman, am personally grateful to a number of individuals that have supported me while writing and doing the research that led to this book. It was a pleasure to write with Clif Conrad, who first asked me to collaborate with him when I was a new professor. Ours has been a collaboration of laughs, serious learning, and frankness. I look forward to many more. I am continually supported by the love and joy that my daughter Chloe brings to my life. Without her I could not do what I do and do it with honesty and integrity. She gives me hope. I am indebted to my research assistants and feel lucky and honored to work with each of them. They are brilliant, committed, and passionate about making a difference in the lives of others—who could ask for more? Lastly, I want to offer a special thank-you to my best friend, Nelson Bowman, for his constant support. Although he was not my coauthor on this project, his insights and humor always inspire me to do my best work.

Educating a Diverse Nation

Introduction

Learning from Minority-Serving Institutions
about Cultivating Student Success

Sara learned about college in elementary school while sitting at the dinner table with her parents. She grew up in Evanston, Illinois. She and her parents are White and upper middle class. Sara attended the Evanston public schools from first to eighth grade and then enrolled in a private college preparatory school favored by her parents. When her cousins, aunts, and uncles visited, they reinforced what her parents told her, as they were all college educated. Sara wasn't exactly sure what college was at that point, but everyone in her family had attended, and they seemed to think that it was exciting and necessary. Her family members and her parents' friends often bought her t-shirts with college names on them. Starting in sixth grade, she attended various summer academic camps. There were camps on architecture, drawing, painting, and filmmaking. Sara is interested in being an artist like her father. Her home is filled with paintings and art from around the world—not the kind of "art and artifacts" you purchase at Pier One or IKEA but the kind you get from extensive travel. By the age of fourteen, Sara was on her third passport, having visited over twenty countries. Sometimes she was even bored in school, having seen so much on her world travels.

As Sara's parents are well educated—her father has a master's degree and her mother a PhD—she spent a lot of time around educated people, often interacting with them at cultural events on college campuses. She attended plays, voice and dance recitals, lectures, and political events. Sara's parents are also politically active, donating to presidential campaigns and participating in local political events. They regularly watch national news as well as satire pertaining to politics. Sara learned to love political satire and has a firm grasp on political issues—a trait that would come to serve her well in college.

When Sara was fifteen her parents sat down with her and had a serious talk about college, asking Sara what kind of institution she wanted to attend. She wasn't completely sure but knew that college was definitely for her. When she was sixteen, Sara went to see her guidance counselor on the advice of her parents. Her counselor spent several hours with Sara, making sure she had taken the right college prep courses and that she knew how to fill out college applications and financial aid forms. Sara took the information home to her parents, and they helped her with everything. The college application process was easy, as both of Sara's parents had ample experience applying to college.

In order to ensure that Sara earned the highest SAT score possible, her parents enrolled her in a test prep program. Although Sara earned an excellent score on the SAT, her parents urged her to take it again; this was what all of the other parents were advising their children. She retook the exam, and her score increased by one hundred points. Having earned a high score on the standardized test, Sara attracted the attention of many colleges and universities. Along with her parents she visited her favorites, flying to some of the campuses and driving to others. Her parents have flexible jobs, so they had ample time to take her on the campus visits. During the visits, her parents reminisced about their college days and felt very comfortable approaching college administrators and asking any questions they had.

Feeling confident, on the advice of her parents and her guidance counselor, Sara applied for early admission to her favorite college and sent applications to eight other schools as well. Her parents paid all of the application fees and helped her with her college essays. Sara's performance in high school and her test scores landed her a place at the early admission college, and as of January, she knew where she would be attending—well ahead of most other students.

The summer before her freshman year, Sara and her parents visited the college so that she would feel at home and comfortable. They also purchased items to decorate her room and new clothes. Sara was excited, felt prepared, and was confident that she would make friends, especially given that eight of her high school classmates were also attending the same college.

Once Sara arrived on campus, she met with her adviser. Her parents told her this was the first thing she should do, as did the orientation counselors. After choosing her classes, which focused on the liberal arts and her preferred major of art, she headed off to the bookstore, where she purchased her textbooks, some pretty notebooks, and a few college tees and sweatshirts. On the first day of classes, Sara was a little nervous to be in a new environment but

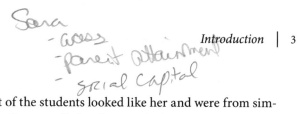

settled in nicely, as most of the students looked like her and were from similar backgrounds. Her professors called on her regularly in class, and she felt valued for her individuality and intellect. One professor even asked her if she would be interested in doing research with him.

Sara did well in college, and even on those days when classes were tough and felt overwhelming, she had her family to fall back on. Going home for the holidays and breaks helped when she got lonely. And Spring Break with her friends at the beach always rejuvenated her. Sara graduated in four years and secured a spot in a master of fine arts program at her top-choice graduate school. She left her undergraduate institution with no student loan debt, as her parents had invested in a college savings fund and were able to pay all of Sara's expenses.

Kareem learned about college from a bus tour organized by his mother's church when he was sixteen. An African American who grew up in a low-income home with a single mother on the South Side of Chicago, near the University of Chicago, he attended a public school in his neighborhood that is notorious for gang violence and poor academic preparation. Prior to the bus tour, which visited some historically Black colleges as well as a few state universities, he didn't think much about going to college, as none of his friends were thinking about attending. Kareem's mom had gone to a community college for one year but had to drop out to work so that she could support Kareem and his little brother. Kareem's dad had not attended college and, while he provided child support, he lived nearly 1,000 miles away.

After making a few connections on the bus tour, Kareem went to his guidance counselor at his high school. It took him four weeks to get an appointment because the counselor was responsible for 1,000 students. Kareem's public school didn't have the resources to support his college application processes. He also approached a teacher and was advised to get a job rather than apply to colleges. Once Kareem secured an appointment, the counselor pointed him to some websites and told him to download the college applications. She also gave him financial aid forms. Kareem took the forms home to his mother, and the two of them tried to figure out what to do next. His mother desperately wanted Kareem to have a better life and was willing to do almost anything to send him to college. Fortunately, his mom's sister worked as an assistant at a nearby H&R Block and secured an accountant to help Kareem fill out the financial aid forms.

Although there were several colleges near Kareem, including a very well-known one, he decided not to apply because he was more familiar with those he had visited on the bus tour. And the local institutions in his city didn't reach out to him. Kareem took the ACT without the help of a test prep course, as his mom couldn't afford it, and he didn't find out that you could take a prep course until he heard some other students talking about it at college. He earned a mediocre ACT score and stuck with it. Kareem applied to four schools and had to piece the money together for the application fees; his relatives and members of his church chipped in because they believed in his potential. Kareem's success would be the success of the entire community and his church. Once in college, he learned that these fees could be waived if there was financial hardship, but no one told him or his mother when he applied.

Kareem was eventually accepted into a state school located about two hours away from his neighborhood and in a rural area. Unfortunately, because he and his mom didn't have enough money, he didn't get a chance to visit the school prior to enrolling. Instead, his first visit was the day he took the Greyhound bus, carrying a duffel bag and a backpack filled with his belongings, to the university. Upon arrival, he was nervous and unsure of his future. Only one other student from his high school was attending the university, and he and the young man weren't very good friends. Kareem attended orientation and felt a bit out of place, as most of the other students didn't look like him. He learned during orientation that he should see his assigned adviser in order to choose classes, and he did so right away. Kareem's adviser helped him but cautioned him that he might not be ready for some of the classes he wanted to take. She suggested that he take a developmental math course. Kareem wasn't happy about this, as he was an A– student in high school and always did well in math. The guidance counselor revisited his ACT score, noting that his math score was borderline and that his high school grades were probably not indicative of his actual knowledge but were inflated given the reputation of his high school. Kareem was confused and somewhat ashamed. He had been one of the best students in his high school and wondered what he was now. His dream was to be a scientist, but he began to doubt himself.

On the first day of classes, Kareem noticed that most students had all of their books and notebooks and appeared ready to get started. He could only

impostor syndrome

realties for low-income

afford the books for two classes and was waiting for his aunt Michelle to send him $150 to buy the rest. Luckily, he had a few unused notebooks from high school, and his backpack was in good condition. Kareem felt awkward in class. The professor had a hard time pronouncing his name, and very few of the students looked like him. After class, Kareem attempted to introduce himself to the professor, but she seemed to look right through him and the other 400 students in the class.

Feeling alone, and struggling in some of his classes, Kareem sought out his adviser, who was helpful. He applied for a campus job—making photocopies in a faculty department—and decided to work fifteen hours per week in order to pay his daily expenses and send his mom and little brother money every month. Kareem also visited the Black Cultural Center, where he found a few students he could relate to, although many were from middle-class families and were not facing the same financial pressures he had encountered. After inquiring, Kareem found that few of the students were working and very few were under pressure to send money from their student loans and campus jobs home to their families. Kareem felt pressured because he hadn't gone home since leaving for college and didn't plan on going home during the summers, as he could earn more money working his campus job full-time than at the McDonald's in his Chicago neighborhood. Kareem was comforted that the students at the Black Cultural Center could commiserate with him around the racial aggressions that they often felt on campus.

After a few months, Kareem became involved in intramural sports and felt a bit more at home; he began making friends outside of those from the Black Culture Center. He also pledged a Black fraternity and made even more friends. With the help of his sports team and fraternity brothers, Kareem started to feel confident about his progress. However, three months into his junior year, a stray bullet in his Chicago neighborhood killed his little brother, and Kareem was forced to leave school to comfort his mother and help support his family. Although he had planned on returning to college, he had to get a full-time job and move back home.

After two years of helping his mother get back on her feet, Kareem decided to enroll in college once again. He didn't return to the state university, but instead enrolled at a local public university. He finished four years later, as it took him twice as long because he was working full-time. Kareem eventually secured a job in sales at a jewelry store in a mall. His earlier aspirations were to be a scientist, but he now hoped he would be able to move up in the management structure at the jewelry company. He had accumulated over $35,000 in student loan debt while pursuing a college degree.

Leticia learned about college from a teacher who noticed how hard she worked on her English class essays. The teacher was surprised that Leticia's writing skills were so strong given that English was not her first language. The teacher talked to Leticia about colleges with strong English programs and encouraged her to apply. Most of these colleges were far away from Brownsville, where Leticia grew up in a Mexican American family on the U.S. border and attended a Catholic grade school and a public high school with only one college prep English course and little reputation for sending students to college. She lived with her mom and dad and six siblings in a two-bedroom home. Leticia took the information she got from her teacher home to her parents and, although they were proud of her, they were concerned that she would be leaving her family. They needed the income from her part-time job and her help watching the three younger children. Despite her family's concerns, Leticia applied to five colleges, including a Hispanic-Serving Institution only a few miles from her home.

Leticia's teacher encouraged her to take the SAT and to take a test prep course to enhance her scores, but Leticia's family could not afford the prep course. Leticia took the test after studying for a few months and doing several practice exams and did fairly well, especially on the verbal section. In order to learn more about the colleges to which she applied, she visited the three closest to her. When visiting a larger, predominantly White university with her teacher several hundred miles away, Leticia felt alone and out of place even though her teacher had gone there twenty years before. Leticia thought she would miss her family and worried about fitting in given the campus racial and ethnic makeup. When she visited the Hispanic-Serving Institution only a few miles from her home, she felt comfortable, and a warm sense of family came over her. The admissions staff asked about her parents and siblings, wondering when they would be coming to campus. They also talked to her about the various clubs she could join and made her feel that she was wanted on the campus.

After some contemplation, Leticia enrolled at the Hispanic-Serving Institution in her border town. She received some scholarship money, as her teacher had made sure that she filled out the financial aid forms. Although Leticia was a strong student in high school with a fairly high grade point average and good SAT scores, she had always had trouble in math. As a result her adviser asked her to take a developmental math course to enhance her skills. At the same time, the adviser registered Leticia for an advanced English seminar, noting her excellent writing. Her adviser also reassured her that her bilingualism was an asset and would make her a stronger student and more marketable when searching for a job.

During Leticia's sophomore year she started to work for the college newspaper, and by her junior year she was the assistant editor. She also joined a Latina sorority and became its president during her senior year, garnering ample service-learning and leadership experience. Her friends in the sorority provided her with support when classes were particularly difficult.

Leticia did well in her classes, and although her grandmother passed away and her little brother had been injured in a car accident, she did not have to drop out of college to help take care of her family. Instead, she worked with her adviser to adjust her schedule and helped her family every day. Taking one fewer class a semester to concentrate on family meant that Leticia graduated a year later than she had hoped. Sometimes having to help take care of her family and postponing her own interests frustrated Leticia. Likewise, she didn't feel that she could relate to her parents or older siblings who had not attended college. Still, Leticia did graduate and enrolled in journalism school so that she could pursue her dream of becoming an investigative journalist. Leticia graduated with $5,000 in student loan debt. She is the only one of her siblings to attend college. Her parents were proud.

Kareem and Leticia are representative of the rapidly growing number of students from traditionally underserved groups—low-income students and first-generation students and students of color—arriving at our colleges and universities. While students like Kareem and Leticia increasingly have access to higher education, many are not fitting easily into mainstream colleges and universities that, for the most part, were established to serve White, upper- and middle-class students, much like Sara, who approach, apply to, and attend college in a fairly standard manner. According to Sara's narrative, students begin learning about college at an early age, and going to college is basically a forgone conclusion for them. Most of these students have the assistance of their guidance counselors and parents in filling out their college applications and, if applicable, financial aid forms. At the age of seventeen, they apply to a variety of colleges and universities because they have been exposed to the merits of the various types of institutions and have had many people in their families attend college. These students, by and large, are accepted by one of the schools of their choice and, if they are more affluent, perhaps even by their top choice of a highly selective college or university.

Once these students get to college, having been dropped off by their parents and typically having all of the "things needed for college" in their possession, their lives are fairly routine. They attend classes with their new textbooks in hand; they join social organizations, often gaining leadership positions in their sophomore or junior year; and they make friends with other new college students like them. If they run into problems during college, they can call home, and their parents are often there to help. If they don't have enough cash to socialize, go on road trips with friends, participate in Spring Break activities, attend conferences, or study abroad, their parents often pay. Many of these middle-class or affluent White students graduate in four years (at the latest six years), eventually securing a job or going on to graduate school. If they don't get a job right away, they often go home and live with their parents in the interim. Of course, this isn't the situation for all middle-class or affluent White students. Some of them suffer depression, feel isolated, have trouble in classes, and have difficulty finding a job after graduation.

Kareem and Leticia cannot approach college in this "standard" manner. As noted earlier, they are part of a growing group of low-income and first-generation college students, many of whom are also students of color. Their parents often do not have prior knowledge of college, and in many cases these students are unfamiliar with the idea of going to college or how it works. They often attend public schools in which guidance counselors have hundreds of students assigned to them and have little time to help students explore various colleges. These students have difficulty completing financial aid applications because the forms are complicated and their parents often have little or no experience with them. As a result, the students make mistakes and often walk around in a fog with regard to applying for college. As few people in their families have attended college, these low-income students of color are often not familiar with their college options. Sometimes they are academically prepared for institutions that are more selective than those to which they apply. But more often, due to mediocre schooling and a lack of access to college prep courses and test prep programs, they find themselves not qualified for the colleges and universities to which they apply.

When students like Kareem and Leticia get to college, they are often underprepared for college courses and must enroll in developmental classes for which they frequently don't receive college credit. These students sometimes cannot afford their textbooks and come to class unprepared and not having read their assignments. And because they are not familiar with the ethos of college, they often don't say anything to their professors, leading many professors to think that these students don't care about learning or are not intelligent. When these students enroll at mainstream colleges and universities, they are often left out of social activities or don't feel comfortable engaging in majority culture, especially if they are the only student of color participating in an activity. And if anything unfortunate happens while they are at college, they often cannot call home for assistance because their parents, although willing to listen, may not have the funds to send them or the money to plan a campus visit. These students are rarely able to go home during campus breaks, and when their parents can visit, they have to drive back the same day because they can't afford to stay in nearby hotels. Often these students drop in and out of college because they are busy taking care of issues at home, preventing them from graduating in four to six years.

More often than not, professors and administrators at mainstream colleges and universities make the assumption that all of their students come from similar homes and backgrounds without considering the vast diversity among students with respect to race, ethnicity, and class. Professors teach to "general" students who come to class fully prepared, actively participate, and don't have outside forces interrupting their classroom work. Because many faculty members and staff in mainstream higher education know little about the history, challenges, strengths, and perspectives that traditionally underrepresented students bring to college, they expect all college students to assimilate into traditional higher education and adapt to the norms of the dominant culture.

Many students now entering college are not eager to adopt the norms and values of the traditional college-going culture, which is often oriented toward middle- and upper-class Whites. Instead, they come with their own aspirations and interests as well as those of their home communities. When many of these students begin college they are asked to leave behind their individual identities and their ties to their own cultures, and they are often asked to learn in ways that are disconnected from many of their personal and cultural resources. Because these students do not match up well with what many colleges and universities demand and offer, too many students like Kareem and Leticia who start college are not persisting in college. Viewed one way, these students are simply not ready for college. We take a different view: too often the educational opportunities available in college are not serving students like Kareem and Leticia.

At the same time that many mainstream colleges and universities are falling short of adequately serving many low-income and first-generation students and students of color, the United States is rapidly becoming a much more diverse nation. In response, there is a growing and widely shared consensus that our colleges and universities need to identify and explore ideas for helping to ensure that traditionally underserved students are provided with the educational opportunities that will support their learning and their persistence in the pursuit of a college education. To address this challenge, we conducted a study at Minority-Serving Institutions (MSIs)—Historically Black Colleges and Universities, Tribal Colleges and Universities, Hispanic-Serving Institutions, and Asian American and Native American Pacific Islander–Serving Institutions—aimed at identifying programs that are using practices that are making significant contributions to the success of diverse college students. We chose to study programs at MSIs for two reasons. First, MSIs are serving many of the increasingly diverse students who are or wish to come to college. In 2011, MSIs enrolled about one-quarter of all undergraduate students in the United States and a disproportionate percentage of students of color. Second, at a historic moment when our colleges and universities need to attract and graduate a greater proportion of students in our increasingly diverse society, MSIs—institutions that have long served underrepresented students—have rarely been studied, even as the White House and major foundations have placed college success for a diverse America at the center of the nation's higher education agenda. With funding from the Kresge Foundation, Lumina Foundation for Education, and USA Funds, in 2011 we began a three-year national study focused on what our nation's colleges and universities might learn from MSIs about programs using practices that are enhancing the learning and persistence of traditionally underserved and underresourced students. Using a purposive approach to selecting programs to study at MSIs, we began the study by facilitating a nationwide competition to identify promising programs that were using practices to help students begin college, stick with college, and benefit from it. We invited MSIs to nominate programs based on two criteria: (1) these programs are experiments in supporting diverse students, and (2) there is evidence that these programs are significantly contributing to student learning and persistence. From the 185 programs submitted from over 160 MSIs, we selected programs at 12 MSIs that are using effective practices for cultivating student success. The programs we selected at the twelve MSIs were scattered across the nation, reaching from Norfolk, Virginia, to Dallas, Texas, to Keshena, Wisconsin, to Seattle, Washington, to the Republic of the Marshall Islands in the middle of the Pacific Ocean. The colleges and universities in the study include public, private, two-year, four-year, large, small, religiously affiliated and nonsectarian, and stable and financially struggling MSIs.

We conducted in-depth case studies of programs at each of the twelve MSIs, which included three Tribal Colleges and Universities, or TCUs (Chief Dull Knife College, Salish Kootenai College, and the College of Menominee Nation); three Hispanic-Serving Institutions, or HSIs (La Sierra University, El Paso Community College, and San Diego City College); three Historically Black Colleges and Universities, or HBCUs (Morehouse College, Norfolk State University, and Paul Quinn College); and three Asian American and Native American Pacific Islander–Serving Institutions, or AANAPISIs (College of the Marshall Islands, California State University–Sacramento, and North Seattle Community College). At each campus we worked with an on-campus representative to collect relevant program documents and arrange interviews with a range of faculty, staff, students, and administrators who had direct experience with the program. During our multiday field visits to each of the twelve campuses, we engaged in campus observation and conducted interviews. Following our visits we gathered additional documents that were referred to in interviews and, as needed, conducted follow-up conversations with various stakeholders via phone or e-mail or in person.

Although we have both attended and worked at many different types of colleges and universities, we had rarely experienced the welcoming and supportive environments we encountered at the twelve institutions in our study. Faculty and staff members not only expressed respect for their students, but many could relate to students' experiences, having gone through a similar journey and learned the coping skills needed to succeed in college and in life.

Staff members were patient with students, allowing them to make mistakes and bounce back. And faculty members worked hard to make course work relevant to students' lives and the lives of their families. Instead of teaching to the archetypal student—which, in the words of Lumina Foundation president Jamie Merisotis, "no longer exists as we know it"—they made efforts to understand the diverse backgrounds of their students and to take account of these backgrounds in their teaching. Faculty members drew upon cultural traditions and markers and, in turn, were nimble and flexible about the way they taught their courses. Staff members walked hand in hand with the students, guiding them along the way, and making sure that their families understood the value of a college education as well as how college works. While we both had some wonderful professors and staff members throughout college, nearly all the professors and staff members we encountered at the MSIs in the study pushed themselves to great lengths to take care of their students and to push and pull them along their college journey. They not only cared about their learning; they cared about students as human beings. We witnessed examples of personally checking in on students' well-being and family situations, pushing students to challenge themselves and their peers in the classroom, and high expectations coupled with remarkable levels of support. We saw many faculty and staff members push themselves beyond the normal comfort zone of a professional position, inviting students to their homes to learn about family life, driving students to jobs, paying for textbooks and clothing, and demonstrating genuine affection for students. In short, in our study of promising programs at MSIs—institutions that have long been invisible across much of the landscape in higher education as well as in the literature on our colleges and universities—we learned that they are pursuing practices and offering valuable lessons about how to enhance educational opportunity for all students.

The driving purpose of this book is to share what we learned at these twelve Minority-Serving Institutions about cultivating student success. We hope that others across our nation's colleges and universities can learn what these institutions are doing to serve their diverse students, students like Kareem and Leticia. We begin the book by elaborating on the challenge of educating a diverse America and, in turn, on the contemporary place of MSIs in educating diverse students for the rapidly changing and diverse world in which we live. For each of the four types of MSIs, we then devote a chapter to elaborating on the practices in the programs we studied that are contributing to student persistence and learning through college. Drawing on these stories of success at TCUS, HSIS, HBCUS, and AANAPISIS, the concluding chapter identifies six major practices for empowering traditionally underrepresented students across our nation's colleges and universities along with educating a diverse America.

We close this introduction by accenting that at the time that this book is being published there continues to be a widely shared conviction across our nation that our institutions of higher learning need to graduate far more students than they currently are and, in so doing, provide students with learning opportunities that will prepare them to flourish in their workplace, public, and personal lives. This agenda can be accomplished only if our colleges and universities are prepared to support and educate students who are diverse not only with respect to race, ethnicity, and socioeconomic status, but also in terms of their life experiences and their expectations of college. Minority-Serving Institutions, which are now serving a large share of minority students— students who in the near future are expected to make up more than one-half of our college-going population—are already playing and positioned to continue playing a major role in helping us realize this agenda. As we learned in this study, all of us throughout higher education—and beyond—can learn much from MSIs about approaches to cultivating student learning and persistence. And in so doing, we can learn much about educating students to embrace the responsibility to contribute to their communities and the lives of others while also preparing them to thrive in their personal and workplace lives.

We invite readers across all colleges and universities to join with us in reflection and spirited dialogue about how the MSIs in this study are advancing equal educational opportunity not only for traditionally underserved and minority students but for all students. All of higher education can learn much from Minority-Serving Institutions—institutions that have long been at the margins—about how to better serve the evolving needs of our diverse and multicultural society.

1 | The Challenge of Educating a Diverse America

The 2010 census made clear that the United States is becoming more racially and ethnically diverse.[1] For now and the foreseeable future, our nation is drawing much of its cultural, social, and economic vitality from "new minorities"—particularly Hispanics, Asians, and people of two or more races—while continuing to depend on the contributions of others, including American Indians and Alaska Natives, Blacks, Whites, and the dozens of other racial and ethnic communities that make up the United States.

The rapidly increasing diversity in this country is grounded in two demographic dynamics. First, immigration continues to have a major influence on both the size and the age structure of the American population. Although most immigrants arrive as young adults, when they are most likely and willing to assume the risks of moving to a new country, U.S. immigration policy has also favored the entry of parents and other family members of these young immigrants. Second, racial and ethnic groups are aging at different rates, depending on fertility, mortality, and immigration within these groups. According to projections based on the 2010 census, by 2050 we will be a nation in which people of color will outnumber the White population.

Evidence of this growing diversity is already apparent. According to U.S. Census data, between 1980 and 2010, as the nation's population grew by nearly 40 percent, Asians and Pacific Islanders increased by 335 percent, followed by Hispanics (246 percent), American Indians / Alaska Natives (106 percent), and Blacks (nearly 50 percent). In contrast, the White population grew by 29 percent. As a result, the distribution of the White population in the United States declined by 11 percent, while Asian Americans and Native American Pacific Islanders, for instance, increased from less than 2 percent of the population to 5 percent, and Hispanics[2] from just under 7 percent to 16 percent. And between 2000 and 2010, the nation saw a 32 percent growth in individuals who identify with more than one race.[3] By 2012, more babies of color were born than White babies, and ten states and thirty-five major metropolitan areas had minority White child populations. This growing racial and ethnic diversity is made even more complex by differences in cultural and socioeconomic backgrounds in a nation where declining overall segregation is coupled with increased residential segregation for minority children and continued differences in social and cultural experiences by socioeconomic status.[4]

The students who come to college now are increasingly matching the new demographic realities of the United States.[5] In the first decade of the twenty-first century, not only did fewer minority students drop out of high school, but they also made up an increased share of the students who took Advanced Placement exams as well as the SAT and the ACT.[6] Despite historically lower academic preparation and lower graduation rates than their White peers, over the past two decades most groups of minority students have increased their rates of immediate transition to college, and the overall rate at which they enroll in college has remained steady or increased. The growing desire of minority students to attend college is reflected in undergraduate enrollments.[7] Between 1980 and 2011, total undergraduate fall enrollment increased by 73 percent, with minority student enrollment increasing by almost 300 percent.[8] Specifically, Hispanic enrollment increased a little over 500 percent, Black student enrollment increased by 165 percent, that of Asian and Pacific Islanders increased by 336 percent, and that of American Indians and Alaska Natives rose by 118 percent. Over the same period, the share of the undergraduate student body that is White declined by more than 26 percent. Minority high school graduates are now enrolling in college at parity with White students.[9]

The racially and ethnically diverse American student body arrives at college from different social origins as well. Between 1992 and 2002, the immediate transition for students from the lowest family-income quintile grew steadily, increasing eight percentage points, from 42 percent to 50 percent, nearly one-fifth. By 2012, more than 50 percent of children from the lowest family-income quintile and slightly less than 65 percent of children from the middle family-income quintile made the transition immediately from high school to college, joining the more than 82 percent of children from the top family-income quintile who do so. As college attendance becomes the rule rather than the exception for Americans who complete high school, students navigate classes and degree programs drawing on a wide spectrum of norms and experiences as well as educational and occupational aspirations and information about college.[10]

Like previous generations, the majority of diverse students now entering American colleges are seeking degrees and credentials,[11] and they are more likely than their predecessors to view college primarily as a "workforce-development system."[12] Even though for many students the link between their college education and occupational development is indirect, they rightly view some college as giving them greater access to jobs that provide further training and access to technology at work, both of which are associated with a range of benefits and higher wages.[13] For them, college appears to function as a gateway to training.

Increasingly, the choices American undergraduates make about majors and even the educational options that are available to them are linked directly to occupational growth and labor market demands for particular skill sets. White House Scorecards and guidance counselors inform students that people with different degree levels and kinds of degrees have different opportunities, and higher degrees are not always leading to higher earnings.[14] American undergraduates now make educational choices in a setting where almost a quarter of those who hold occupational or vocational associate degrees earn more than the average bachelor's degree holder, and certificate and license holders with no degree earn on average more than a quarter more than bachelor's degree holders.[15] For many of these students, a college education means completing "some college" so they can earn more than high school graduates (though not as much as degree holders) in occupations that are hiring where they live.

The Challenge: Providing Diverse Students with Opportunities to Learn

While differences in access to college by race, ethnicity, and social class continue to exist, the opening of American colleges and universities to a diverse society is something of a success story. By 2011, historical gaps in the immediate transition from high school to college for different racial groups had closed substantially—70 percent of Whites, 66 percent of Blacks, and 62 percent of Hispanic high school completers made the transition.[16] These students have come to college in search of degrees and capabilities that will enable them to take their place in a diverse society. In turn, our nation's colleges and universities find themselves facing a formidable challenge: ensuring that the diverse Americans who are now coming to college have equal access to educational opportunities that will lead not only to degrees but also to developing the capacities they need to thrive in their lives.

There is no question that colleges and universities in the United States have long struggled to provide equal access to educational opportunities. Students from low-income families, for example, have been schooled to have lower college aspirations and are less likely to enroll in college regardless of their academic achievement. For Native Americans, schools in the United States played explicit and implicit roles in the religious and cultural conversion of Indians; as a result, Native Americans have long had reason to distrust educational institutions as well as teachers and to view a college degree as yet another exercise in forced assimilation. Once forbidden to learn to read and write, Black Americans could be legally denied access to public schools until 1954. Hispanic students have contended with the stereotype of being newly arrived, non-English-speaking "illegal aliens" with an interest in short-term jobs rather than education. Asian students, when they have been permitted access, have often been viewed as "inherently alien" students who either overachieve or fail to learn English. Lumped into often misleading groups, minority students often begin their college education having to prove they deserve a place in an American school, in some instances in the explicit presence of racial and ethnic slurs.

Consider the case of Native American students. Many come from communities marked by low levels of high school graduation and high unemployment, communities compromised by economic and social isolation and high rates of drug abuse and suicide, and so they begin their pursuit of a college degree with few options.[17] On average, Native American students are older and more likely to be financially independent and to have dependent children than the typical American student; they are the smallest, poorest, and most underrepresented group of college students in the United States.[18] A glance at enrollment and attainment rates confirms that few Native Americans find their way to college and that few finish degrees.[19] In 2011, nearly half (48.6 percent) were enrolled in a public two-year college, and 15.4 percent of those in four-year colleges were at a Tribal College or University. The stories of other groups—and those of individual American Indian tribes—vary, but these stories share a common struggle in finding meaningful access in colleges designed for other people's children. The diverse people who now make up the United States are coming to college, but the attainment of low-income students and most students from most minority groups continues to lag behind their representation in college. They do not yet have equal access to educational opportunity.

As difficult as it is, ensuring equal access to college is only half of the challenge of providing equal access to educational opportunity in a diverse society. Twenty-first-century colleges and universities have to do more than assimilate students into preexisting academic and social communities on campus and help them successfully pursue degrees. Our nation's colleges and universities also need to provide a heterogeneous student body with equal opportunities to learn. To begin with, this means that institutions need to understand and value the cultural, social, and educational resources that each student brings to college. The students now coming to American colleges have been socialized in diverse contexts. They cannot be assumed to share common academic preparation, educational habits, or first languages. Meaningful opportunities to learn will provide diverse students with resources to integrate new information with their prior experience and their individual social or cultural senses of self as well as opportunities to experiment with new ways of knowing that are foreign to their experience.[20] In turn, institutions need to document and respond to students' reasons for resisting learning because of perceived threats or insults to their already existing identities.

Nowhere is the challenge of providing equal access to educational opportunity more clear than in the case of undergraduate minority students. These students have historically had limited choices. Hispanics and Native Americans have long enrolled in greater numbers at public two-year institutions, whereas Black students have been more likely to attend four-year institutions than other minority groups. Black and Hispanic students enroll in for-profit institutions at higher rates than White students. And even though many academically well-prepared minority students have increasingly become the target of intense recruitment by majority institutions, many minority students continue to be drawn to institutions relatively close to home where they value the presence of other minority students and a welcoming culture in an affordable setting.[21] Some minority students choose a particular college to avoid potentially racially and ethnically hostile environments at majority institutions.[22]

Once enrolled, minority students often face formidable challenges on the pathway through college. Many not only struggle to make use of campus resources but find that becoming actively engaged in college can be challenging.[23] Why? They may arrive on campus not fully prepared to do college-level academic work, with limited knowledge about higher education and with significant obligations to family and community. At majority institutions, minority students often find that campus cultures deem their experiences and even their identities as inferior and, in turn, they may struggle to maintain relationships with friends and family while they forge new relationships with faculty mentors and their college-going peers.[24]

Let us be clear. The difficulty in providing every adult in a diverse nation with equal access to educational opportunities does not involve convincing diverse students to come to college. They are coming. It lies in providing students with access to institutions that understand and value their experiences and resources, challenging them with the obligation and the opportunity to learn what really matters to them, and getting them to a degree. The undertaking is formidable.

The Need for New Ideas to Serve Diverse Students

A diverse student body is now knocking on the door of American colleges and universities. Many institutions are not providing diverse students with a fair opportunity to learn. Based on data reported by institutions to the National Center for Education Statistics' Integrated Postsecondary Education Data System (IPEDS), the six-year graduation rate for the cohort of full-time degree-seeking students who started college in 2003 was 57.4 percent. Just over 60 percent of Whites and 68 percent of Asian Americans and Pacific Islanders who started college in 2003 had graduated by 2009, whereas for Blacks, Hispanics, and American Indians and Alaska Natives the six-year graduation rates were 39.1 percent, 48.7 percent, and 38.3 percent, respectively.[25] Students in this group who came from families with low incomes and students who themselves are financially independent graduated at lower rates than students who are financial dependents in higher-income families.

To date, American colleges and universities have largely ignored this problem. In the keynote address to the Institute for New Presidents sponsored by the American Council on Education in 2013, Kevin Reilly, the outgoing president of the University of Wisconsin system, made the case straightforwardly:

> We [United States] have now slipped to the twelfth most widely-educated country in the world in the proportion of our 25 to 34-year-olds with a college degree. Until as recently as 1995, we were ranked first. In a highly competitive global economy, and with our relatively high wage rates, Americans will succeed only if we can get more of our people to higher order knowledge and skills. To get to the numbers of graduates we need, many more students of color and those from disadvantaged backgrounds, groups we have not served particularly well until now, will have to be handed hard-earned diplomas.[26]

We need, Reilly argues, colleges and universities in which diverse students have fair opportunities to learn. We are working with mainstream institutional models that are often indifferent to the needs of a diverse society that includes students from a vast array of backgrounds and communities. Minority-Serving Institutions constitute a set of institutions within our colleges and universities that are addressing the challenge of educating a diverse society. Before turning to what we have learned from them, in Chapter 2 we provide a brief overview of the emergence of these institutions as well as their contemporary role in higher education.

2 | Minority-Serving Institutions

Educating Diverse Students for a Diverse World

Minority-Serving Institutions (MSIs) are a diverse collection of colleges and universities. Although they continue to remain invisible to many both within and outside of higher education, MSIs—Historically Black Colleges and Universities (HBCUs), Tribal Colleges and Universities (TCUs), Hispanic-Serving Institutions (HSIs), and Asian American and Native American Pacific Islander–Serving Institutions (AANAPISIS)—have become an increasingly important part of American higher education, especially as a gateway to higher education for many traditionally underrepresented students across our country.

In 2011, degree-granting MSIs enrolled 3.6 million undergraduate students—one-quarter of all undergraduate students in the United States and a disproportionate percentage of students of color. While HBCUs represent just over 2 percent of all colleges and universities, they enrolled over 11 percent of all African American undergraduates; TCUs represent less than 1 percent of higher education institutions yet enrolled 10 percent of Native American undergraduates; HSIS represent less than 6 percent of postsecondary institutions but enrolled nearly one-half of all Latino undergraduates; and AANAPISIS represent less than 3 percent of all degree-granting colleges and universities yet enrolled one-third of all Asian American and Pacific Islander undergraduates.[1]

MSIs also serve a disproportionately large number of low-income students: 98 percent of African Americans and Native Americans who attend HBCUs or TCUs qualify for federal need-based aid. Moreover, more than one-half of all students enrolled at MSIs receive Pell grants, compared with only 31 percent of all college students. These high rates of Pell grant eligibility exist even though tuition rates at MSIs are, on average, 50 percent lower than those of majority institutions. Students at MSIs are also more likely than those attending Predominantly White Institutions (PWIS) to have lower levels of academic preparation for college and are more apt to come from high-stress and high-poverty communities. And not surprisingly, almost one-half of all

MSI students are the first in their families to attend college, compared to only 35 percent of students attending PWIs.

By way of elaboration, it is important to note that the student bodies at MSIs cannot easily be reduced to simple categories such as Black versus White or Hispanic versus Asian. While a majority of MSIs draw their identity from a single minority group, in some MSIs minority students constitute a "minority." And a handful of HBCUs and a majority of AANAPISIS are majority White institutions. Significantly, some HSIs enroll not only large numbers of Hispanic students but also substantial numbers of Black, Asian, and Native American students; a dozen HSIs enroll roughly equal numbers of Hispanic and Black students; and at least one HSI has a student body with roughly equal proportions of Hispanic, Black, and Asian students. MSIs also differ from majority institutions with respect to the extent to which their students are "nontraditional"—age twenty-four or above, financially independent, single parents, or part-time students. For example, Hispanics at HSIs are more likely than their peers in comparable non-MSIs to have delayed entry, work full-time, and ascribe to a nonstudent identity. In four-year HSIs, Hispanic students are less "nontraditional" than their peers in four-year non-MSIs.

This chapter situates MSIs on the contemporary landscape of higher education. We explore how MSIs—through their missions, environments, programs, and practices—provide culturally relevant educational opportunities for their students. Then, for each of the four types of MSIs, we describe their students, their distinctive institutional characteristics, their programs and practices, and their contributions. We end the chapter by suggesting that MSIs share a dual mission: first, to provide minority students with a supportive environment that enhances their individual growth and development and, in so doing, prepare them to contribute to their communities; and second, to afford minority students the credentials that will contribute to their public and workplace lives.

MSIs: Culturally Relevant Institutions

Designed with the needs of minority students at the forefront, MSIs provide culturally relevant opportunities for students who have historically been marginalized in our nation's mainstream colleges and universities. In so doing, MSIs have called out, disrupted, and questioned the historical roles of race and class with respect to student access and success in higher education. As institutions that are relevant to the students who matriculate at them, their relevance finds expression in their missions, environments, programs, and practices.

&

Missions

The long-standing mission of MSIs has been to increase the capacity of higher education to serve students whose earlier educational experiences have been shaped by such life experiences as poverty, immigration, and life on reservations.[2] In turn, MSIs have been designed to play a major developmental role: to provide a sound education and, in so doing, call attention to the barriers that communities of color face as they seek to participate in American social institutions as equals. In recent years, many MSIs have begun to play that role for communities other than the one for which they were originally designed.

MSIs span the sectors of higher education in the United States. Although minority students are more likely than other groups of students to attend public two-year colleges, MSIs are distributed across institutional types. Across the four major types of MSIs, HBCUs are most likely to be four-year and private institutions; HBCUs, HSIs, and AANAPISIs include several doctoral institutions; and all TCUs began as two-year community colleges.

The diversity of their institutional missions notwithstanding, MSIs share an overarching commitment to ensuring access to higher education and making college a meaningful experience for minority students. To begin with, their campuses are often cost-effective. With student bodies composed of substantial numbers of minority students, MSI campuses provide an option for students who consider racial and cultural identity a central dynamic in education.[3] In identifying and engaging the educational aspirations and needs of the students they serve, MSIs are heavily focused on teaching and on the active involvement of faculty and staff members in student development both within and outside of class. Some MSIs place major emphasis on students' self-determination of their pathways and overtly challenge conventional educational practices that exclude the students they are designed to serve.[4]

Central to the shared mission of MSIs is a widely shared assumption about postsecondary education: not only can all students succeed, but faculty, staff, students, and surrounding communities share an obligation to see that all students are successful. This assumption grounds educational opportunity in two defining characteristics of MSIs. First, many minority students choose

MSIs because they believe they will have a sense of belonging at college without sacrificing their cultural identity or their educational goals.[5] Once at an MSI, minority students often find a range of opportunities that support their academic growth and racial identity development. For example, some MSIs reframe the college curriculum, such as offering an explicit mediation between non-Western and Western cultures. Many MSIs provide students with diverse community- and service-based learning opportunities and invite students to reflect on ways in which ongoing contact with their home community as well as their college experiences can enrich their education.

The second characteristic grounding educational opportunity at MSIs is an explicit focus on guiding minority students to obtaining degrees.[6] Despite historically lower rates of funding and a commitment to serve those students who face significant challenges in completing their degrees, some MSIs still match or outperform comparable non-MSIs.[7] The thorny issue of overall degree completion rates aside, MSIs work to assure that their graduates accrue the major benefits of a college education: higher earnings, access to additional higher education, access to the professions, and STEM career opportunities. Graduates from many public two-year MSIs find their way into local labor markets, and graduates of more selective four-year MSIs have a well-established history of moving on to graduate school and the professions.

In short, MSIs embrace educational relevance to minority students as their defining touchstone. They offer accredited, transferable college degrees that in many ways are indistinguishable from the degrees offered at majority institutions. At the same time, MSIs make explicit to historically marginalized students that attaining a degree does not at the same time require them to assimilate fully into a society that has often marginalized them.

Environments

Across institutional types, MSIs invest in creating inclusive and welcoming environments that are relevant to the needs of minority students. In many instances, students view MSIs as promoting racial self-development, academic development, and social opportunities.[8] Although MSIs are designed for minority students, White students have often found them to be open and friendly environments with supportive faculty. More broadly, researchers have found MSIs to have inclusive climates and nurturing environments that are satisfying to students.

MSIs cultivate communities that call attention to race, local involvement, and the importance of actively promoting the success of minority students. Such communities are accompanied by the widely shared belief that MSIs must be relevant to all students, including students of color who come from poverty, and must be committed to hiring faculty and staff that reflect campus demographics.[9] To that end, MSIs often take initiatives to involve faculty and staff members in designing curricular and cocurricular activities for specific groups of minority students. Not surprisingly, then, minority students often view MSIs as inclusive and empowering and, in turn, MSI students often arrange and pursue their college-going activities with an explicit concern for their peers' success and persistence.

Programs and Practices

In concert with creating educationally relevant environments, MSIs develop programs and practices relevant to the minority students they serve. Reflecting their respective histories of promoting access and empowerment, MSIs have developed widely shared and distinctive understandings of student success, support services, and methods of outreach that support the entry of underrepresented students into higher education.[10] More specifically, MSIs have long-standing commitments to providing supportive services, remedial education, and inclusive student affairs programs to serve students who have historically had inadequate preparation for college and often conflicted experiences in school.

In attending to the dynamics of race and ethnicity, MSIs develop academic and student support programs in ways that make understanding and managing those dynamics part of both the curriculum and the cocurriculum. For example, MSIs infuse the minority experience into the curriculum via programs that emphasize students developing as persons—academically and socially as well as emotionally and spiritually. More often than not, this emphasis on developing character includes a commitment to service learning and community service. MSIs also have a long history of serving as sites for researching and teaching subjects and traditions that are relevant to minority experiences in the United States and also for preserving and enriching the cultural traditions and practices of minority groups.

At the same time that MSIs seek to accelerate and support the academic growth and development of their students, they seek to build the social capital of students. Many MSIs offer a guided introduction to college and provide programs that help students identify and pursue their educational goals—from obtaining their degrees and/or certificates, to transferring to other institutions, to pursuing graduate education. MSI classrooms provide supportive learning climates that are free of many of the barriers minority students often encounter at majority institutions. Perhaps not surprisingly, scholars have found that the supportive academic environments of MSIs are related to higher student motivation and engagement, and that such climates foster community, enhance the quality of interaction among students, and strengthen interactions between faculty and staff. MSIs have also been found to offer opportunities for rigorous academic interaction between students and faculty—often with higher expectations than in majority institutions.

In addition to preparing students to be successful learners, MSIs provide opportunities to put students' learning to use. Many MSIs provide students with opportunities to engage in community-centered research projects and to attend conferences and interact with scientists. And many MSIs provide undergraduate experiences that promote deep involvement in students' home communities and prepare students to contribute within their communities through programs that are keyed to regional and group needs—programs that are staffed by faculty members who are committed to local and regional development. Not surprisingly, the opportunity to be involved with their communities often begins on campus in social networks that contribute to student learning, persistence, and retention.[11]

Within the context of the overarching MSI mission, faculty members play a critical role in developing programs and practices relevant to minority students. Not only do many MSI faculty members come from the dominant minority group of the institution, but in some instances MSIs recruit faculty with nontraditional credentials consonant with their minority-serving missions. For the most part, MSI faculty members choose to work at institutions with an orientation to teaching and in many instances to the success of a specific group of students. And more often than not, faculty members view themselves first and foremost as teachers. Several decades of research, particularly at HBCUs, have found MSI faculty members not only to be encouraging of students, but committed and able to build relationships with students that help the latter to realize their potential and participate more actively in the institution. To that end, HBCU faculty members are often recruited and developed to have such an orientation, and faculty members at HSIS, AANAPISIS, and TCUS are increasingly coming to see their roles in terms of engaging the minority students who have chosen to come to their institutions.[12]

While programs and practices at MSIs often express a widely shared mission, individual MSIs sometimes fall short of realizing their mission for several reasons. First, MSIs sometimes develop programs and practices with insufficient funding and place excessive reliance on fickle federal money. While MSIs provide minority students with access to higher education and strive to cultivate their success, these institutions are often more successful at promoting access than graduation, or better at promoting transfer readiness than successful transfer. Second, in those instances where institutions choose to adapt their educational programs to prepare their students to at once succeed in and challenge the dominant culture, such a position can paradoxically lead them to take an accommodationist stance. Thus, even when MSIs develop specific practices—such as dress codes or articulation agreements with regional PWIS—as bridges between cultures, these practices have the potential to narrow the engagement of the students MSIs seek to serve or impose restrictions on what and how MSI faculty can teach. In short, there is a growing awareness of the challenge of maintaining fidelity to the MSI mission both because the mission is often conflicted and because most MSIs have insufficient resources.[13]

Four Major Types of MSIs

Tribal Colleges and Universities

The Indian Civil Rights Act of 1968 gave power to tribal communities. Soon after passage of the act, the Navajo nation created the first tribally controlled college.[14] Although many at the federal level thought that the college (as well as the primary and secondary schools started by the Navajos) would fail, this institution—originally named Navajo Community College but now called Diné College—served as an impetus for the establishment of many more tribal colleges across the West. Tribal colleges offered curricula from a Native American perspective, including tribal languages and the history of tribal communities. Likewise, tribal elders and what could be viewed as nontraditional faculty with local and practical experience taught classes.[15] These institutions served as learning centers for all those in their surrounding communities, providing library and archival services to local tribes. And in addition to education, these new tribal communities actively sought to boost local economies with their small-business development centers. From their beginnings, tribal colleges have sought to break the "destructive cycle of poverty" present on most reservations throughout the country.[16]

Today the nation's thirty-four TCUs are spread across twelve states and include nine four-year and twenty-four two-year colleges.[17] With over 180,000 students enrolled in 2010, TCUs have grown significantly since Diné College in Arizona opened its doors over four decades ago.[18] Predominantly public institutions (over 75 percent), TCUs vary in enrollments from under 100 to nearly 2,500 students.[19] Most TCUs are located on reservations: among the thirty-four TCUs are four urban or suburban campuses, three campuses located in distant or remote towns, and twenty-seven rural campuses (sixteen of which are classified as remote). Established for Native American students and communities, TCUs are community colleges and centers that offer accredited degree programs; they also host cultural events and house critical social services and often function as business incubators.[20] Compared to traditional students, TCU students are older and more likely to be financially independent and have dependent children, and are among the poorest American college students, often coming to college from challenging social settings, and often having family obligations that take priority over their personal academic progress.[21]

Findings from research on TCUs suggest that these institutions are defined by sensitivity to students' varied levels of preparation and time constraints, relevant degree programs and teaching, support for developmental education, and highly supportive faculty.[22] As such, these colleges and universities retain students who are otherwise unlikely to remain in higher education and bring resources to marginalized communities while sustaining tribal-related knowledge and practices.[23] And not least, TCUs continue to experiment with ways to make the concerns of minority groups part of the mainstream conversation about development: shared authority, shared accountability, collaborations, alternative programs and credentials, and education for self-determination.

Hispanic-Serving Institutions

The Higher Education Act of 1965 authorized the support and designation of Hispanic-Serving Institutions. In many ways, this designation was different from the federal government's relationship and support of other MSIs, such as HBCUs and TCUs, because it was not based on a compensatory rationale, but instead on a demographic increase and shift.[24] The growth in HSIs is the result of four important influences in American society.[25] First, the civil rights movement and corresponding activism opened up higher education to students that had historically been excluded. Second, in the decade leading up to the designation of HSIs, the Latino population grew very rapidly—a full 3.9 million-person increase in the early 1960s alone, with a birthrate that was a two-to-one ratio compared to other immigrants.[26] Latinos made up 4 percent of the overall U.S. population. Third, the Latino population was moving to larger urban areas, forming clusters throughout the nation in California, Arizona, New Mexico, Texas, New York, and Florida.[27] And fourth, Latinos, seeking cultural support and closeness to family, tended to enroll in colleges and universities that already had significant populations of Latinos, increasing the population and pushing it toward an HSI designation.

The vast majority of HSIs were not founded as Hispanic-Serving Institutions. Their not being established for the purpose of educating Latinos can have important implications for the students at these institutions. Basically, an institution can be designated an HSI but have no established commitment to educating Latinos. This inconsistency has led some scholars to differentiate between Hispanic-serving and Hispanic-enrolling institutions.[28] In the absence of an official list of Hispanic-Serving Institutions, the HSI designation refers to institutions that meet the federal institutional and enrollment criteria for eligibility to receive funds under Title V of the Higher Education Act: 25 percent or more total undergraduate Hispanic full-time equivalent student enrollment. Based on these criteria, 311 institutions in the fifty states, Puerto Rico, and the District of Columbia qualified as HSIs in 2011. Scattered across fifteen states and all institutional sectors, these 254 institutions—just over 6 percent of all degree-granting institutions—enroll almost 4 million undergraduates, including one-quarter of all minority undergraduates in higher education in the United States, and nearly one-half of Hispanic undergraduates. These institutions are predominantly public, two-year, urban, and significantly underresourced.

Research has found that HSIs serve an important role in providing access to college for diverse students. HSI students have historically been less likely to complete degrees than students at non-HSIs, in part because HSIs enroll students—many of whom are Hispanic—who have nontraditional enrollment patterns and strong ties to communities away from campus and who at the same time receive less aid and are less prepared.[29] Hispanic students at HSIS who make it to senior status experience the same levels of satisfaction and engagement and also gains in development as Hispanic students with similar backgrounds and experiences at majority institutions.[30] Serving diverse students has led HSIS—as individual institutions and through the Hispanic Association of Colleges and Universities—to advocate for additional resources and to cultivate organizational cultures and degree programs that are relevant to Hispanic students in particular and needy students in general.[31] HSIS include in their numbers some of the most diverse institutions in the United States. Many of these institutions are experiments in minority-majority education and often serve as desperately needed points of access to technology, information, and public space for communities with few such resources.[32]

Historically Black Colleges and Universities

With the end of the Civil War in 1865, the federal government, through the Freedmen's Bureau, and many northern church missionaries shouldered the daunting task of educating over 4 million newly freed Blacks. As early as 1865, the Freedmen's Bureau began establishing HBCUs, which were made up mostly of male staff and teachers with military backgrounds. During this time, most HBCUs were colleges in name only; these institutions mostly provided primary and secondary education, as Blacks needed basic education after years of oppression. Religious missionary organizations—some affiliated with northern White denominations such as the Baptists and Congregationalists, and some with Black churches such as the African Methodist Episcopal (AME) Church— were actively working with the Freedmen's Bureau. One of the most prominent White organizations was the American Missionary Association, but there were many others as well. White northern missionary societies created HBCUs such as Fisk University in Nashville, Tennessee (1866).

Although HBCUs benefited greatly from the benevolence of White missionaries, these individuals often operated with their own interests in mind and with a pejorative attitude toward Blacks. Many established colleges in an attempt to bring Christianity to the freedmen, to instill northeastern Victorian values, and to rid the country of the "menace" of uneducated African Americans. White missionaries treated Blacks much like the early colonists treated Native Americans, as savages who needed to be inculcated with White values.

Among the colleges founded by Black denominations, specifically the AME Church, were Morris Brown College in Atlanta, Georgia, and Paul Quinn College in Dallas, Texas. These institutions are unique among HBCUs, as Black churches and mission societies founded them for Blacks.[33] Because these institutions relied less on support from Whites and more on support from Black churches, they were able to design their own curricula. Still, they remained vulnerable to economic instability.

A few public HBCUs resulted from the 1862 Morrill Act, such as Prairie View A&M University. With the passage of the Second Morrill Act in 1890, the federal government took a more assertive interest in African American education, establishing seventeen public HBCUs throughout the South. This act stipulated that those states practicing segregation in their public colleges and universities would forfeit federal funding unless they established agricultural and mechanical institutions for the Black population.[34] Despite the wording of the Morrill Act, which called for the equitable division of federal funds, these newly founded HBCUs received considerably less funding than their White counterparts and thus had inferior facilities and more limited course offerings. Among the seventeen new "Agricultural and Mechanical Colleges for the Benefit of Colored Youth" was North Carolina A&T University in Greensboro, North Carolina (1891).

Spread across twenty states largely in the South, the District of Columbia, and the U.S. Virgin Islands, the 105 HBCUs remaining today are nonprofit institutions, roughly split between public and private, and predominantly four-year institutions (nearly 90 percent). In 2010, HBCUs made up roughly 2 percent of the degree-granting Title IV institutions and enrolled nearly 290,000 students—including 1.6 percent of all undergraduate students in the United States, 3.7 percent of total minority undergraduates, 0.3 percent of White undergraduates, and 11 percent of Black undergraduates.[35] Overall, the 105 HBCUs are predominantly Black institutions—in 2012, over 75 percent of the undergraduates served by these institutions were Black—with students who have profiles similar to those of Black undergraduates enrolled in institutions other than HBCUs.[36] Although Black undergraduates as a national cohort attended relatively poor high schools that were in many instances urban and predominantly Black, they continue to improve their graduation rates and reap the benefits of a college education.[37] In 2008, HBCUs made up less than 3 percent of all degree-granting postsecondary institutions but accounted for nearly 18 percent of bachelor's degrees awarded to Black students.[38]

A growing body of research on HBCUs has shown that while for some students an HBCU is a local and cost-effective path to a desired degree, many students choose HBCUs because they offer a supportive environment in which they feel they belong and at which they believe they will find cultural support, a sense of belonging, and a feeling of pride, as well as an opportunity to develop a racial identity. These institutions are distinguished by close relationships between students and faculty.[39] HBCUs pay explicit attention to race as a factor in development and cultivate faculty cultures that are focused on teaching and helping students be successful.[40] Black students at HBCUs tend to be more engaged, more satisfied, and better adjusted than their peers at majority institutions.[41] HBCUs stand out in the system of colleges and universities in the United States, which is now almost 30 percent for-profit and 40 percent two-year.[42] Distinctive in institutional type, they are also distinctive as champions for access to higher education for underresourced and underprepared students, notwithstanding the challenges this mission creates with respect to enrollment management, finances, and the recruitment of faculty.

Asian American and Native American Pacific Islander–Serving Institutions

In 2001, on the heels of a fight against the pervasive "model minority myth," which says that all Asians are academically successful, the White House Initiative on Asian Americans and Pacific Islanders recommended that a new college and university federal designation be given to institutions that have significant percentages of Asian American and Pacific Islander (AAPI) students. The White House Initiative hoped that the designation would serve as the impetus for new ventures among the federal government, AAPI-serving institutions, and local communities.[43] In 2002, Congressman Robert Underwood introduced H.R. 4825, an amendment to Title III of the Higher Education Act of 1965, but with little success. In 2003, Congressman David Wu introduced a bill into Congress focused on AAPI-serving institutions, and he did so again in 2005. During the same year (2005), Senators Daniel Akaka and Barbara Boxer introduced a Senate companion bill: the Asian American and Pacific Islander Serving Institutions Act.[44] The legislation proposed establishing a special designation for institutions that enroll a student body in which (1) AAPI students make up at least 10 percent of undergraduate students and (2) at least 50 percent of AAPI students receive federal financial aid, or the Pell grant eligibility of the AAPI students should be at the national median. Much like the other funds designated under the Higher Education Act of 1965, funding for institutions that serve high numbers of AAPI students could be used for operating costs such as student success programs, community partnerships, research on AAPI students, labs, and library facilities.[45] One of the most important aspects of the legislation supporting these institutions (H.R. 2616) is that it rejected efforts to align AAPI students with Whites and those claiming that AAPI students are victims of reverse racism and affirmative action. The legislation pointed out the great diversity among AAPI groups, showing that although AAPIs overall have the highest rate of degree attainment, when broken down by subgroups many AAPIs have much lower degree attainment rates. In particular, Vietnamese, Laotian, Cambodian, Hmong, and Pacific Islanders struggle with very low rates of attainment, ranging from 5.1 to 13.8 percent.[46] According to Robert Teranishi's 2011 CARE Report, the federal program supporting institutions that serve large numbers of these students is important for at least three reasons: "First, it acknowledges the unique challenges facing AAPI students in college access and completion. Second, the [federal] designation represents a significant commitment of much-needed resources to improving the postsecondary completion rates between AAPI and low-income students. Third, it acknowledges how campus settings can be mutable points of intervention—sites of possibilities for responding to the impediments which many AAPI students encounter."[47]

Today, a group of institutions identify—through a federal designation and funding program—as AANAPISIS.[48] At these 116 institutions, 10 percent of undergraduate students are low-income Asian Americans or Pacific Islanders. Scattered across the country, with most on the West Coast, these institutions serve a diverse group of AAPI students—forty-eight different ethnic groups that speak 300 different languages. While these groups do not have a common language or culture, they share the history of immigrant groups;[49] many have needs that are similar to those of other underrepresented racial and ethnic populations.

A still-emerging body of research suggests that, like HSIS, AANAPISIS are evolving as they and their communities come to terms with demographic shifts in student bodies. As they become aware that many low-income AAPI students arrive on college campuses unprepared to pursue college-level work, AANAPISIS have implemented programs focused on developmental skills and academic success to serve their needs. Some AANAPISIS are infusing their curricula with AAPI history and culture so as to empower students and build their self-esteem in terms of their development and identity, and are also working to increase the presence of AAPI faculty on their campuses while they conduct professional development workshops with existing faculty to help these individuals better understand the complexities of the AAPI student population.[50]

Place of MSIs on the Contemporary Landscape of Higher Education: Dual Mission

Notwithstanding their differences, MSIs share a dual purpose across types and sectors. First, regardless of the group of students from which they draw their identities, MSIs provide students with an accredited pathway to a degree or certificate. Situated largely in regions where the students they serve are concentrated, MSIs educate students and provide them with credentials that are linked to social, economic, and cultural opportunities. Second, at the same time that they provide students with credentials, most MSIs are involved in building, reinforcing, and exploring the cultures and communities from which minority students come.

In this chapter we have explored the rise of MSIs, including how changing demographics have shaped our colleges and universities and the way they operate. Through a combination of religious missionaries, philanthropists, the federal and state government, and individual contributions, MSIs have survived and in many cases thrived over the course of their existence. MSIs have taken on a major role in educating the nation's rapidly growing and increasingly diverse population.

3 | Tribal Colleges and Universities

Culturally Responsive Places

Tribal Colleges and Universities (TCUs), from their contributions to local economic development to providing college access to students in remote rural areas, play a prominent role in communities that are often defined by cultural, social, and economic isolation. Committed to teaching Native American students about their cultures and to solving the social problems faced by their communities, TCUs have cultural identities that are infused throughout their institutions. Their charters and missions as well as their status as land grant institutions mandate that TCUs develop educational programs needed by local reservations, from providing basic education and social services to degree programs that prepare students to contribute to local economic and social development. In this chapter, we share stories of programs in three TCUs that use practices that are providing students with access to college and entry into professional communities that contribute on the reservation and beyond. We begin with the story of the developmental math curriculum at Chief Dull Knife College (CDKC). We then explore two initiatives at Salish Kootenai College (SKC): the Department of Academic Success, which is facilitating the transition of underprepared students into college, and the STEM Education Center, which is educating students for careers in science, technology, engineering, and mathematics. At the College of Menominee Nation (CMN), we discuss the STEM Scholars program and the STEM Leaders program, initiatives that are creating educational opportunities in STEM for American Indian scholars.

Chief Dull Knife College: Making Math Relevant to the Lives of Students

We can no longer live the way we used to. We cannot move around any more the way we were brought up. We have to learn a new way of life. Let us ask for schools to be built in our country so that our children can go to these schools and learn this new way of life.

—Chief Dull Knife

Situated on the Northern Cheyenne Indian Reservation in southern Montana, Chief Dull Knife College is located on the sun-drenched prairie of the Great Plains over one hundred miles from Billings, the closest city. After flying into Billings, we drove the hundred miles to Lame Deer and were greeted by Montana's Big Sky—distant mountains in an expansive landscape. The tribe is the largest employer on the reservation. According to U.S. Census Bureau estimates, unemployment hovers at just above 20 percent, and nearly one-half of the people living on the reservation aged twenty-five years and older have not gone on to postsecondary education.[1] As we learned from people we interviewed, this is manifest on the reservation in both physical and psychological ways—including drug abuse, alcoholism, and lack of access to health care.

During our visit we became increasingly aware of the economic isolation in which the Northern Cheyenne lived. One faculty member observed that for many people who live on or near the reservation, grocery shopping often means putting a cooler in the trunk of a car and making the long drive to Billings. At first glance the campus consists of only a few modest buildings; a sign outside CDKC marks these buildings as a college. There are no hotels or restaurants in the vicinity. Access to food in Lame Deer is a convenience store, and the people in the community have little access to fresh, healthy food. We stayed in a small house located on a hill overlooking the campus. The house was built by students as part of an engineering project, and one of the professors had lived there for several months. It was a simple building, insulated with straw.

A Native American tribal community college and land grant institution, CDKC is situated in a local economy driven mostly by ranching and coal mining. Lame Deer is a community of roughly 3,000 residents, many of whom have lived in impoverished circumstances their entire lives. Chartered in 1975, the college was named after the chief of the Northern Cheyenne—Morning Star, also known as Dull Knife—who, in the late 1870s, led his people on a courageous trek from confinement in Indian Territory in Oklahoma back to Montana. Like many tribal colleges, CDKC was chartered because few Northern Cheyenne high school students were attending college by the 1970s, and those who did often did not graduate. Of those who went away to college, we learned, many had encountered culturally challenging environments—a few had been called "prairie nigger"—and the expectation that they would need to leave behind their tribal identity. Students often had to overcome such challenges while assuming major family responsibilities such as caring for aging grandparents who lived on the reservation or family members who had been overtaken by drug abuse. Nearly all of the students we met had limited access to computers, cell phone signals, and even groceries.

Under the leadership of the tribal president, CDKC originally operated in army tents and educated students in mining, construction, and forestry, preparing them for jobs in the surrounding area. Funding by the Bureau of Indian Affairs helped provide permanent facilities, and by 1978 the college was granting a small number of two-year degrees as well as vocational certificates. Today the campus remains a modest facility, with CDKC having limited program offerings and serving relatively small numbers of students. While the campus includes a few ancillary facilities such as a library and a cultural center, the primary facility on campus is a single, bare-bones, multipurpose building that includes classrooms, a learning center, administrative and faculty offices, and a cafeteria. The roughly 300 students enrolled in 2012 were over 90 percent American Indian, and about three-fifths female, a ratio that holds up in the mathematics and sciences courses on campus. CDKC then employed about fifteen full-time faculty members.

To incorporate Northern Cheyenne culture across the college, CDKC observes indigenous cultural holidays and events and provides culturally related educational opportunities for tribal members to increase their options for work, public life, and further education. CDKC offers courses in Cheyenne Studies and Native American Studies and regionally relevant degrees and certificates—such as in the field of mining—as well as courses in traditional fields upon which a student can build an associate degree that transfers to a four-year institution. Off-campus classes serving the Northern Cheyenne Indian Reservation and surrounding areas are offered in K–12 classrooms in Lame Deer and nearby communities.

In the nearly four decades since it was founded, CDKC has faced major challenges in providing higher education on the reservation. Along with poverty, many students have challenges ranging from problematic family situations to poor study environments and drug abuse. More often than not, students can afford to enroll in only one or two classes at a time. Perhaps the most significant challenge facing CDKC is that the majority of students are under-prepared for college, ranging from deficits in study skills to not being college-ready in terms of academic preparation. Nowhere is this more apparent than with respect to mathematics: more than one-half of first-year CDKC students are enrolled in developmental math classes.

"Choke Point"

Mathematics has long been considered the subject most feared by American Indian students. As we heard repeatedly during our visit to the campus, they often grow up hearing that American Indian students are unlikely to succeed in mathematics. Rejecting this belief as a myth, administrators and faculty at CDKC see Native American underperformance not as a lack of *capability* but as a lack of *opportunity*. As we came to understand, most students have had uneven exposure to elementary mathematical concepts such as fractions, decimals, and percentages and to learning opportunities that connect mathematics to their everyday lives.

Preparing students for college-level algebra by introducing innovations in developmental mathematics, which began to be addressed a decade ago at CDKC, grew directly out of faculty dissatisfaction with completion rates for students in these courses. From 1997 to 2003, although more than three-quarters of each entering cohort of students was placed into remedial math, enrollment in remedial mathematics courses averaged no higher than forty-five students per semester, with an average completion rate of less than 46 percent. Students in college-level mathematics courses fared only slightly better. In 2002, less than one-third of the students placed into remedial education went on to complete any of the CDKC lecture-based three-credit remedial math courses. Fewer than one-tenth of students who started in re-medial math completed a degree or certificate. Many of those who passed remedial math classes could not use the math they had learned in college-level STEM courses.[2]

In 2004, CDKC faculty members in mathematics and the sciences began discussions based on these alarming data and agreed that the mathematics challenge had to be addressed, for several reasons. For one, a successful experience in developmental mathematics was important if many Northern Cheyenne were even to consider college in the first place. For another, basic competence in mathematics was pivotal if students were to be successful in college. As one faculty member told us, mathematics had become a "choke point" for many students. Still another reason was that faculty felt strongly that more CDKC students needed to be prepared to consider majoring in STEM fields, which require a solid foundation in mathematics. In turn, CDKC faculty considered the fundamental challenge in developmental mathematics—a challenge that has consumed the energies of several faculty members for nearly a decade—to be "How should CDKC teach developmental mathematics to students who lack the basic mathematics skills they need to successfully pursue two-year degrees and beyond?"

When this question became an institutional focus in 2004, the CDKC approach to remedial math, like that at many colleges, was a sequence of three-credit semester-long courses: Basic Mathematics, Introductory Algebra, and Intermediate Algebra. Some students were placed at the beginning of the sequence and were uncertain of their timetables; others were placed into the final course and needed only a refresher on linear equations before they were ready for college algebra. All students with remedial placement needed to complete at least one three-credit course before they could take any college-level math. Given the confluence of inadequate preparation, low expectations for academic success, and everyday lives that were interrupted by their jobs and the needs of their families, the odds that any CDKC student who enrolled in a remedial course would pass it were low.

To address this challenge, CDKC faculty members began modifying instruction in science classes and shortly thereafter redesigning developmental mathematics. In 2005, they began experimenting with a series of innovations aimed at ensuring that all students have the opportunity to acquire the basic mathematics capabilities that they need to move forward in college. The first step in the experiment was a new sequence of three three-credit developmental math courses that were anchored in a common computer-based math learning system and a self-paced and ungraded approach to remedial education. Instead of being required to attend lecture-based courses, students worked primarily on an individual basis at the computer and, as needed, received feedback directly from a "tutor" built into a computer program. When students chose to attend class and asked for feedback, they received it from the instructor. When they reached the 80 percent mastery level in a section in the course, students proceeded to the next section.

This approach to remedial education guided more students to completing part of the remedial math curriculum over the next several years.

Data gathered by the math learning system show that, by 2008, 80 percent of students were completing at least one segment of the remedial math course in which they enrolled. Still, many students struggled to complete three credit hours of mathematics in a single semester. Ironically, many of these students found themselves starting over and working their way through material they already understood. Students and faculty members alike found the process frustrating. In 2008, faculty and staff began experimenting by breaking the three-credit courses into one-credit courses focused on specific mathematical concepts. Drawing on data collected in the math learning system and by means of a more appropriate placement test, they increased the precision of the placement process to ensure that no students needed to cover material they already knew, and linked progress to mastery as determined by common assessments that were part of the computer-based learning system instead of to course grades given by teachers. Most noteworthy, faculty in mathematics and science decided that most CDKC remedial math students needed a more structured environment and, in turn, designed a hybrid course that blended self-paced work on the computer with teacher-led instruction and inquiry-based learning. Students who test into the developmental math sequence are now advised either to start with a one-credit class that prepares them for a math skills seminar or to start the math skills seminar at a point that matches their needs. They can also pick up additional one-credit courses focusing on topics that have turned out to be critical to student success—such as basic number theory and graphing and linear systems—when needed. Students leave the sequence as soon as they demonstrate that they are prepared to take college algebra.

The Chief Dull Knife Math Emporium

The developmental mathematics challenge at CDKC is being addressed through what an administrator labeled a "highly hybridized emporium." In so doing, CDKC has embraced the conviction that all students can learn mathematics if they become "engaged in the math" and get the feedback they need about their progress when they need it. This overarching message was echoed across all of our interviews. But what is at the core of this math emporium that is making such a difference? We identified two themes that cut across the developmental courses in mathematics at Chief Dull Knife College that were having a significant impact on student learning and persistence: (1) creating safe spaces for students to learn mathematics, and (2) challenging students with real-world problem solving that connects mathematics to their everyday lives.

Safe Space

At CDKC we found significant differences among the students enrolled there—from their foundational skills in mathematics to whether they lived mostly according to tribal customs or mainstream American society or both. One faculty member described CDKC students as a "huge mix. . . . I will see students who have very traditional behaviors and beliefs and so forth that at the same time will be using iPods and cell phones and clearly being influenced by rap music and so on. There's an awful lot of melting pot, but most of the time there's traditional undertones."

Woven among these undertones stands a common denominator across CDKC students: a fear of mathematics, an anxiety they need to overcome if they are to become competent in mathematics. As an administrator at CDKC put it: "Many students have never had academic success. It's nothing but anxiety causing and . . . think of all that anxiety, confusion and frustration that they've got to overcome to even walk in the door. . . . Now that you have them in that classroom you have some pretty fragile students right off the bat." Faculty and staff at CDKC have successfully employed two major strategies to create the kind of safe spaces that students need to successfully overcome this challenge: blending self-paced, computer-assisted learning with collaborative learning, and cultivating personal relationships with students.

Through a computer-based curriculum, faculty support self-paced learning that requires students to achieve mastery of each topic. While they have incorporated computer-assisted learning into developmental studies courses for some time, in the last several years faculty have used a more "blended" approach. Students work their way through the computer-based curriculum, which provides them with instant feedback from an intelligent computer-based tutor. At the same time, they are able to get information and feedback from an instructor in the classroom—often one on one—along with assistance provided by students who serve as math tutors in the learning center. Their teachers can see when they are stuck and when they are ready to move to new topics. Central to this approach is the shared use of a computer-based math learning system so as to standardize the math topics that every student encounters and the assessments that indicate when each student masters each topic. Using the computer, students practice their mathematics, do practice tests, work with an adaptive tutor, and take tests—moving on to the next topic only after they have "beaten" the computer at the 80 percent level.

Faculty members also integrate computer-assisted learning into their classroom instruction. For example, faculty members often begin class with a minilesson that is followed by students' practicing a particular mathematical skill or concept via an online computer. In other instances, students come into class and pick up with the computer where they left off the previous day, and the instructor checks in with each student. Students then complete the lesson at home or in the mathematics lab, which is kept open and staffed by an on-duty instructor throughout the day. As we learned from students and faculty alike, this system works very well. According to faculty, the mini-lessons promote deeper understanding of course material than the computer alone can provide. At the same time, working individually with the computer enables students to be engaged in doing math, reduces anxiety, and frees the instructor to work with students on their individual problems. The tutor and the online practice problems provide flexibility for students who miss class and relieve anxiety for many students. Since the math learning system is always available, students can use it to catch up on what they may have missed in class.

Most of the students we interviewed emphasized the value of self-paced, computer-assisted learning. As one student told us: "[The computer] just shows you how do it without actually asking somebody. It shows you how to work with the problem yourself by just looking at it and seeing an example.... I loved how they give you a CD and you just take your time on it, because some students can't keep up with the pace, and some are behind, and some are way up there." Another student described it this way: "There have been times when the online instructor has gotten me through a problem, like when I'm stuck at home or stuck at work . . . and it seemed like a real person." While computer-assisted learning is not the first preference of all students, it is highly valued by most. As one student told us: "It's slower than having the instructor there. I think he can explain it quicker and more realistically than having to read through the steps on the computer. But I appreciated having the tutor program on there for when the instructor was busy."

Elaborating on the value of the CDKC math emporium, several students told us that in the face of personal challenges—such as having a grandfather who was ill and in need of attention at the expense of their attending class—the "tutoring button" on the computer program was invaluable. In the words of one student, the tutoring button shows you "step by step how to do the problem" and, in so doing, teaches you "all the conceptual steps to get the answer." Several of the students we interviewed told us that the computer allows them to work on their mathematics in ways that accommodate their schedule. As one student put it, it "has been a big help because I have it at work, I have it set up at home . . . and showing you that it's okay to work at your own pace is a huge thing."

Students also told us that faculty members designed classes in ways that enabled them to move forward at a pace they could manage. One faculty member, for instance, begins class with a mini-lesson, followed by an opportunity for students to work together to make sense of the ideas initially presented. Students settle in to do math either individually or in collaboration with one another or with the instructor. Another instructor begins class by inviting students to continue to work on math problems encountered during the previous class session; meanwhile, the instructor circulates through the room, checking in with each student and providing feedback, motivation, and advice.

One student described how her professor began class with an "opener"—a math problem—and simply asked students to work on the problem. Students then had a choice whether to work individually or in a group. As this student told us: "The instructor gives you a choice. Sometimes she'll put you in a group, and if you want to do it by yourself you can." In reflecting on their experiences with this approach, all of the students we interviewed were highly appreciative of the hybrid approach—regardless of who was teaching. Another student told us that he found that "learning that math isn't as hard as I thought it was . . . . Now I don't have to be scared of math. It makes it a lot easier, because I tried to avoid math."

Along with this approach to teaching math, faculty members establish personal relationships with students. As we learned from a faculty member at CDKC, one of the challenges faculty face is creating spaces for students to reconcile the practices associated with learning college mathematics to Cheyenne cultural traditions. As one faculty member told us, "A teacher in

Cheyenne culture is an authority figure, and it kind of goes against their cultural background to question an authority figure in that way." Expanding on this idea, another faculty member described it this way:

> The traditional way of educating a younger Cheyenne is to just have them observe and practice quietly on their own whether it's housekeeping or dressing an animal or whatever they're doing. They learn by watching and kind of practicing on their own out of sight. Then when they're ready they do it in front of the family or out in public or when it's their turn to take over that role. So they don't ask questions. They're not supposed to ask questions and say "Do that again" or "How did you do that?" They're supposed to watch and let it sink in.

Learning about CDKC students led faculty to rethink why they were struggling in classes that are so crammed full of content that students "don't have time to just sit and let it sink in." As several faculty members observed, students who are prone not to ask authority figures questions are often stuck on a single math problem for a long time.

Personal relationships have served as a "work-around." From the beginning of each class, teachers told us that they modeled talking in class, often encouraging students to ask questions of the instructor and talk with their classmates. As one faculty member described it:

> So right from the beginning of a class, students realize it's okay to talk to their neighbors and ask questions and help each other. So it sets up an atmosphere of collaboration to where then it kind of lasts throughout the semester. . . . For our students I think that's important because sometimes they don't feel comfortable asking the teacher or they don't want to ask the teacher all the time because then other students see them raising their hand and they don't want to sound dumb.

As this faculty member elaborated: "If you can make a cultural connection with a student, they will work because they'll feel like they owe it to you. . . . Whatever success I have had with the students I attribute to being able to connect with the students, and it goes back to treating them as fellow humans."

The importance of establishing meaningful faculty-student relationships at CDKC cannot be overestimated. As one professor emphasized to us: "The thing we do better [than most institutions] is we know every one of our students. They're precious to us and we nurture that." Again and again, faculty and administrators said that their relationships with students were critical to helping students get beyond believing that they were lifelong failures at mathematics.

A CDKC administrator shared what it is like feeling "math shame." As she described it: "I know intimately what it's like to be an adult trying to be an academic and be ashamed that you're not brilliant when it comes to math. . . . I've got to tell you that you may not realize what it feels like to have 'math shame.'" This administrator, like many of the faculty, staff, and students we interviewed, saw the solution to this as faculty creating safe spaces in which each student feels comfortable asking questions and the instructor having the time and patience to respond directly to each question. By way of illustration, she described an instance in which she observed this in a mathematics class: "At one point this one lady . . . I can't remember what she asked, but it was like, everybody was going, oh brother, I know that. . . . He came to her defense and he said, 'That's a really a good question.' You see his body language. . . . The message to everyone in the room is: 'I can never ask a dumb question that he won't come to my defense for having asked it.' That's just an experienced teacher knowing their subject and knowing how to handle students that, you know, as opposed to some college professors who are all ready to say 'You're stupid, get the hell out of my class.'" Another student described the same professor this way: "For me the biggest thing is he doesn't condemn or demean me in any way. . . . He just explains math without making you feel stupid. . . . He's just so accepting and inspiring and helpful."

The students we interviewed emphasized that CDKC faculty make connections with students in diverse ways. One of these is using play and laughter to relieve stress and facilitate learning. To illustrate, a student invited a faculty member to participate in a local cultural event known as a clown dance—a modified powwow in which people dress up in costumes and dance to powwow music instead of wearing traditional regalia. In reflecting on her participation, this faculty member told us, "So I don't know, I just try to do stuff like that when I can just so students see that you're out there, and I think that helps break down some of the mistrust or discomfort or whatever it is they feel between White teachers and themselves." She added:

> There have been times when students would come and talk to me about their personal problems and I do what I can to help in those areas. If a student will come to me with reasons or excuses or explanations why they weren't there I make it pretty clear that my first concern is their welfare, and their welfare in my mind includes them learning math, but it's not limited to that. It matters to them.

Again and again students told us how much they valued relationships with their instructors. As one student put it, "Faculty always help me out, and they understand when you have something to do, too, because I have children and I don't have very much time on my hands." A faculty member told us that she felt strongly that faculty members "have to know [their] students. I mean you have to be able to read them, read their body language, and it's something that occurs over time."

Faculty emphasized to us that knowing their students helped them make math fun. One faculty member said:

> One of my goals in the class is to eventually get everybody there to smile. That way at least you know that you've connected. So yes, there are some people that take most of the semester before they ever smile. But you know if you're watching their eyes and stuff you can see to some degree if they're connecting. But if they actually smile when you make a comment, then you know that they're listening to what it is that you're saying. You know some of them will even be looking down and away, and you just see the corners of their mouth come up and it's like they're smiling. . . . Math isn't this big demon that I've got to someday slay. I am managing to do it right now.

Faculty repeatedly told us about the importance they placed on one-on-one relationships with students. As one faculty member said, "We've become kinder, gentler, more encouraging, more mentoring, more nurturing, and more aware of how they're actually progressing through." A professor who had observed a colleague in his classroom told us, "If you ever watch him in the classroom, he is always sitting next to a student and working with, col-laborating with, the student."

Real-World Problem Solving

In concert with the hybrid approach to mathematics, one of the most dis-tinctive features of developmental mathematics at CDKC is a widely shared commitment among faculty to place problem solving—especially real-world problem solving—at the center of developmental math courses. Faculty have defined this, as expressed by one faculty member, not as a

> textbook type of thing, but rather . . . a "real-world" type of thing, how are we going to solve this, how are we going to work it over, you know, looking at the process of problem solving apart from actual skills. So basically in math there's two components. You have your skills, add, subtract, mul-tiply, divide, that type of thing. But then you also have problem solving. There is I have these skills, for example, I'm building a house, it's like learning how to hammer and use a saw, and a drill, and all that kind of thing. Now the question is can you make a cabinet now and how are you going to go about making it? And problem solving is kind of akin to that.

Early in our visit to CDKC we learned that most entry-level students do not see a direct connection between mathematics and their everyday lives. As one professor told us, "Students are looking at math from the standpoint of why do I have to know this?" To help students see the relevance of mathematics, math and science faculty use real-world problem solving to connect mathe-matics to students' everyday lives. One math faculty member, for instance, described opening a class by having students examine a basic floor plan for a house. They read through the dimensions and begin to calculate the cost of replacing flooring in the kitchen and living room. A follow-up problem might ask students to decide how many boxes of flooring to buy. Another in-structor explained how he taught number theory using cultural artifacts from Native American cultures:

> What I would do is I would start out by actually giving them this bone, just a cow bone I found in a field somewhere. I found a diagram of a wolf bone from I think it was 40,000 years ago that had carvings on it. I

duplicated the carvings on the bone and used that as a way of introducing the idea that the numbers that they've known and hated ever since kindergarten started out as an invented idea essentially, and work up from there.

The approach, he admitted, is "no magic bullet," but for many students it grounds math in a context outside of school, a context they understand and value.

Problems rooted in the everyday lives of students seem to promote their engagement with the mathematics they are learning. In a class one student addressed the problem of the rapid growth of nonnative vegetation, a group of students used various techniques to identify cabin sites where elders used to live on the reservation, and another group of students addressed challenges concerning reservation culture. While problem-solving activities do not work for all students, one professor told us that "occasionally after these exercises people come up to you and say I hate to tell you this professor, but math matters." As one student put it: "Problem-solving activities are teaching us to solve problems in life. It doesn't matter what kind of problem it is. It teaches us to look at it from start to finish and see what the result is going to be, and check and see if that result is the result you want."

While engaging students in problem solving, faculty members emphasize the importance of being collaborative. Students collaborate in group problem solving—more often than not, instructors ask students to divide themselves up naturally, a practice that is woven into Cheyenne culture—and faculty actively participate in this process as well. As one professor described it:

You're the math teacher and everybody is busy with something, but you can still move around the room and stop and help individually. That's huge, I mean it has to happen that way in terms of resources, but it's also a huge benefit to that student. Because now when the student has kind of got over their stuck spot, they're still engaged, so it doesn't require you as the instructor to go back and keep prompting or doing something from the board for instance, because they're engaged by the program.

Faculty members at CDKC encourage and support students in their problem solving through what they refer to as "organically forming cohorts" that address real-world problems. While they unfold in diverse ways, cohorts often form around a shared question, and then students work together until the skill has been mastered by all participants and the question has been successfully addressed. Throughout this process, faculty members interact with students, offer just-in-time feedback, and manage organically forming cohorts—cohorts that keep changing as students move through their developmental mathematics courses.

In challenging students to solve real-world problems, all of the faculty members we spoke with at CDKC emphasized the importance of helping them to be more critical thinkers. As one faculty member said:

My entire approach is to promote the idea of thinking about the problems, thinking about what information you have to start with, what is relevant, what is it possible to deal with right now. If I ever see a student who does nothing more than trying to apply a formulaic approach, that's an issue that I see as needing to be worked with, worked on and corrected rather than "Oh, good, you know how to do that problem." I think that entire approach of doing nothing other than "this is how to do this problem" is what's killing their ability to develop this abstract thinking.

Faculty members at CDKC continue to experiment with regard to developmental mathematics. Along with tinkering with the sequence of one-credit remedial courses, faculty are experimenting with having two instructors teach the entire remedial math curriculum together in larger classes—they trade off, working with small groups as well as individual students who are engaged with the same topics at the same time. As one faculty member described this: "With two instructors in the room I think there is going to be much more opportunity . . . where the instructor is moving from hand to hand and another is able to keep an eye on the individual students and what they're doing and be able to move in even when they haven't asked for help." Meanwhile, institutional research—aided by the data collected through the math learning system—is beginning to show a greater percentage of students remaining active in classes throughout the semester. In the spring and summer 2013 semesters, nearly 80 percent of the students who began remedial courses were still actively engaging the learning system during the last two weeks of the semester.

This experiment in making math relevant to the lives of students who live on or near the Northern Cheyenne Indian Reservation goes on. To be sure, faculty and administrators told us, the college has not fully solved the remedial math challenge: many students avoid math altogether and leave without degrees. While more students are becoming prepared to take college algebra, relatively few who successfully complete the remedial math sequence ever make their way into credit-bearing STEM courses. Nevertheless, the college has established a process for iteratively adapting math curriculum and instruction in response to evidence of student persistence and learning. Moreover, evidence of progress is becoming more precise as new tools permit data mining that shows levels of student engagement and progress on criterion-based assessments through content that is aligned to CDKC STEM programs.

Salish Kootenai College: For Self and for Community

The traditional values that served our people in the past are embedded in the many ways we serve and invest in our people and communities, in the way we have regained and restored our homelands and natural resources, in the ways we have built a self-sufficient society and economy, in the ways we govern our Reservation and represent ourselves to the rest of the world and in the ways we continue to preserve our right to determine our own destiny.

—"Vision," Confederated Salish and Kootenai Tribes

As we drove toward Salish Kootenai College from Missoula, Montana, all around us were snow-capped mountains. In the midst of this beauty were windows into life in Indian country. Lining the interstate was a large billboard that said "Meth Sucks," a reminder of the serious drug issue that is killing many Native Americans. The houses and trailers along the highway looked worn out. To our eyes the signs of poverty were everywhere—trailers, trash along the roads. We began to wonder how students could afford to attend college—even one with low tuition.

Once we entered campus, large metal sculptures of Indian warriors, representing the various tribes indigenous to the area, greeted us. We gained an immediate sense of the culture and a grasp of the values that are held in high regard. While the campus itself has few trees and few buildings, there is a serenity that extends across the college that invites self-reflection. Throughout our visit, we felt this calmness and took pleasure in this opportunity to step out of our everyday lives and take in the surroundings and culture of Salish Kootenai College.

The tribal college on the Flathead Indian Reservation is an integral part of the unfolding story of the restoration of the homelands and natural resources, along with the self-sufficiency, of the Bitterroot Salish, Upper Pend d'Oreille, and Kootenai tribes. As expressed in their tribal statement, this story is anchored in how each tribe has developed its ways of life through generations of respectful "observation, experimentation, and spiritual interaction" with the seasons, lands, and biology of western Montana and parts of Idaho as well as British Columbia. Beginning in the mid-nineteenth century, when they were forcibly removed to a reservation, each tribe has had to defend both its way of life and its homeland. To illustrate, with the passage of the 1855 Hellgate Treaty, the Bitterroot Salish, Kootenai, and Pend d'Oreille ceded 22 million acres and were granted the Bitterroot valley; in violation of the treaty, they were subsequently forced onto the Flathead Indian Reservation (1.25 million acres) two decades later. Targeted for termination as late as the 1950s, the Confederated Salish and Kootenai Tribes have often had to take aggressive actions to maintain and secure their land on the reservation.

As American Indian leaders across North America reflected on tribal higher education during the self-determination movements of the 1960s, SKC began to invest in higher education on the reservation. The tribes began leveraging local educational resources and hosted a branch campus of Flathead Valley Community College that offered up to forty-five credits to students at seven sites on the reservation. By 1977—only five years after the founding of the American Indian Higher Education Consortium and a year before the federal Tribally Controlled Community College Assistance Act was passed—the tribal council passed a resolution to formally establish a college on the Flathead Indian Reservation.

After formally separating from Flathead Valley Community College in 1981, Salish Kootenai College was established in Pablo, Montana, on a wooded campus across a central highway from the administrative offices of the tribes. The initial class of 142 students could choose from over one hundred courses, three associate degree programs, and four certificate programs. A decade later the college was accredited—the first TCU in the Northwest to receive full accreditation—and soon afterward was serving over 500 students in fourteen associate degree programs. In 1998, SKC introduced its first bachelor's degree program. Today, the 128-acre campus includes student housing, a day-care center, and state-of-the-art science laboratories and enrolls over 1,200 students, including over 800 Native American students representing more than five dozen tribes. SKC students—many of whom arrive by regular bus service from across the reservation and from Missoula—can choose from over thirty degree and certificate programs. Most students plan to work in the skilled trades or become teachers, scientists, or health-care professionals.

SKC has many of the same challenges that other TCUs are facing. Not only do a substantial number of students come from challenging home situations, but many students matriculate with little understanding about how college relates to what they wish to do and who they hope to become. Many SKC students, a faculty member told us, "are just trying on education." More often than not, this tentativeness is rooted in uncertainty about academic preparation and negative experiences in school. We learned that many SKC students have good reason to be concerned about their college readiness. Historically, nearly three-quarters of entering students test into developmental education. Many of these students have never mastered such basic college-going skills as note taking and asking questions. In 2009, less than one-half of students who completed their developmental courses went on to take college-level classes. Given this history, it is not surprising that even some of the well-prepared SKC students we interviewed were haunted by uncertainty about whether they belong in college.

Prepared or unprepared, many SKC students start college—in the words of a staff member—"bruised by a system" that has never "cared about what they think" and has often been indifferent to their prior knowledge and experience. As a result, they lack "the kind of confidence" that will enable them "to overcome whatever they need to in order to be successful." In the words of a STEM faculty member, many students begin college "with an expectation of failure." The Department of Academic Success (DAS) and the STEM Education Center at SKC are two major approaches designed to respond to students' uncertainty about college-going and their concerns about whether they can succeed in college. The first program is designed to help them gain a foothold; the second launches them into STEM careers. Each is elaborated on in what follows.

The DAS: People and Resources to Prepare Students for Success

The Department of Academic Success, which has gained considerable recognition in public media as a model for moving underprepared students who are "trying on college" into the college curriculum, grew out of a series of conversations among staff and faculty in the Adult Education Center. In reviewing the course-taking behavior of students who place into remedial education, this group learned that over three-quarters of SKC students started college underprepared and that less than one-half of these students ever took a college course. One staff member recalled that these findings gave birth to a mantra: "'We cannot afford to continue to lose 60 percent to 80 percent of our students.' We've become famous for repeating that mantra." Fueled by these findings, a developmental studies task force was established, and in 2009 the DAS became the hub that coordinates teaching and support for students who begin their college career in developmental studies. Staffed by Adult Basic Education (ABE) and General Education Degree (GED) prep faculty and retention coordinators, the DAS guides students who are on academic probation and students from ABE and GED programs into developmental studies courses and then into college-level classes.

To facilitate the entry of developmental studies students into SKC, the DAS manages developmental education programs for adults with little academic experience who are seeking a way into higher education. The DAS is also directly involved with students who have high school diplomas but limited academic preparation for college and with students who are on academic probation. The DAS works to ensure that underprepared students are placed accurately, that the college offers the classes these students need, and that students meet with DAS counselors after placement. While the DAS mostly coordinates and streamlines academic support for at-risk students, DAS faculty members also design and teach modular, credit-bearing DAS academic success classes that students take either in a summer boot camp or during the semester in a series of mini-courses or a three-credit course. This academic success curriculum does more than introduce students to college. Academic success workshops and courses also provide opportunities for students to assess their academic skills and to learn and practice new academic skills as well as to refresh their reading, writing, and math skills. The curriculum includes formal opportunities for students to talk with tribal leaders about the purpose of a college education and opportunities to reflect on who they are as learners. Since 2011 the DAS has also offered a two-week intensive Summer Bridge program to students who test into developmental studies.

The DAS also serves as a point of physical contact for students and faculty. Students can meet with counselors and have access to a suite of support services including career counseling, an online tutoring program, and the campus math and writing labs. The DAS has also become a site of faculty professional development. Through DAS facilitation, faculty who teach developmental studies and introductory discipline-based courses come together to develop strategies for integrating "soft skills" into college-level courses and course work in developmental studies as well as the college-level curriculum.

Along with providing classes, workshops, and consultations, the DAS plays a significant role in transforming the ways that underprepared students enter and pursue college. In the words of one staff member, "Our role is really to coordinate and support and streamline and really spearhead institutional change." As we talked with students, staff, and faculty involved in the DAS, we identified two interlinking strategies that are key to its success: (1) the DAS provides the point of entry into college for underprepared students, and (2) the DAS serves as the hub through which students connect with the people and tools they need to succeed in college.

A Point of Entry to College

SKC students come to college from tribal and non-Native communities with a wide range of expectations and prior academic experience. While some students arrive the fall after they graduate from high school, others arrive years later with GEDs and through ABE programs. In the words of a DAS staff member, many students start college not yet "on a track that really meets their interests and their ideas" and with habits "that are counterproductive toward the pursuit and completion of their goals." Most students enroll, a developmental writing teacher told us, without proper funding and ill prepared to take college-level English or math. The DAS is designed for students who are not ready for access into the institution by focusing on the identities and skills they need in order to succeed in college. To that end, the DAS provides two points of access for students: a point of access to college and a point of access to the college classroom.

The DAS has transformed the way Salish Kootenai College is readying underprepared students for college. Historically, SKC brought underprepared students onto campus through a set of disparate services—including advising and counseling, GED preparation, and ABE services—that were separated from the academic programs in the college. Few students ever made the jump from these services to degree programs. The DAS centralized these services and aligned them with curriculum and instruction in SKC academic programs.

Three critical aspects of this institutional transformation are noteworthy. To begin with, the DAS has helped to cultivate an institution-wide belief that students' successful transition from developmental education into the college curriculum is an obligation of everyone at the college. "It takes a village to solve this problem," as one administrator told us. As she elaborated, the DAS has its roots in a task force that gathered faculty from ten academic departments, student services, developmental education, and institutional research to talk about the "60 percent or 75 percent of our students" who were leaving without degrees. This group came to the conclusion that the success of students who started in GED, ABE, and developmental studies was closely linked to everyone assuming full responsibility for taking actions to ensure that students have a viable pathway that moves them from developmental education to degree programs. The DAS was established to support the campus in taking up this responsibility.

From its founding the DAS has focused on an institution-wide investment in developmental education that has included widespread faculty engagement with underprepared students. Faculty members do not always know how to work with developmental students, as one person noted, but they often "have a clear idea of what it takes for the students to succeed in the next level." The DAS scaffolds the collaboration between disciplinary experts and student developmental professionals in programs that these professionals have developed. This individual also told us about a department chair who taught in the DAS Summer Bridge program: "In working with students technically at the developmental level, it really resonated with him that it's not just academics that are getting in the way. In the summer he started experimenting with different ways to incorporate study skills, note-taking skills, all of those things to reinforce those in his class." This department chair now teaches students in his "normal" classes how to read a textbook and what productive note taking might look like. DAS staff members continue to reach out to draw more faculty members into this kind of engagement with the most vulnerable students on campus.

The DAS has transformed two other aspects of how underprepared students enter SKC. Most significant, the process of getting into college is coordinated by a single department. As a staff member told us, raising academic success to the departmental level (DAS) has legitimized campus professionals with expertise in working with developmental learners and, in so doing, brought increased attention to developmental students campus-wide as well as providing a vehicle for investing in their success. This investment has led to DAS becoming the home of a bridge program, credit-bearing courses in academic success, and the Academic Improvement Waiver program—an innovative approach to supporting students on academic probation. A single Department of Academic Success has meant that students who are uncertain about being in college in the first place will have consistent guidance and support and streamlined access to the services they need. In addition, by co-locating the instructors who teach developmental education and aligning the curriculum they teach, the DAS has begun to make the transition from developmental studies to college classes more transparent and less intimidating.

A renewed interest in the importance of conducting institutional research is the third major component of the institutional transformation that is helping to ensure that underprepared students are being prepared for college. As staff repeatedly told us, research played an important role in the initial meetings of the Developmental Studies Taskforce. This group established a tradition of looking at the course-taking patterns and completion rates of students with different placement profiles and also sharing information about the experiences of specific students. Considering both numbers and stories, they began to be able to predict which students would need help before they were in trouble. These predictions are shored up the regular review of additional information—attendance at DAS classes and workshops and meetings with counselors as well as conversations with faculty about students.

Along with tracking student progress, DAS staff members are deepening their understanding of how developmental students learn. One staff member recalled being told, "Hey, you need to take this online class." Two years later, his study of noncognitive factors that affect learning had an impact on the SKC academic success curriculum. DAS staff told us about the work of staff members who are using research to develop interventions for visual stress syndrome and a developmental math instructor who is investing "a lot of energy and a lot of imagination and a lot of courage . . . trying to figure out why our students aren't succeeding better in math." This faculty member gathers data about students' responses to math instruction and feeds that information back to the math department.

In addition to transforming the ways that underrepresented students are provided with a point of access to college, the DAS provides a point of access to the college classroom. This includes the academic skills curriculum that is taught in the Summer Bridge program and, during the academic year, the quarter-long Academic Skills 101 course and one-credit workshops. Staff and students point to two aspects of the curriculum that "really matter." For one, the DAS has helped align developmental education programs with college certificate and degree programs. Through a collaborative process, DAS staff ask faculty who teach gateway courses to be explicit about the knowledge and skills they expect their students to have mastered before the course begins. The DAS faculty members explain to them what they expect students to know already, the pace at which they expect students to read course material, and the kinds of projects they expect students to complete, as well as the technologies they expect students to use. In its coordinating role, the DAS ensures that existing SKC developmental education curricula prepare students to meet these expectations, and through their direct contact with students, DAS faculty members make sure that students understand what is expected of them. Students we talked to explained why this alignment matters: it makes them confident. The DAS Summer Bridge, one student told us, "kind of got you up and ready." Because this student had used the precalculus skills—and even the textbook—expected by SKC mathematics faculty, he tested into and passed Calculus 1 in the fall. Another student attributed making it through English 101 to writing and editing practices she learned in a DAS academic skills workshop. She told us that she was continuing her DAS studies as she progressed toward a degree in the field of education.

In addition to aligning developmental education and degree programs, the DAS teaches students how to enter the college classroom. One DAS staff member told us that the major contribution of the DAS to the success of underprepared students is an academic skills curriculum that intentionally "facilitates an environment where students can talk" with one another and with faculty about who they are and how and why they learn. You get a chance, one student told us, to "get to know yourself, . . . your learning styles, . . . and the fears and anxieties that you have that you didn't know you had." A person who has taught the academic skills curriculum explained how faculty invited students to enter the college classroom. In his words:

> In Academic Success 101 we spend two and a half class days talking about identity and all the things that contribute to identity and whether identity is something that's stagnant or whether it's malleable. We spend a

lot of time going through things with students on a deeper level because what we're finding is that oftentimes the limits to their success aren't really academic issues. Academic issues become symptomatic of some underlying issue that we're really trying to address.

Students in DAS academic skills courses and workshops also read about and reflect on Native and non-Native views of ways of knowing and communicating, learning styles and preferences, and self-regulation and goal setting.

As one DAS student told us, a faculty or staff member "observes and watches each student" and customizes feedback and, in so doing, is able to help "students get involved" in the subject at hand—whether the course is on note taking or college algebra. Another student noted that faculty who teach academic skills are able "to see what's working for people." A DAS faculty member supported this student's observation and suggested that the academic skills curriculum works because it is designed so that teachers can "observe a student's needs automatically and . . . adapt to those needs." DAS faculty members also serve as role models. The final academic skills workshop is often a session in which faculty and invited tribal leaders talk about their own struggles with education and their strategies for putting education to work.

A Hub for Success

The DAS not only guides underprepared SKC students into college. The department also serves as their initial safety net or home base. We came to think of it as the hub for a network of relationships and resources that challenge students to take on the identities and habits of college students and, at the same time, support their peers. Through interviews and observations, we became increasingly aware of the importance of this hub for entering students. As a staff member framed the challenge: "A lot of our students . . . they're just trying on education and I think that's a really good way to put it. Instead of coming here committed to college . . . it's more like many of them never thought they were going to go to college and it's sort of this, 'Wow, I'm in college! What does that mean?'"

Many of the students we talked with spoke openly of describing themselves as Indians, as members of a tribe, and as members of extended families who need to support their families. At the same time, they recalled not believing that they were likely to be successful in college. One student went so far as to say: "It's just kind of weird thinking of myself as intelligent. I don't know." While he has successfully made the transition from GED preparation to developmental studies at SKC, he remains uneasy about whether he can succeed. Other students acknowledged that their basic approach to learning—listening rather than asking questions, waiting for someone to ask if they need help, avoiding faculty and staff—often made them wonder whether SKC or any college was for them. A faculty member told us that many SKC students "haven't done very well in high school and they've been put down or whatever, and so then it's scary to go talk . . . [with someone]." Still others told us that their identity as a college student is rooted in their deep commitments to families and communities that often view college success as a "good thing," but who fear that successful offspring might "pass their families up and . . . become more educated than them. [Some] families cut them down for it."

The DAS maintains two distinct networks of relationships and resources that make the college a supportive and welcoming place for developmental learners. First, the centrally located DAS serves as the physical hub for an institution-wide commitment to the academic success of students who have not been successful in school thus far. Second, for students who remain uncertain about college, the DAS provides a home base where they find college professionals who are eager to guide and support them while also pushing them as they work out what it means to be a successful college student—a successful American Indian college student.

As a hub for students in developmental education, the DAS is the space where students and faculty access developmental education, even though academic skills courses, developmental studies courses, and other services provided by faculty and staff are located in other buildings and departments. In the words of a faculty member who serves on the Developmental Studies Taskforce, "The DAS serves as a space where the SKC faculty can sit down and discuss [developmental] students." This faculty member emphasized that the DAS provided a range of activities for faculty who value personal investment in their students. "Our students aren't numbers," she explained. "Our students are our family, our neighbors, our friends. We know them by name when we see them."

The DAS provides a range of opportunities for faculty to connect with—to teach, co-advise, and recruit—students who are preparing to enter degree programs. As one administrator put it, in a department focused on developmental student success, faculty and staff design developmental education curriculum and learn about supporting students "from our own angles—from an English point of view, from a reading point of view, from a social needs point of view." These faculty and staff become colleagues in what a DAS staff member called an "active role" in teaching students "how to be students"—even though students are not yet enrolled in any of their home departments.

In addition to providing a central location for faculty to invest in the development of underprepared students, the DAS streamlines student access to key resources. One student described discovering through the DAS "things you never knew you could get": tutoring and academic skills workshops, social services, student groups, books to rent, and cultural events. Another student told us about how conversations with her DAS teacher and adviser helped her arrive at her purpose for being in college, identify a major, and find funding to make it all possible. Other students emphasized the wide range of assistance provided to them. Their DAS contacts help them fill out applications for aid and scholarships, refer them to support services, and even walk with them to the math laboratory to make sure they meet the right tutor. "Formalizing the steps" is critical, one staff member emphasized. Food is critical as well. "We have food here, always."

As a hub for developmental students, the DAS also provides a forum that serves as a space for establishing relationships. In the words of one staff member, in the DAS suite students see their adviser as a "mother duck," and then follow their DAS adviser into college. Over time, students, along with their DAS advisers, "quack their way over" to their academic advisers and move on from the DAS to their degree program. Students explained how this imprinting process works. Rather than waiting for students to realize what it means to be underprepared in college, DAS staff members make contact with them. They send letters, make phone calls, and send text messages to students. One student contrasted her interaction with DAS staff with her experience at a majority institution: "So here [at SKC] they do, they do, they say, 'Do you need help? This is what we're going to do.' So it was a little bit more structured for me, whereas at the university I was just kind of off on my own and it didn't work there for me."

Anchored in their dedication to student development, staff and faculty who encounter students in the DAS invest heavily in relationships with them. One staff member told us that this commitment was an integral part of the SKC culture:

Faculty members are personally invested in students, and that is not just Department of Academic Success. I think that is campus-wide. It is a community here. It is its own community outside of the towns and outside of the tribes, and I think that the support is here for students. A student walks in and they want to earn that degree, then they have that network of people supporting them.

The DAS staff embodies this network of support. Asked how she approached her students, one DAS faculty member said simply, "Every student that I come in contact with I try to know their name and their story and something about them so that I can touch them, work with them, help them in whatever it is that they need; every one of them is different." Students made it clear that the willingness of staff and faculty to know and invest in them helped them on their journey. As one student put it: "I know all of my instructors by name. They know me by name. And I'm able to go to them as a mentor and talk with them on more of a different level." Another student recalled being able to take risks in classrooms and engage in emotionally challenging topics because she knew that "every one of the teachers knows my story and they really support what I'm doing."

Relationships between staff and students in the DAS keep students moving through developmental studies. Why? In the DAS, students encounter college professionals—from the director to faculty to advisers—who believe them to have the capabilities to be successful and who are ready to talk with them about how to be students. Reflecting on her Summer Bridge experience, one student told us that it's "the communication between the teacher and the student. . . . They want to know what we don't understand or what they need to explain further." DAS staff and faculty want to know "what you're not understanding," not to assign a grade but to help the student understand it. This same student added, "I enjoy immensely being able to go to their office and talk with them." Another student told us that entering SKC through the DAS and then going on to study in the field of education obligated her to become part of a "unit" that was committed to move forward together. A veteran DAS staff member summed up the ethos of staff relationships with students as interactions in which students "have the opportunity to take the content we're delivering and make it relevant to themselves, somehow, if it is."

This dedication proves to be infectious. The students we interviewed see being dedicated to the success of other students as part of their own education.

To illustrate, one student who had benefited from a DAS bridge experience told us that informally tutoring students led him to help others master algebra and, in turn, made him a better calculus student who was planning to pursue a four-year degree and then medical school. The story of another student clarified for us, albeit indirectly, how the hub contributed to helping underprepared students. She told us that for a time she lived with two of her nieces and all of their children in her apartment. In her words:

> One apartment, three-bedroom apartment, but I knew if I didn't help them that they would never come here. They'd never take that step and so I made it as easy as possible. I paid all the bills. They just had to help clean and cook, and so once they each started kind of getting used to the college, eventually they got their own apartments and they're all living separate[ly] now. We actually have another niece coming this fall and she is going [to] transition over here.

A Native American STEM Education Center

In addition to guiding underprepared students into college, SKC is also becoming known as a center for science education that emphasizes a Native worldview and the use of STEM to address issues of concern to indigenous peoples. SKC students pursue degrees in a cluster of science programs—including bachelor of science degree programs in secondary education, forestry, environmental science, information technology, computer engineering, hydrology, and life science that do double duty. At the same time that these programs prepare students to further their education and careers, they introduce them to Native American views of natural systems and human responsibilities and invite students to apply the science they are learning to problems on the Flathead Indian Reservation. Providing this kind of STEM education has meant restructuring traditional STEM programs and reallocating resources to small classes with faculty mentors, student externships, and laboratories that support applied research in such fields as environmental chemistry and cellular and molecular biology.

The science programs at SKC share an overarching commitment to increasing the number of American Indian students prepared to pursue STEM degrees—a commitment that has led to a distinctive approach to STEM education. Two faculty members explained to us that the educational experiences in STEM programs at SKC are designed to show TCU students how STEM is relevant to their lives and at the same time to stimulate their interest in using STEM—especially environmental and life sciences—to sustain their communities. Students in these programs do more than learn science and math. They conduct original research that has led to presentations and publications on such topics as risk assessment of mercury in fish in tribal lakes and rivers and the genomics of bacteriophages that live in soils around the reservation. In short, SKC invites STEM students to learn and do science in a program that at once incorporates a Native worldview and focuses on solutions to the problems faced by indigenous peoples around the world—such as sustaining local ecosystems—as well as by the Flathead Indian Reservation.

The SKC faculty we interviewed repeatedly pointed out that their commitment to STEM education comes with the challenge of serving students who are often uncertain about college. Many STEM students arrive at college unable to imagine themselves as potential scientists or engineers. One student we met came from a community that "really didn't . . . see STEM or Native STEM professionals" making a difference in people's lives. Uncertainty about the relevance of a science education to their lives and communities is often compounded by limited exposure to STEM education and little success in science and math courses. "When I first started," one student recalled, "I wasn't sure, one, that computer engineering was for me and, two, there's a lot of math involved and math is a very old enemy of mine. And so I was very hesitant because of the amount of math required." Other students spoke of coming to SKC from high school classes that rarely asked them to explain their own understanding of scientific and mathematical concepts and provided limited practice in "getting ahold of concepts." These students recalled an education that seemed to present math in particular as a skill set to hold onto fearfully rather than as a tool to support inquiry.

STEM programs at SKC have adopted two strategies to address these challenges. First, math and science are introduced in ways that are relevant to the lives of Natives in the Northwest and the Central Rockies. Faculty teach math and science through topics such as energy development and health in western Montana, which stimulate students' interest in how STEM can be relevant to their communities and their careers. Moreover, as several of the students we interviewed told us, STEM education is infused with a set of ethical values that resonate with SKC students. In one of our group interviews, students reflected on the impact of collecting specimens with a respect for living things, publishing findings about local environmental health issues, and taking courses such as Indigenous Science, Native American Women, and Issues in American Indian Health. In the words of one student, a SKC STEM education provides "a pretty encompassing worldview."

Second, STEM faculty members provide formative feedback to students. The students we interviewed emphasized the central role that faculty input plays in their education. One student recalled with surprise the amount of time and energy that faculty invest in students' individual progress, and another described the central role that honest and respectful faculty feedback played in her ability to make connections between concepts and also between her education and future goals. Faculty members are willing to make that commitment because they are convinced that their personal input helps students decide whether a STEM career is right for them and what steps they need to take in pursuit of such a career.

Functioning as a tribal center for science by creating opportunities for Native American STEM students to seize their own education, SKC is educating students who are prepared do STEM on a reservation. In addition to providing relevant and responsive education, STEM programs are anchored in two strategies that help make this opportunity a reality for SKC students. Each STEM program connects each student to (1) a supportive network of peers and STEM professionals, and (2) an academic apprenticeship in STEM for Native professionals.

Networking STEM Professionals

When they told us about what mattered most in STEM programs, students often started with their participation in a network of STEM professionals. As they interact with STEM students from across the country, SKC faculty, and researchers from other colleges and universities who collaborate with SKC, students have the opportunity to talk about their work with faculty and peers who often serve as role models. The story of one student serves as an illustration. When she graduated from high school, she told us, she "didn't see [herself] in college":

I was kind of way over school. I didn't really have that motivation to kind of continue on because I didn't know what I wanted to do. I felt like I was going to waste credits or money and time into figuring out a major to go into. So I kind of solved this and I actually applied . . . kind of late and I was accepted. I initially came over here, to be honest, because of the basketball program.

While science classes stoked her interest in addressing some of the problems with nutrition that she had observed while growing up on a reservation, she discovered that while she loved science, it was the environment at SKC, particularly the community of scientists, that led her to continue her studies and become a scientist herself. She went on to identify three major aspects of the network of relationships. Foremost, she felt she was being cared for as a person. As she elaborated:

> I feel like especially in the life science department—and I am not saying every one of my instructors was this way or wasn't this way—but there is a different level of caring here. . . . They care about our success. They are not worried about what we put in their surveys or if we like them or whatever. They are worried about helping us get a good education and reach our goals. They care about us as a person. They can relate to us as a person, and a lot of times you don't always find that, and so it is just really something grand, that level of caring.

Moreover, her personal access to experts meant that she could ask a lot of questions. As she recalled, she and other students were "able to access our professors," and an open door policy made her and others believe that they were at an appropriate level with their science and math. Finally, and perhaps most importantly, her interaction with faculty made her confident that she could do a summer internship at the University of Washington and then go on to medical school. In the lab and in the field, she had "a PhD right next to my side saying, 'This is what we did in my post-doc,' or things like that." It was because of that one-on-one experience in state-of-the-art facilities, she explained, that she was confident that she could do science:

> It feels like professional almost. You feel really cool doing these things that these professionals are doing, and here, we are students, and we are right by their side, and we are doing the same experiments as they are. Even like when I went and did an internship at University of

Washington . . . I knew techniques that they didn't think; I knew what some of the grad students didn't know about. And so it just kind of . . . it felt really cool, like, "Oh, here I am learning these techniques. . . ." Yeah, it made me feel confident. . . . And empowered.

She subsequently won an American Indian Higher Education Council science competition, became a Native Youth Leadership Alliance fellow, coauthored a publication with an SKC faculty member, and began pursuing a career in the medical sciences. As important as was the quality of personal interactions with her peers and faculty, what she valued most was how those relationships empowered her. She described her purpose in college in terms of the "seven generations" tradition: "So it's like, well, I am here, this college is available to me, so I am going to take all of these opportunities because I know people fought for these opportunities for us. And so it just feels important, like we have to honor that, our ancestors, even the first Native American science students; it is like we are kind of honoring them by striving for success."

This student, along with several of her peers in a group interview, talked through two other versions of the tradition—traditions they had encountered at home and then read about at SKC—that elaborated how a STEM education might be understood as the preparation of individuals to contribute to their communities. Together as a community of STEM students, they described their educational and career goals, explaining how their interactions with faculty and researchers prepared them to accomplish those goals, and at the same time made them increasingly aware of why those goals were relevant to their lives and their communities.

Faculty and other students we interviewed went on at length about the importance of faculty networking with students. STEM faculty share the understanding, a department head explained, that establishing "relationships with students is the most important thing that we do." These relationships are grounded in concern and validate the contributions of the students. In intentionally small classes and cohorts, students are not just a number: they are known and valued by professors who help them seize their own purposes in STEM. In a group interview, students confirmed this emphasis on connection and caring. Most of the students we interviewed said that their faculty and peers "know you by name" and, as one student noted, they "know your skill sets."

Our student interviews deepened our sense of why a network of caring relationships mattered. Two students explained that students in the STEM programs move fluidly into the role of formal or informal tutors. "Giving back what I can," one student noted, supports peers, "helps to reinforce my learning, and makes STEM fun." Another student described coming to SKC after leaving another TCU without a degree due to personal problems. He is succeeding at SKC, he explained, because of "the level of connection you get not only with other students but [with] the instructors that you are working with and the professors that you are learning from." Support and the invitation to join a community of working scientists—"So far I have been able to get two internships"—made school exciting and purposeful for him. Another student described leaving two Predominantly White Institutions when he ran out of other options. He then came to SKC to study nursing and chanced upon the STEM community, where STEM faculty noticed his potential and invited him to be a teaching assistant and later a tutor. It was the opportunity to contribute to the community and to do research, he emphasized, that turned him into a successful college student.

SKC students told us that they find this network very supportive because it makes STEM education accessible and helps them balance becoming a STEM professional with continuing to be members of traditional communities. The University of Montana in Missoula is not an attractive option for many SKC students. Not only is Missoula two hours from SKC, but it is disconnected from social networks and obligations on the reservation. For many students far removed from Missoula, a faculty member told us, "it might as well be on the moon." At SKC, on the other hand, in STEM classes and labs faculty members invite students to connect academic topics to potential applications in Native communities. In addition to making STEM culturally relevant, SKC faculty make it socially relevant. One faculty member described connecting a student who was ready to take a temporary leave from the reservation to take an internship at the Goddard Space Center, as well as creating opportunities for place-bound students who can be successful only if they are able to live in and contribute to their home communities—and in many instances support their families financially.

While a web of relationships provides STEM students with "a sense of belonging . . . a sense that we care about them," the faculty members we interviewed were clear that caring was "not enough." Faculty members often described their relationships with students in terms of "tough love," a combination of "hand-holding and ass-kicking." In validating students' potential to be STEM professionals, faculty members sometimes give them a rude awakening about their need to develop skills and step outside of the campus to find new opportunities to develop: "We keep trying to . . . raise the bar." One faculty member told us about being willing to "force them, pry them out after their junior year" to complete an internship away from the comfort of SKC and the reservation. This challenge was not lost on a group of students we interviewed. Every student in this group mentioned the high expectations of faculty—especially in relation to math and research skills—and a sense of obligation to both faculty and peers to meet those expectations. As one student put it, "Our instructors, our mentors . . . help us to be prepared . . . but it is up to us." Another student added that the STEM program opened doors and taught each student that it is "your own passion that drives you through those doors." The SKC network makes a STEM education accessible in part by challenging students to make good use of open doors.

These open doors have two major effects on students. First, the network helps students who arrive on campus with uncertainty about college to seize their own pathway to a STEM career. Reflecting on a student preparing to graduate and go on to a job with NASA, a faculty member said that collaborating with SKC faculty and internship directors at NASA "focused his goals" and that "once he decided that these were his goals then you could see the path of what work he would have to do to reach the goals." Second, interacting as a member of a STEM network frees SKC students to adapt STEM tools and careers to their lives and communities. A faculty member spoke of one student developing the "freedom to kind of figure things out on his own" and becoming able to "integrate knowledge across all the different sorts of subfields" and "to see the connections between different areas." Students agreed that they were able to use math and science creatively, but for them a more fundamental freedom was related to their futures. They described how a graduate degree or an internship could move them toward a career that made sense at home or toward solving a problem that plagued their community. STEM students at SKC, one student told us, "kind of make our own doors." As members of a STEM network, they are learning firsthand both what STEM careers can mean for their communities and what it takes for SKC students to be ready to pursue a career in STEM.

An Apprenticeship Model

The STEM degrees awarded at SKC are designed to enable students to move off the reservation for more education and to pursue careers, but they are also an expression of SKC's intention to develop a set of professionals who can manage the civil infrastructure on the Flathead Indian Reservation and contribute to the economy. The four-year degrees offered—secondary education, forestry, environmental science, information technology, computer engineering, hydrology, and life science—all are relevant on a reservation that is home to Mission Valley Power electric cooperative, S&K Technologies, S&K Electronics, and various other tribal businesses. Located in modular facilities that can be modified as new opportunities and interests emerge, these programs aim to produce STEM professionals who are prepared to ply their trades on a reservation whether they chose to live on one or not.

The students and faculty in these programs described a highly supportive model of STEM education that is anchored in an academic apprenticeship in STEM for Native professionals. The programs have been designed to be relevant for students who are, as an administrator explained, often going to "have to go off and work elsewhere for a while but midcareer are going to come back home and be business entrepreneurs and either work in these tribal technology businesses or start their own businesses." The teaching and learning in the STEM apprenticeship rest on a basic principle as expressed by a faculty member: "trying to really actively engage our students in research pretty quickly." All of the SKC STEM faculty members we interviewed brought up this principle, often noting that this approach was different than that used in many STEM programs. As a faculty member elaborated, the institutional commitment to a hands-on, laboratory research-based approach required SKC programs to teach STEM concepts and processes in the context of real research projects, always in small classes and frequently by way of year-round, credit-bearing paid internships. The rationale for an academic apprenticeship approach to teaching STEM, suggested another faculty member, is simple: as students build robots or study mercury levels in local fish and wildlife, they find personal educational and career goals that stand a better chance of motivating them to learn STEM concepts and processes—especially in overcoming issues with the "old enemy," math.

The students we interviewed elaborated on this approach to teaching and learning along with its impact. One student, for instance, reflected on what it was like to enter the program: "One of the first things that we did when we walked in the door in this program is we built a robot." This approach, he assured us, was different from the kind of education he and his peers had expected. They were applying what they learned across three different programs on "the very first day." Suddenly, course content feels like building blocks and students become interested in leveraging resources to make the process work: "Not only does it keep you interested, which is really important in STEM fields, which can be very difficult, but you really learn the process of defining a problem and building the solution to meet the requirements of the problem."

In another interview, an environmental science student who had wandered unsuccessfully through two other colleges before landing at SKC emphasized that he learned STEM as he worked on projects that enabled him to "see the effects of what I am doing." Beyond taking tests and doing lab exercises, the apprenticeship took him to conferences and required him to write up findings for the local professionals who set guidelines for safe levels of environmental toxins. Before he had finished his first degree, he was in the field, helping "people become more aware" of environmental contaminants and having an impact on "the way that people see the world and how they interact with it."

While the academic apprenticeship is infused into every aspect of the STEM programs, we came to appreciate that student internships are the ultimate embodiment of this approach to teaching and learning STEM. Internships—ideally a formal part of SKC students' sophomore and senior experience—advance student participation in the network of STEM professionals not only by connecting students with campus STEM professionals but also by challenging them to be ready to move into a STEM career off campus. A faculty member with deep ties to NASA elaborated on how STEM internships work at SKC. Faculty members maintain contacts—often as principal investigators or co-investigators on active projects—with labs across the country and especially with researchers who have "a desire to keep connected with tribal colleges." When students enter their program, an SKC faculty member assigns them to teams that are parts of projects the faculty member is managing, either in an SKC lab or at a remote site. Along with studying the content that is part of traditional credit-bearing classes, students also work on these projects for internship credit. They receive a stipend and regular invitations to attend lectures and conferences where the salient advances in the field are being discussed or where their project is being presented.

Faculty and students repeatedly told us about what participation in an academic apprenticeship in general, and an undergraduate internship in particular, contributes to a STEM education. Initially, the apprenticeships simply open up new possibilities. Internships mean, as one faculty member noted, that students have "the ability to go somewhere that they would have never been able to go." Students concurred, telling us that without their internship they would not have been able to attend conferences and, in the case of two students we interviewed, that they would no longer be in school. They added that in addition to enabling them to go places, their apprenticeship helped them to interact with people they would never have met otherwise. Several students told us about shadowing STEM professionals at work. And another student explained that he had lined up two summers of paid internships because his work with an SKC faculty member led him to attend a lecture and, more importantly, enabled him to talk to a biologist after the lecture "as friends or as colleagues in that kind of a respectful fashion."

The apprenticeships also contribute to students' ability to seize on new possibilities. They provide "a key motivational experience that triggers that 'here's what I want to do,'" as one faculty member explained to us. As this faculty member elaborated, the demands of contributing to a collaborative project lead students to decide whether they are willing to fill in the gaps in their preparation and, if so, to focus on their educational purpose and the steps they need to take to achieve that purpose. After his first internship experience, one student recalled returning to SKC and saying to his adviser, "You have to sign me up, I have to be in this full-time. This is amazing."

Faculty and students also emphasized that the apprenticeship approach cultivates important habits of mind. Foremost among these, an environmental science professor told us, were the habits of a researcher. Especially in internships, his students developed the capacity to do research and also to present their findings at professional meetings, where they make connections and network. The apprenticeship, he mentioned almost in passing, provides a transition to graduate school or professional life. We also came to appreciate that the STEM apprenticeships at SKC produce, in the words of a faculty member, students who have the capability to

integrate knowledge across all the different sort of subfields that they're getting exposed to where they're learning somewhat in a segmented way in the individual classes as they're going through their course curriculum.... Really having to do that sort of on the fly on a research project, I think that really helps them to see the connections between different areas and [become] innovative thinkers.

One of his students confirmed and extended his assessment of the impact of the SKC academic apprenticeship: "When I'm down at NASA, one of the things that I notice that I bring to the table that a lot of engineers don't is I can definitely seem to understand how the system over here and the system over there will eventually need to interact with each other.... I seem to have a bigger view." Other students we interviewed elaborated on this view. They told us that their programs led them to see physical and social worlds as interacting and interconnected. One added that his view of science now emphasizes the implications of "real impacts." Another said that because of her SKC apprenticeship, which intermingled scientific and tribal views and traditions, she felt as if she was "developing as a better person alongside of being a better student." Still another described using the scientific method to guide his own thought experiments and explorations, and he then summed up the impact in a way that resonated with the three other students in the interview: "It is a pretty encompassing worldview that I have come to know.... [I know] how my actions affect the planet and what we can do to fix those sorts of things and remedy them."

Faculty members at CDKC continue to experiment with respect to both the DAS and science education. To be sure, underprepared students continue to struggle. But the DAS has structured the first year of college so as to ensure that underprepared students have immediate access to resources and a network of caring people who guide them through the process of learning how to navigate college. As importantly, the DAS has made visible for the campus community the "step" that underprepared students must take in order to enter college. Staff and faculty members are becoming accustomed to talking about the rates at which different groups of students complete courses and enroll in the next course in a program. They are paying attention to institutional research, and there is good news. A 2010 retrospective study showed that in fall 2008, prior to the establishment of the DAS, the pass rate in developmental math was 46 percent. In the fall of 2010, 70 percent of students who took a developmental math course passed.[3] The college has evidence that it is no longer losing 60 percent to 80 percent of its students in the first math class they take. Instead, the college is beginning to achieve what one administrator referred to as its ultimate goal: "We want to see a trickle-up effect from developmental study success in the gateway courses and then on to degree attainment and then beyond to job placement, all those things eventually."

The cluster of SKC science programs is educating STEM students to enrich their own lives and the lives of those in their communities. One of the STEM faculty members offered this anecdote regarding student success:

> I just had one of my students, one of my graduates from several years back, send me a message that said "I just got published in a waste water treatment operations manual that's going to be used all over the country and, look, here's my name and I just want you guys to know that one of your SKC graduates did this." . . . To me, the biggest source of satisfaction that I think I have right now is . . . that I know that I have a bunch of graduates out there working.

As of 2011, SKC enrolled a high proportion of Native American students—73 percent in 2011, including 71 percent of whom were eligible for Pell grants. Its graduation rate—55 percent in 2011—substantially exceeded the national average. More to the point at hand, of 1,175 students enrolled in the fall of 2009, 259 were enrolled in SKC's STEM associate and certificate programs and 42 in STEM bachelor's programs. In the previous year, all of our nation's colleges and universities conferred fewer than 2,500 associate degrees and fewer than 1,500 bachelor's degrees in these areas to Native American graduates.[4]

The college is making a difference.

College of Menominee Nation: Scholars and Leaders in STEM

Chartered by the Menominee Tribal Legislature in 1993, the College of Menominee Nation (CMN) serves the people of the Menominee Nation, members of other tribes, and the people of northeastern Wisconsin. The main campus in Keshena is located on the southern edge of the Menominee Indian Reservation, while a branch campus is located near the Oneida Reservation in Green Bay. Although it is home to one of the most sustainable logging enterprises in the world, the Menominee Indian Reservation sits in one of the poorest counties in Wisconsin, and employment opportunities on the reservation are limited. Still, throughout our visit we were struck by the friendliness and warmth of everyone we met and by the pride that everyone took in Native American culture.

In this setting CMN is building new opportunities for students who seek to begin their education at a tribal college. The college brings together students, staff, and faculty on a reservation that is home to working forests and in a metropolitan area that is fifty miles from the main campus. Drawing on the ideals of the Menominee Nation, CMN provides the Menominee people, other tribes, and surrounding communities with a wide range of opportunities for higher learning that are infused with American Indian culture. In the words of the college's founding president, Verna Fowler, "At the core [of the college curriculum] are respect for the land, water, and air; partnership with other creatures of earth; and a way of living and working that achieves a balance between use and replenishment of all resources."

CMN does more than embrace rhetoric about sustainability and American Indian culture. They are built into the fabric of the institution. To begin with, every degree-seeking student studies sustainable development and either American Indian history or language. The CMN Sustainability Institute, which has existed for as long as the college, houses the Center for First Americans Forestlands. At the college library and cultural center, students and community members can easily access the CMN Menominee language program on the web as well as elsewhere on iPads and iPods. In collaboration with the tribe, the college brings together elders whose first language is Menominee and CMN students who are learning the language to create instructional DVDs that have been distributed to every household on the reservation. Since 1999 CMN students have studied Native American theater and produced and staged an original play, a major contribution to Native American theater. In 2012, the college opened a community technology center to make cultural materials and communication technology more available to all communities served by CMN, Indian and non-Indian alike—not only the Menominee Nation.

True to its founding mission, CMN is a twenty-first-century expression of the Menominee tradition—the people of the wild rice (mahnomin)—of nourishing its members, its culture, and its region. Anchored in this tradition, CMN has developed degree programs to meet the diverse needs of students, the tribe, and the region. Some programs focus on preparing students to transfer, pursue four-year degrees off the reservation, and seize career opportunities wherever they may find them. Others, like the Transportation Alliance for New Solutions (TRANS), focus on immediate job preparation by helping students cultivate the skills and acquire the knowledge—along with the self-confidence—needed to pursue workplace opportunities. CMN has infused American Indian culture across the curriculum, ensuring that undergraduate education is relevant for American Indian students as well as their communities.

CMN provides on-campus jobs for many students along with opportunities for students to explore their tribal identities. Today, the college employs over 200 people, most of whom work on the Menominee Indian Reservation. The Campus Grind, a coffee shop located in the library at the center of the main campus, interconnects learning, working, and building community. Working out of the Campus Grind, members of two student organizations applied for a grant several years ago from the Scott Zager Venture Fund. The American Indian Business Leaders (AIBL) wrote a business plan to market fair-trade coffee brought to campus by Strategies for Ecology, Education, Diversity, and Sustainability (SEEDS). Managed by students and staffed by volunteers, the Campus Grind serves as a community center, provides an ongoing internship for AIBL members, and operates an outlet for the fair-trade coffee that SEEDS is bringing to the region.

With over 150 faculty and staff members, CMN now serves more than 600 students each semester. CMN offers three bachelor's degree programs, fourteen associate degree programs, five one-year technical diplomas, and three certificate programs. Along with integrating American Indian cultures and sustainability into the undergraduate curriculum, the college has become a point of access to higher education for many Menominee and Oneida tribal members in particular. CMN has also become the college of choice for students from over two dozen other tribes and many non-Native students. More than one-half of the staff and faculty who serve this diverse student body are American Indians.

In 2003, the same year that CMN was accredited, the college began to develop STEM as part of an institutional commitment to prepare students for "careers and advanced studies in a multicultural world." While the primary aim was to produce Native American STEM graduates, college leaders reasoned that STEM programs also served an ancillary purpose. By studying STEM, CMN students would also come to understand "Western science tendencies" and be able to use that knowledge along with STEM capabilities and credentials to sustain and enrich tribal lands, cultures, and peoples.

CMN leaders, faculty, and staff early understood that the expansion of STEM programs—which included opportunities for students to study the biological and physical sciences, computer science, engineering, math, natural resources, and sustainable development—came with a formidable challenge: historically, many Indians, along with many other minority students, have not pursued careers in STEM or succeeded in STEM education. Anchored in this challenge, both CMN and the Menominee Nation "wanted STEM," in the words of a CMN administrator.

In this section we highlight two initiatives—the STEM Scholars program and the STEM Leaders program—that are creating educational opportunities in STEM for American Indian scholars. After discussing the CMN approach to STEM education, which includes creating opportunities in STEM for American Indian scholars and designing practice spaces for learning, we elaborate on the STEM Leaders program before turning to the STEM Scholars program.

The CMN Approach to STEM Education

The CMN staff and faculty we interviewed offered insight into why few American Indians have succeeded in STEM fields. Most noteworthy, they told us that for Indians, pursuing advanced study in any field has often meant working against cultural assumptions and practices. As an administrator put it, many Indians are told throughout their schooling that they are "good for technical things" but not "good for college"—and especially not suited for STEM fields of study. Even Native students who are willing to push against such assumptions often find themselves unprepared for the rigors of STEM because they have come from schools with few resources or because, as another administrator recalled from personal experience, they have been tracked into remedial education simply on the grounds that they are Native American. Preparing Native STEM professionals, one leader emphasized to us, meant preparing a new kind of STEM education.

Since taking up this challenge, CMN has been experimenting in developing a rigorous STEM education that is at once relevant and accessible. The college began by building facilities and recruiting faculty. Meanwhile, staff and faculty traveled around the country to explore promising practices for supporting STEM students. But rather than simply adopting programs in place at other institutions, CMN staff adapted various practices at the college as they were developing their own STEM Scholars program to draw underprepared students into STEM careers and then a novel STEM Leaders program for well-prepared Native STEM students.

With funding from the National Science Foundation, CMN began in 2006 to recruit students into its STEM Scholars program. Along with engaging CMN faculty and staff with teachers and students in local schools, placement data and student interviews were used to identify and recruit students who, while often placed into remedial courses in mathematics and English, were prepared to make a commitment to a STEM education. For the ten to twenty students selected each year, the STEM Scholars program provides incentives in the form of a stipend that they can earn through attendance at class and cocurricular activities and maintenance of an acceptable grade point average.

Faculty and students told us that the two signature features of the STEM Scholars program are the structure and personal relationships. With respect to the former, the program defines students' schedules in two ways. First, students enroll in seventeen credits each semester and complete their remedial course work and their introductory general education requirements in one year. Second, the program structures their pathway through college, as students do not choose any elective courses while in the program. While students and faculty members consistently observed that this structure contributes to high rates of completion, they emphasized that the experience of being in a cohort with a faculty mentor is even more important. Why? Most STEM Scholars arrive at CMN having had limited success in school, much less in STEM fields of study. In a cohort, they work closely with a single faculty mentor who teaches two of their first-semester courses and collaborates with faculty who teach their other courses for purposes of coordinating assignments and feedback. During both semesters of the program, a faculty mentor facilitates a required lab session in which STEM Scholars work as a cohort to ensure that assignments from other courses are completed—and also to develop a better understanding of the meaning of college, how learners can support one another, and what STEM means for their local community. Between 2006 and 2011, these full-time students persisted at rates twenty points above the persistence rate for CMN students overall.

As the STEM Scholars program got under way, the college secured Nuclear Regulatory Commission funding to develop a separate STEM program for high-achieving Native students. This program—the STEM Leaders program—grew out of the experiences of student services staff members who had watched local high school students graduate with high grades and ACT scores, head off to research universities, and often return to CMN without a degree. CMN faculty and staff knew that these students could "do the math" but also that they were too often unable to negotiate a distant campus where they were typically one of only a handful of students who were American Indian. In turn, the STEM Leaders program was designed to recruit academically well-prepared STEM students to prepare to pursue four-year degree programs and STEM careers—all while infusing STEM courses with American Indian culture. In an aside, a STEM leader we interviewed recalled being a nervous and shy but high-achieving high school student without much educational purpose who was "basically forced . . . into the program" by his family and CMN faculty. Four years later, he was—with a full measure of enthusiasm—on his way to graduate school to study earth sciences.

Like the STEM Scholars program, the STEM Leaders program gathers students into a cohort and connects them with resources—a stipend or scholarship, support to attend conferences, and faculty mentors—while also requiring them to take a full course load in fall, spring, and summer along with a summer internship. Reflecting on their experience, the alumni we spoke with highlighted their rigorous academic preparation, the opportunity to attend and present findings at American Indian STEM conferences, and the obligation to talk with elders and their local community about the relevance of STEM to their nations and their world. The success of this program mirrors that of the STEM Scholars program. Between 2006 and 2011 all fourteen STEM Leaders (100 percent) completed an internship, and only one STEM Leader did not continue on in college.

In our conversations with STEM Scholars and STEM Leaders, as well as with the staff and faculty who supported and taught in both programs, we learned that CMN had redesigned STEM education as a means of establishing paths between worlds. Specifically, faculty and staff build ties between the world of the Menominee Nation and worlds such as graduate school at a majority institution, being an engineer at a paper plant in a nearby city, or working as a scientist in a biomedical start-up in a science park in Madison, Wisconsin. On the basis of our interviews and observations at CMN, we identified two themes that cut across the STEM Scholars and STEM Leaders programs that are significantly contributing to student learning and persistence. First, CMN is redefining schooling as creating opportunities for the development of American Indian scholars in STEM. Second, CMN is designing spaces for students to practice STEM learning. Each theme is elaborated on in what follows.

Opportunities to Discover STEM Pathways

It is widely acknowledged that relatively few mainstream colleges and universities provide environments that American Indians find welcoming. A CMN administrator who was also a longtime faculty member sighed repeatedly as she told us stories about Native American college students—especially Native students who, like the Menominee, have strong ties to their historical homeland—having to learn how to claim space for themselves and their culture at majority institutions. Far too often they had to learn how to learn from people who implicitly or explicitly dismissed their way of life. They are sometimes asked to speak for all Indians or to share details about private traditions and rituals or their experience as a subjugated people. In addition to learning calculus or European history, these students have to learn how to say respectfully to an authority figure, "No, that's not accurate" or "This is not something we should talk about" or "You haven't approached me in an appropriate way." A staff person described how most students returned to the reservation exhausted from studying at campuses where they did not feel like accepted members of the college community. Too often, one leader noted, on facing a hostile educational environment at a PWI, American Indian students vote with their feet and leave college.

As they recruited students into a tribal STEM experience, CMN staff and faculty came to better understand that students had little confidence in their academic ability, including students who had been told in high school that they weren't any good. One staff member recalled a prospective student who later completed the STEM Scholars program telling him: "I was never good at [math]. My mom was never good at it, and I can't do it." For some Indians, another staff member stressed, coming to college is "scary" because it is a major step toward radically changing their lives. One staff member elaborated on

> the challenges that a lot of our students are facing, where they may not
> have a mom or dad, or whoever is in their life, because our students have
> all kinds of life situations going on. They may not have that background,

and maybe their life has been the reservation, and they haven't had a lot of exposure to other things sometimes. So, I can understand that fear of starting.

Staff and students reminded us throughout our visit to CMN that even American Indian college students with histories of academic success in high school often struggle in majority institutions. From their perspective, a major challenge is finding a social network to help them catch up when they need to or simply to help them make sense of why they are in school. One staff member defined the challenge that STEM Leaders confronted in developing a STEM community this way:

> They haven't seen a lot of chemists. They haven't seen a lot of things that biologists do. They may have seen it but they don't realize that is what it is, so I think they have a hard time envisioning what they are working toward. . . . I think they don't really have a sense of everything that being in a science or a math field can lead to.

An administrator at CMN told us that the STEM Leaders program was created in large measure to serve high-ability students who failed at majority institutions because they struggled socially in college.

Nested in this context, the STEM Scholars and STEM Leaders programs have been successful in part because they have redefined STEM education for students and faculty. This distinction begins with how CMN recruits students into each program. With respect to the STEM Scholars program, this means recruiting potential students whose mathematics placement scores predict that they are unlikely to study STEM but are nearly ready to take college-level courses. Each summer, CMN staff contact students who place just below college-level mathematics and invite them to interview to be a STEM Scholar. The interview committee looks at placement scores as indicators of preparation rather than static and unchangeable ability and, in turn, selects students who are hungry to change their lives rather than those who already seem likely to make it in STEM. The testimony of students, faculty, and staff suggests that this approach results in a cohort of students who, despite their need for some remedial education, feel that they belong in college and in STEM.

STEM Leaders are eligible for the program because they already have a "good STEM skill set." CMN invites students with strong math skills and a strong interest in STEM who are considering attending majority institutions to stay at home and become STEM Leaders before they go off to finish their education. STEM Leaders are also selected because they are prepared to learn STEM in order to contribute, to protect the land, and to care for the tribe. As with the STEM Scholars program, a committee of faculty and tribal elders chooses the STEM Leaders, and they become a group of which much is expected.

During the academic year, both STEM Scholars and STEM Leaders take a full load of classes and meet regularly with mentors. The STEM Scholars become a cohort committed to entering STEM programs; the STEM Leaders meet with tribal elders and leaders, participate in field trips, attend regional and national conferences, and arrange a ten-week summer internship. In both cases, these students become part of a group in addition to achieving as individuals. The purpose of the programs, one of the founders explained to us, is not to single out individuals but to invite them to become part of a group. In his words: "It is kind of hard to single people out, Natives more so than anyone. We . . . are a different breed of cat." Students confirmed the importance of a sense of obligation to others. One STEM Leader explained, for instance, that it is a routine matter for a STEM Leader to tutor a peer who is struggling in a course the leader has completed or even to write a grant to fund a project that meets a need on campus.

Participation in both the STEM Leaders and STEM Scholars programs is accompanied by "frank talk" about preparation and expectations. Staff and faculty described avoiding what one staff member called "a sort of paternalistic attitude toward students that says, 'We're not going to tell you, but we're going to help you here.'" Put simply, both programs are forthcoming with respect to program requirements as well as challenges that students are likely to face. And once they arrive at CMN, STEM Scholars not only take a full load of challenging classes but are expected to confront directly their fear of math. STEM Leaders early become aware that they will be presenting themselves in regular interactions with tribal elders and visiting scientists, and also at regional and national conferences and in internships far from the reservation.

While the courses in both programs—including topics covered and textbooks used—parallel content at the institutions to which students are most likely to transfer, the educational experience comes with what one administrator called "a certain frame." The programs infuse American Indian culture into STEM not by replacing STEM curriculum with culture but, as one administrator explained, by going a step further than traditional STEM curricula in two distinct ways. First, the programs embed an emphasis on the advancement of the community in the educational experience. By way of illustration, STEM Leaders have established a local chapter of the American Indian Science and Engineering Society, written grants to develop new STEM opportunities for CMN students, and been engaged in volunteering as well as talking with tribal elders and legislators about the need for leaders, science and technology, and economic development on the reservation.

Second, STEM Leaders interact with a national cohort of what one CMN leader called "brown eggheads." Recalling a national conference STEM Leaders had attended, one staff member recalled student participation in a "talking circle," a poster presentation, and social networking. Students, she observed, felt a camaraderie with other Natives who were STEM professionals and were challenged to play the role of a STEM professional by "dressing the part" and "talking the talk." CMN students often left the experience feeling, in the words of a student we interviewed: "Hey, it's OK that I'm an intelligent student. It's OK for me to want to do well." STEM Scholars, on the other hand, enter a community of learners that is challenged by an accelerated curriculum, often confronted with new things, and persuaded by mentors and peers to keep moving on, keep working out problems even to the point of exhaustion. As a community, these scholars discover together that "yes, I can do it."

CMN staff members who have worked with both programs expressed a common educational purpose. The programs were conceived of as opportunities for Native students to take ownership of their future and, in the words of one staff member, to "find their niche to see where . . . they want to go . . . what program they want to do." At the same time, both programs offer futures infused with tribal traditions, namely, preparing STEM the student who "by his actions and his words shows ability and . . . shows what we need for our tribe." In the words of another leader, the two programs give expression to the Menominee tradition: "For the Menominee, to send people out and to learn what was going on beyond their boundaries, and then have those people come back is a traditional way of doing things."

A Matter of Design

To advance their shared agenda of educating American Indian STEM Scholars who will give back to their communities, both the STEM Scholars and the STEM Leaders programs have established educational spaces for CMN students to remain actively engaged in their STEM studies. The programmatic emphasis on scholarly practice has been grounded in two interrelated challenges. First, placement and retention data showed students entering the college with a wide range of preparation: some were ready to enter calculus and college composition, some needed to work one on one with tutors in the CMN Skills Builder Lab to get prepared for college, and some were on the cusp but not quite college-ready. In turn, a major challenge was to provide opportunities that would at once challenge each group of students while also supporting their learning. Second, staff and faculty knew very well that many CMN students—especially those who had initially enrolled in majority institutions—struggled in traditional STEM classes, which required immediate access of prior knowledge, unfolded at a relentless pace, and emphasized individual achievement and learning abstract knowledge. As CMN staff and faculty told us, they had learned that students were capable of thriving in rigorous STEM classes if they were provided with engaging learning environments where their questions were answered and where they could represent with confidence their own growing understanding of STEM course material.

In response to these challenges, both the STEM Scholars and STEM Leaders programs engage students in purpose-driven and challenging educational experiences. For STEM Scholars, the first semester is composed of eight-week courses, with students taking only three courses at a time, and focuses on the skills and dispositions students need. The pace, one staff member observed, can be exhausting for students. To give students direct support, the program establishes time for scholars to interact with a faculty mentor, places a tutor in one of their classes, and puts their peers—who are all working on the same assignments—in the Math Center to take a second look at their work. In addition, STEM Scholars become a pool of volunteers, serving as tutors on campus and as STEM advocates in local schools and at community events. Staff and faculty suggest that a major consequence of this is a shared obligation to keep moving forward. By year's end, students who started on the cusp of college readiness are done with all their remedial course work and a handful of introductory classes as well.

The STEM Leaders program focuses students not only on becoming scholars—STEM Leaders begin college academically well prepared—but on the skills and dispositions they need to advance the tribe. As noted earlier, along with taking a full load of courses in fall, spring, and summer, the STEM

Leaders participate in field trips, attend conferences, arrange a summer internship, and participate in service-related and other activities. The program also requires a monthly meeting with a staff mentor—"food and talk," one staff member noted—and guests. One STEM Leader told us that at every meeting a scientist, tribal elder, tribal legislator, or other community members would push the STEM Leaders to think about how leadership was structured on and off the reservation, what STEM expertise offered to a Native community, and what they could do to become leaders themselves. The STEM Leaders, as one staff member recalled, began to understand that "you can't swing a dead cat without hitting some sort of math and science around you," and that what they did in school, with their stipends, and with their free time was preparing them to run boards and councils and make decisions with and for their community. One student told us directly that the STEM Leaders program raised for him the possibility "to go through college, or to seek a bachelor's degree, or to want to go to law school or to a graduate program." Not insignificantly, required participation in conferences and internships has opened up the academic world to many STEM Leaders.

Second, both programs operationalize the CMN approach of infusing higher education with American Indian culture. STEM course syllabi and academic expectations are, one leader noted, indistinguishable from those at Predominantly White Institutions. But the approach is different. CMN faculty and staff meet to share information about student progress and needs so that interactions with students can focus on developing skills and dispositions needed for STEM programs and limit the stress of being in college. In interviewing staff members who advise students, we heard stories about their helping students choose courses that would build the skills and dispositions they needed for the STEM program. Faculty—especially those connected to the STEM Scholars program—described a curriculum designed to provide not only the knowledge and skills but also the confidence students needed to move to the next level. In no small part, the capacity of CMN faculty and staff to build student confidence rests on trust. Again and again, Native staff and faculty told us about sharing with students stories from their own educational experiences and, at the same time, inviting students make use of their personal gifts and abilities and the opportunities that CMN provides.

Finally, STEM Scholars and STEM Leaders engage in real-world practice. For STEM Scholars, the "real world" is CMN and the experience of navigating college. They attend classes together and engage one another in the STEM Lab or in the Math Center or over a game of pool or lunch. In short, they get down to the work of the first year of college and often lean over and remind one another of what they learned in class. They do not just complete assignments but gain practice in asking questions about whatever they need help with from faculty and peers and giving help as they are able. Students, one staff observed, learn about negotiating college and team building and then make it a habit of asking one another what is due, how to address assignments or fill out financial aid forms, and whether everyone has assignments done on time. STEM Scholars and faculty told us matter-of-factly about calling students at home or at a hospital to find out how they are doing and whether they need a ride or child care or help with an assignment.

STEM Leaders engage a world beyond the campus in monthly meetings with STEM professionals and tribal leaders and at conferences. As one STEM Leader put it, faculty are invested in "getting you out there," such as putting questions to engineers from NASA in a busy conference hall. This individual described reading a conference agenda and circling sessions that were relevant to his career goal and intellectually interesting as well. Summer internships pushed many STEM Leaders even further into the real world. As one administrator put it:

> They had to get out, live out on the campus and socially they had to see it. They had to start understanding the science labs and working at some of the bigger labs. They had to see other students who are also interning there. They had to get used to that social component of it, but they knew it was short-term. "Ten weeks, oh, we can last."

Students confirmed over and again the importance of opportunities to practice STEM skills outside school. For example, one student talked about the opportunity he had to intern in a biomedical engineering lab where he "got to apply [his] chemistry and stuff." Another student described arriving at her internship feeling like "everyone else was smarter than me, everyone else knew more science than me, and everyone else was more interested than I was." But she went on to explain that her ten weeks of working in a lab and making presentations resulted in a relationship with a mentor and the sense that she too could go on to study STEM at a research university if she wished to.

As elaborated on earlier, the STEM Scholars and STEM Leaders programs share two overarching themes that contribute to student learning and persistence: creating opportunities in STEM for American Indian scholars, and designing spaces for students to practice STEM learning. While they have much in common, these two programs embody these themes in distinctive ways: the STEM Scholars program provides a pathway through the first year of college, and the STEM Leaders program cultivates a cohort of Native American scholars in STEM who are becoming leaders of their tribes and in their professions. Each of these is discussed in what follows.

New Pathways for STEM Scholars

As we talked with students at CMN, we became increasingly aware of what it might mean for a Native American student to make the transition from a high school on or near a reservation to a college STEM program. While they were aware that the transition to college would be challenging, not least because their rural or tribal schools often had limited programs and resources, students repeatedly talked instead about beginning to believe that they could do this. For example, one young woman said that she had not been initially confident that "a little girl coming from a little family can do this" even after graduating second in her high school class and earning good grades in her first college classes. Well aware of this challenge, CMN staff and faculty designed the STEM Scholars program as an interactive pathway into college that links the development of basic skills to relevant information about college. This approach works, one leader told us, because of structure and relationships.

The structure is not, on first glance, revolutionary. The cohort of STEM Scholars is guided through a fixed curriculum into degree programs, and support is comprehensive and based on attendance. For a year, STEM Scholars work closely with program faculty and academic staff. As the academic year unfolds, faculty and staff work together to facilitate a sequence of interactions that, in the eyes of one of the designers of the program, empower STEM Scholars to begin to make their own choices about how best to pursue their aspirations. The program gives students room to make sense of how they are progressing and where they are going and, at the same time, manages the STEM Scholars' transitions to college so as to open for students the possibilities of STEM careers. One faculty member, for instance, developed in partnership with the tribe a display that linked pictures of people who work for the tribe with job descriptions and descriptions of the kinds of math they use every day. As the year progresses, staff and faculty wean students off and ensure that the STEM Scholars—who by that time are a tightly knit campus cohort—are connected with campus resources to support their continuing success.

This basic structure works, we came to appreciate, because of the relationships with which it is infused. STEM Scholars initially encounter an instructor who teaches most of their first semester classes and becomes a mentor. Faculty involved in the STEM Scholars program collaborate to develop and facilitate carefully sequenced opportunities for the students who participate to ask questions, to be successful in completing their college assignments, and to reflect on what made them successful. STEM Scholars become accountable first to their mentor for meeting class requirements. Staff and faculty also made clear to us that the program is not simply a mentoring program. STEM Scholars early become accountable to their peer group, "so the group itself begins to move them forward," in the words of one faculty member. She went on to describe friendly competition and support across ages and levels of competence that emerge as STEM Scholars become highly supportive groups. These cohorts also become a significant campus resource. One teacher noted that STEM Scholars were the obvious choice for tutors in the Math Center, and she thought of them as students ready and able to do "community service, as ambassadors, and volunteers."

The web of relationships that supports STEM Scholars is not, we learned, circumscribed by the program. The STEM Scholars program is nested in the College of Menominee Nation. All programs at the college, one leader explained, provide preparation so that students—whether they are American Indians or not—are educated for their community even if that means that "they have to go out and get their master's or their Ph.D. someplace else to come back and serve the community." A tribal college education comes with the obligation to use that education "to go back into the big world and make some changes." Many of the faculty who teach at CMN, this leader went on, came "to this little one-room college . . . well, one-building college . . . because it was a movement more than an institution."

It became very clear to us during our visit to CMN that faculty and staff involved in the STEM Scholars program are deeply committed to cultivating scholars. As one faculty member put it, "I try to get them to see that they have strengths that other people need." She then described an older student who, despite limited experience in math, realized that she had "experiences and wisdom" that her cohort needed. She was able to make sure the group got assignments done on time, and the group made sure that concepts were explained and reexplained to her until she understood them. Students moved together as scholars. Again and again, staff and faculty told us that STEM Scholars are not only learning math and science but, in the best tradition of STEM, learning how to frame and solve problems using math and science. To illustrate, as part of a required Critical Literacy class that they happened to be taking together, one group of STEM Scholars analyzed local transportation problems and proposed an alternative approach to getting students to campus, ultimately involving Green Bay Metro and making a presentation to the CMN vice president who manages the Green Bay campus of CMN.

Cultivating Native American Scholars in STEM

In our interviews and observations, students spoke confidently about STEM fields of study, national organizations and conferences, and theories of leadership and organizational behavior. At the same time, they described themselves as unlikely leaders when they first entered the program. To a person, they recalled all the options they were exposed to in the STEM Leaders program. One student described all of these as a kind of "culture shock." Another STEM Leader recalled that all the STEM opportunities at CMN made him nervous: "I wasn't sure if I was qualified for it, and so that made me nervous because I didn't think I was qualified for it at the time because I was more of a . . . I'll stay in the back, I don't really want to be out there like that." Still another STEM Leader described the challenge of soaking in the possibilities he encountered in his classes and at a professional meeting. Without exception, the young men and women we interviewed were forthcoming that the STEM Leaders program had opened to them a pathway different from the one they had imagined for themselves—and also that taking that pathway required them to change.

The STEM Leaders program has been successful in moving Native students on to advanced study in STEM because it scaffolds for students the development of a new identity as a Native American scholar. We identified three features of the STEM Leaders program that significantly contribute to the development of this identity. First, entrance into the program means accepting an obligation. The initial staff mentor tells each group of new STEM Leaders: "We chose you. You didn't go out asking to be in this program. We came to you. . . . Now you have got to show us. . . . You have a responsibility. The Spirits gave you a good skill set." One STEM Leader described being pushed into the program by two CMN faculty members who had worked with him when he attended college classes as a high school student. He was in the program because his community saw potential he himself did not believe in. Other STEM Leaders had similar stories and saw the fun they had in the STEM Leaders program, their study of STEM, and their choice of careers as part of a community investment.

STEM Leaders—who were grateful to have financial and social support—identified a second program feature that contributed significantly to their developing a sense of who they were and who they could be. The STEM Leaders found themselves part of a cohort that included not just STEM Leaders and the faculty and staff who support them but also a national network of elders, community leaders, faculty, and staff who were committed to the development of Native American scientists and technologists. Leaders frequently recalled the impact of seeing other American Indians from their high school or their reservation performing well in college classes and their growing sense of what they could achieve. The same STEM Leader who found that the opportunity made him nervous remembered thinking of a fellow STEM Leader: "I went to school with her. I got better grades than her. . . . So yeah, I can do this." Program staff emphasized the value of requiring STEM Leaders to participate in conferences and internships as the STEM Leaders program took them off the reservation and exposed them to other students—often other Native students—who were pursuing STEM at other colleges and universities. One STEM Leader talked about learning how to apply for an internship and then connecting with a Native American mentor through an internship at the University of Wisconsin–Madison. Another described going to a conference and meeting successful students from other institutions who "were Indian; they came from reservations." STEM Leaders successfully become STEM Scholars to a great extent because the program introduced them to other Native Americans who were or were becoming STEM Scholars.

In describing another dynamic, most of the students and staff we interviewed made it clear that the program led to changes in what high-achieving

Indian students believed they could do because it takes a tribal approach to STEM. That approach begins with an invitation to take delight in science. One student described how a stipend, supportive peers and faculty, and the expectation that she would do STEM—obtain internships, participate in conferences, talk about STEM with local high school students—turned her into a "nerd. I fell in love with microbiology." STEM inquiry at CMN is purposeful in several ways. For STEM Leaders, inquiry involves challenging oneself. Another student described the impact of CMN faculty teaching small classes and the commitment of STEM Leaders to make 200-level classes into 400-level experiences. These faculty members said, as one STEM Leader put it: "You're going to have to work harder. If you want to succeed, you're going to have to work harder. . . . If you want to succeed in school, you're going to have to work twice as hard as White people work." He described how difficult it was for him to become a STEM Leader and then leave the reservation for a regional Predominantly White Institution; at the same time, he ascribed much of his success at CMN and at that regional campus to being pushed by the program to be a leader. In his words:

> I found it extremely important for myself as a Native American person to try to achieve the highest degree of education, and try to interpret the methods of science to regular people. I just found it really important, you know, to be a person from my position and where I come from. It's important for me to continue school. It's important for me to continue being challenged.

The purpose of inquiry for STEM Leaders is also vitally linked to ensuring the future of the tribe. As one STEM Leader put it, it means being a scientist or an engineer in ways that align with "the way we were brought up. It's not individually; it's community. If the community is successful, you're successful. So we, as STEM Leaders, were a community. So if one was having trouble, we were all having trouble, so we'd try to help that one out." Toward the end of an interview, this student, on his way to another region to continue his education, noted in passing that he was the lead author on a grant to establish the Young Forest Keepers, a youth forest monitoring program on the reservation. Writing grants, establishing and sustaining formal and informal STEM organizations, contributing to research, attending national meetings, addressing local needs—all of these activities are an integral part of the education of a STEM Leader at CMN.

A decade after CMN committed to developing STEM programs, the college has gained national recognition, and STEM enrollment quadrupled from fewer than 50 students majoring in STEM or allied health in the fall of 2003 to 208 students (one-third of total enrollment at CMN) in the spring of 2010. As of this writing, students, staff, and faculty have been involved in developing a wind turbine prototype and engaging in climate change and biodiversity research. And across multiple STEM programs, the college contributes to the care and harvest of one of the Menominee forests, with CMN continuing to operate the Center for First Americans Forestlands within the Sustainable Development Institute. As we learned in our visit to CMN, the STEM Scholars and STEM Leaders programs are designed to link being an Indian with being a scholar. As one administrator put it, founding CMN president Verna Fowler has been unwavering in her message that visitors to the college should expect students and scholars, and not simply "beads and feathers."

Stories of Success in TCUs

The three TCU institutions highlighted in this chapter all are successfully engaged in experimenting with innovative ways of preparing students, including underprepared students, to pursue and succeed in college. And in so doing, these institutions are providing higher education relevant to the needs of communities that have been left behind by many mainstream colleges and universities. Specifically, each of these institutions has established points of entry to college that affirm the potential of every student to be a college student while at the same time providing the support and guidance students need to persist on their journey through college. Chief Dull Knife has a hybrid developmental math curriculum that links the study of math to students' lives through real-world problem solving. Through the Department of Academic Success and its STEM programs, Salish Kootenai College has established networks of students, staff, and faculty that challenge and support each student to seize her or his educational pathway. And at the College of Menominee

Nation, the STEM Scholars program has created opportunities for American Indians to become scholars and professionals in STEM.

Through providing culturally responsive learning spaces and networks, all three TCUs are supplying exemplars of initiatives that are having a significant impact on student persistence and learning. Albeit in different ways and in different contexts, each of these institutions is inviting, supporting, and obligating students to become not only college educated but committed to contributing to the learning of others and engaging in problem solving with and for their communities. The hybrid developmental math curriculum at CDKC and the Department of Academic Success and the STEM programs at SKC are scaffolding educational success for underprepared students. And the cluster of STEM programs at Salish Kootenai College and the STEM Scholars and STEM Leaders programs at the College of Menominee Nation are providing students with educational opportunities—such as problem-based learning and internships—that prepare them to use STEM to enrich their own lives as well as contribute to the lives of others.

4 | Hispanic-Serving Institutions

Designing Pathways for Student Success

Our nation's Hispanic-Serving Institutions (HSIs) are on the front line of educating a diverse America. These nonprofit institutions were designated as a point of access to higher education for Hispanic communities that believe in the importance of education but often have limited success in education in this country and limited economic resources. Many of the students HSIs were formed to serve arrive at college as part-time students who need to work away from campus to support their families; many start college with limited English skills.

Located mostly in urban communities that have large concentrations of Latino populations, most HSIs themselves have limited economic resources. Defined as much by their student enrollment as by their missions, HSIs are establishing new paths to college access and success for students who often have limited academic preparation and limited information and understanding about what college is and how to succeed in college. Put simply, HSIs are responding to the needs of students from diverse cultural, linguistic, and economic backgrounds while at the same time ensuring that an HSI education leads somewhere—to living wages or to more education. In this chapter we highlight three approaches to empowering diverse, first-generation students to negotiate college—from what a college education involves to how to successfully pursue a degree. We begin with the story of the First-Year Experience program at La Sierra University. We then turn to a portrait of two programs at El Paso Community College: the College Readiness Initiative and the Early College High School. We conclude with the story of the First-Year Experience program at San Diego City College.

La Sierra University: Trailblazing Individual Pathways

Located in suburban Riverside, California, not far from San Bernardino and about sixty miles east of Los Angeles, La Sierra University (LSU) is one of the most racially and ethnically diverse institutions in the United States. The highly diverse population includes not only large numbers of Hispanics but also substantial numbers of Asian Americans and African Americans. As reflected in recent undergraduate student demographics at La Sierra, about 34 percent of undergraduates are Hispanic; 18 percent are Caucasian (non-Hispanic); 16 percent are non-U.S. citizens; 16 percent are Asians; 7 percent are African American; and 3 percent are Native Hawaiian / Pacific Islander. In no small measure, the religious diversity at La Sierra is reflected in the distribution of Hispanics; roughly one-half are Adventist and one-half are Catholic. The diversity with respect to the academic preparation of students is no less noteworthy. In the words of an administrator we spoke with: "Some of our students are so smart they slept through high school and they got good grades anyway. Some of our students . . . barely made it through high school but they got here somehow."

The beautiful campus of La Sierra University is perfectly manicured, with cactus and fruit trees spread throughout the campus. The sun shines brightly on the vast diversity of the student body. Because it is a Seventh-day Adventist institution, students are often reminded of their obligation to give back to others and to live a life of purpose, including by the use of banners that fly above the campus walkways. Health is also emphasized, and we appreciated the institutional commitment to health while on campus, from the dried fruit and nuts we were served throughout visits, to the cafeteria with its vegetarian offerings.

Established in 1922 as La Sierra Academy, La Sierra subsequently became a junior college and, in 1946, was accredited as a private four-year liberal arts college. While La Sierra became a university in 1990 and began offering undergraduate programs and graduate programs outside the liberal arts, the institution continues to be an undergraduate-focused liberal arts institution. Along with serving large numbers of minority and low-income students at the undergraduate level, La Sierra maintains relatively small classes, with a 16:1 student-to-faculty ratio.

Anchored in its affiliation with the Seventh-day Adventist Church, La Sierra's mission is "to SEEK truth, enlarge human understanding through scholarship; to KNOW God, ourselves, and the world through reflection, instruction and mentoring; to SERVE others, contributing to the good of our local and global communities." With a long-standing tradition of graduating students who become educators, health-care providers, and contributors to the public good, La Sierra's commitment to an ethos of social justice runs throughout the culture of the institution. Echoing the voices of many students and faculty we interviewed, one person told us what he often said to entering students: "Some day, if we do this thing right, what we call this La Sierra University education [will lead you to have] your name on the path of the just, someone who is recognized around the world as a person who's made such a difference in the lives of people, made life so much better for people that you will take your place on the path of the just."

Because LSU is a Christian university, the Seventh-day Adventist influence finds expression throughout campus life—from meat not being served on campus to classrooms being closed on the Sabbath. At the same time, La Sierra has a great deal of diversity with respect to both religious and faith communities. As we learned during our visit, students are not only comfortable with but also appreciative of this diversity. As one student put it, "I've encountered quite a few people who are non-Adventist and I think it's pretty cool because in a couple of the religion classes I've taken we've had some people who are like Muslim or just Protestant or even we've had a couple of atheists, which I think it's cool because you get different opinions."

Notwithstanding its commitment to serving a highly diverse group of students, by the 2005–2006 academic year there was growing concern among faculty and administrators at La Sierra regarding the first-year retention rate (60 percent) and the graduation rate (34 percent) in particular; students who placed into developmental math and English courses persisted at even lower rates. Moreover, there was widespread agreement that La Sierra had become challenging for entering students because various aspects of students' lives were organized into separate silos: recruitment, admissions, registration, campus life, and instruction. In 2006, a university-wide task force was established to identify ways to improve the retention of first-year students. Building on their recommendations, a pilot program was implemented during the 2006–2007 academic year. Along with introducing a general education course entitled Strategies for Academic Success, the pilot program included tutoring for students in remedial mathematics, an early alert system for faculty to request intervention for students at risk of failing remedial English and mathematics, and the collection and analysis of student retention data.

La Sierra defined the overarching challenge addressed in the first year of college as providing an education for students who not only were differentially prepared for college but also had a wide range of life experiences and college expectations. The baseline for admission to the college is passing grades in an academic high school curriculum and ACT and SAT test scores that are below the average at other four-year private and not-for-profit colleges. Some of La Sierra's diverse students arrive with limited proficiency in English or a placement in remedial math, while others matriculate with substantial Advanced Placement credits. For some of these students, simply earning a degree will be a first in their family. Other students start their first year with detailed plans for getting into medical school. A 2005–2006 review of first-year programs revealed that students' first-year experience—from their access to financial aid to their interactions with faculty and course selection—was largely shaped by what they already knew about college. The college itself, reviewers concluded, was not doing enough to ensure that every student had an opportunity to learn. As one faculty member put it, "I don't think we can help them [students] with the typical academic tasks until we get a look at who they are as individuals."

Building on the success of the pilot program, the following year La Sierra University launched a centralized campus-wide program for all first-year students—the First-Year Experience (FYE)—that was placed under the newly established Center for Student Academic Success. The driving purpose of the comprehensive FYE program is to help students successfully access La Sierra University, develop expectations for college, and cultivate the problem-solving skills that will enable them to be successful in college and beyond. Since it was established in 2007, the FYE has come to include a number of key components: summer orientation, academic and personal coaching, mandatory first-year seminar, the Writing Center, math labs, Early Alert, and required workshops on such topics as time management and test-taking strategies. FYE establishes for each student a personal point of contact within a diverse network of peers, coaches, staff, and faculty who guide and support the student's entry into college and along the pathway through the first year of college.

While numerous aspects of the FYE contribute to student success, two features have been critical to the success of the program: (1) personal and academic coaching, with a coach for each student; and (2) first-year seminars, which include team teaching by faculty and coaches. These two aspects of the

FYE reflect the flexibility and individual attention that define the first-year experience.

A Coach for Each Student

To address the wide range of personal and academic challenges that students face in college, personal and academic coaching early became the centerpiece of the FYE. All first-year students—roughly 500 each year—have their own coach. In brief, academic coaches are full-time staff members. All have a bachelor's degree, have had professional training as a coach, and are available throughout the week for students. With respect to being a coach, a faculty member told us: "I mean coach. I don't mean peer. . . . [The coaches] have a real sense of what it means to navigate through a place like this." Along with team teaching mandatory first-year seminars with faculty, each coach works weekly with approximately forty students, conducts educational workshops, and participates in summer orientations.

During our visit to La Sierra, we learned that the developmental model encompassed two major types of coaching. The first type, coaching students in taking on the identity of a college student, is emphasized during students' entry to college and the first two quarters at La Sierra. The second type, inviting and supporting students to become self-directed in their journey through college, becomes more prominent as students become comfortable in college. In what follows we elaborate on each type of coaching before turning to a discussion of first-year seminars that includes the role of coaches in team teaching first-year seminars.

Becoming College Students

Coaches take a proactive role in working with students from the outset. As part of the mandatory first-year seminar, each first-year student meets weekly for one-half hour with the coach who is team teaching the first-year seminar. The relationship between the coach and the student is one in which the coach—as someone who has experience and expertise—offers advice and guidance to the individual receiving coaching. As a guide and mentor, the coach takes a very active role in assisting each student. Coaches help students address such personal challenges as time management, study strategies, and navigating the undergraduate experience. As one coach described the coaching role: "We talk about how classes are going, kind of troubleshoot and help them out if they're having issues, point them in the right direction, kind of try to give them the tools to succeed." As he elaborated: "For me part of coaching is really being proactive about what potential issues could be for them to be successful and keeping track of how they're doing and reminding them constantly. So we have workshops like time management. . . . We might give them some kind of assessment of their skills and that would rate their time management."

With respect to academic coaching, the coach serves as the academic adviser—an academic guide for most of the first year of college—for students. In the spring of their first year, students choose a major and are connected to a faculty adviser. In team teaching first-year seminars and in weekly meetings with each student, the coach works closely with each student in helping him or her address academic challenges and opportunities, including choosing a major and a career trajectory. In short, through both personal and academic coaching, each student at La Sierra is given ongoing support in becoming a college student. As one student told us: "It was just nice to have that extra support. I think coaching was useful just because you have a lot of questions when you do go into college, like which major should I choose, am I taking the right classes, am I on the right route, and . . . coaching allows us to ask those questions and it doesn't put up the awkwardness where you have to feel obliged to talk to a professor or something like that."

To be sure, several students told us that they were initially skeptical about having a coach when they entered their first term at La Sierra. One student said that when he was assigned a coach his first reaction was "Oh, come on, really, one more thing you got to do is a coaching appointment once a week. But after my first appointment I was pretty stoked about it. . . . [My coach provided] borderline therapy/borderline advising." Another student said that when he first came to La Sierra,

it was just like why is there somebody telling me what to do? I thought this was college. I thought you could do whatever you wanted. So I was kind of hesitant and kind of didn't want to do it at first, but after [a while] me and my coach we kind of had a relationships and we grew together. I still talk to my coach and so it's just like . . . now we're friends and we still talk. He pushed me to want something more of myself. So it's kind of like at first I hated the whole idea and then after a while of him, of getting to know him, being in the class, and getting with the whole experience, it kind of grew on me and now it's still a part of me.

Another student described her coach this way:

She's really cool and we connected on more than just a school basis. I was really homesick and stuff and she was always there. She was always like, "If you need anything at all I'm here," and we had e-mail contact and Facebook. . . . I wanted to be able to give up sometimes, but then she was like, "No, you're really bright, keep going, we're here to help you."

One student, who had previously attended a community college, admitted that when she first came to La Sierra she was very skeptical about crossing religious boundaries, as she is not Seventh-day Adventist. But with the support of her coach, she was very glad that she came to La Sierra. As she explained it:

So when I came here I was like, "I don't want to go to this school because it's a different religion and they're going to try to change my religion," and so I was really closed-minded and it made my life kind of difficult because I was trying to shut everybody out and I didn't have any friends for a long time. Then my coach [said]: "Not everyone is going to try to change your ways. You have to let people in." . . . He's like, "I'm Adventist and I haven't tried to change your ways, have I?" And I was like, "No." So it's kind of like they open your eyes. And then so my coach kind of helped me to be more open-minded and be okay with different people and changes and stuff like that. . . . I kind of go with the flow now. It's not so hard to change. So I think that that [the impact of her coach] was a positive way for me.

Another student, who was nearing completion of her first year when we spoke with her, told us:

I'm not going to lie. When I first realized that we had to go to coaching once a week I wasn't happy about it. [I had this] I can handle this all by

myself type of mentality, but during the last two quarters we formed relationships with our coaches. We could talk to them about our classes. . . .
vent to them and tell then what was happening in your personal life they
would listen and give their advice, and they always told us how everything was confidential. It was like advising academically, but at the same
time moral support as well.

Not insignificantly, most of the students we interviewed said that it was helpful
that many of the coaches were alumni of La Sierra. As one student told us,
"They just graduated a few years ago and so they've been through it and they
know how the school works."

In elaborating how coaching had a positive impact on their first year of
college, many students told us stories about how coaches experimented with
their students. One student told us about a coaching session in which students were the coaches and the coaches were the students. Acting as coaches,
students asked questions about "how the day was going, what classes they were
taking. . . . So now I put that into play with my friends. I'm like, how are you
doing in your classes, are you doing good, do you have any troubles, do you
need help? . . . [If] you need help I can help you study. I can take you to places
where you can learn some of the material even more."

One of the coaches we interviewed talked about establishing trust with students. He walks a "fine line" between "hand-holding" and providing direction, exhibiting what he and other faculty at La Sierra called "tough love."
He described one situation: "I had a student that it turned out to be kind of
a difficult student to coach because I don't think he really took the coaching
relationship very seriously. But I noticed that whenever he wasn't attaining
whatever goals . . . there was always an excuse to it." Eventually, this coach
confronted him outside of class about his attitude, and this turned out to be
a wake-up call. From then on, as the coach put it, whenever he started "blaming
anyone then he'd catch himself and say, 'No, it's my responsibility.' I should
actually go to class and I can't blame someone else or my friend told me that
I should take this class and I can't just blame my friend for it."

Their Own Journey

As the first year progresses and students become more fully prepared to navigate college, La Sierra students take on greater independence and become

more self-reliant in their journey through college. Coaches are more likely to ask questions that challenge students to find answers within themselves as they pursue their college-going experience based on their values, preferences, and pathways. Especially as students proceed through their second quarter at La Sierra, the academic and personal support coaches provide is increasingly aimed at helping them move forward in whatever direction they wish to go.

We heard many stories from both students and coaches about how coaches support students in taking ownership over their journey through college. One of the coaches reflected on the importance of providing students with "a chance to sort of think out loud" and "permission" to choose an educational pathway that matches their interests. Coaches, she said, "kind of affirm what [students are] already thinking" and help them find majors and careers that they "like doing."

Engaging Students as Learners

Beginning in the fall of freshman year, each student is required to enroll in two quarters of a freshman seminar (University Studies [UNST] 100 and 101). Co-taught by a faculty member and an academic coach, students—who make a two-quarter commitment to the seminar—choose from a wide range of possibilities. Subjects of recent freshman seminars included critical thinking skills, enriching one's life, the law in American society, becoming a biologist, and telling stories. (Some seminars serve primarily as developmental courses for students who have specific academic needs—such as in mathematics.)

As we learned in our interviews and through various documents, the overarching purposes of the UNST courses are (1) to explore the topic of the course as designated by the faculty member; (2) to engage individual students as problem solvers, thereby cultivating habits of mind along with personal development; (3) to connect students with university resources (such as the Writing Center and the Learning Support and Testing Center); and (4) to assist students in developing personal connections with their peers, a faculty member, and their academic coach. To that end, UNST courses variously incorporate instructor-centered teaching and team teaching with student-centered teaching in which students are invited to "share the stage" with the instructor and the academic coach.

By way of illustration, a recent course offering at La Sierra was Puzzles: Watching How the Mind Works through the Medium of Puzzles. Students in the course worked on a range of puzzles—from lateral thinking and math puzzles to logic and paradox puzzles. Working individually or in groups, students constructed puzzles—along the way recording their mental and emotional states to get a sense of how their minds function with respect to problem solving—and then presented their work. The course instructor explained to us the critical role these presentations played. She recalled a shy Latina who wowed the class with a card trick. Being in front of the classroom initially took her "way out of her comfort zone," but she stepped up, talking and manipulating the cards effortlessly. "It just blew everybody's socks off, including mine."

In UNST courses students often use their own experiences as a tool for understanding. In so doing, students integrate new course content with their prior experience and become more reflective learners. By way of example, a faculty member mentioned that "one of the more touching poems I had this year was [by] a young lady who wrote about four vultures in a cage, and you would think that would be a topic that would leave you cold. But her closing lines had to do with her talking about her own freedom, how those vultures feel in that cage. You can't fly, you can't even spread your own wings."

Coaches also play a significant role in most UNST courses. To begin with, some faculty members invite the coach to take ten or fifteen minutes of class to talk about such topics as note taking and time management; others treat coaches more like teaching assistants. While many faculty members share a considerable amount of course responsibility (both within and outside of class), others engage in a tag-team relationship, with both faculty and coach having specifically allotted time during class.

By way of example, one student told us that in her UNST course her professor would teach the first forty-eight minutes of class and then leave the coach with ten to twenty minutes at the end of the class. Another student told us that both the instructor and the coach would give students feedback on and grade their papers. One professor told us that he and the academic coach would sometimes role play and one would be a teacher and the other a student in the class. This professor said that he and the academic coach would meet every week and address the question "How do you think it [the previous class] went?" He and the academic coach then

> had to figure out what we would do the next time. I mean even though
> I am well organized in a class, I am very flexible depending on how things

are going so that it doesn't have to be my class. It is their class, for them to get their student outcomes, not my student outcomes. And if it is not happening I better go back and fix it because these are a lot of skills that we are trying to do.

A faculty member who had worked with coaches in his UNST courses over the past several years provided an example of how he worked with them. In his class on the American legal system, guests come to class and testify about a fictitious bar fight as he and his coach play the role of prosecutor and defense attorney and students serve as a jury. In addition to reading about eyewitness testimony and jury selection, students enact a case "that is highly explosive, has racial and sexual connotations." The case comes alive, he added, as students watch the coach banter with a faculty person, cross-examining potential jurors and witnesses. Team teaching, he emphasized, is central to the success of the class. Other faculty, students, and administrators elaborated on the contributions of team teaching to the success of the FYE. Reflecting the perspective of many people we interviewed, one professor told us that "what has driven the success of this [FYE] program is *personal attention* [our italics]; that is to say, I think we have . . . brought students out of environments that are not very compatible to the life and expectations of the university." In light of this challenge, the professor went on to emphasize that "students develop a unique relationship with both their academic coach and the instructor in their 101 class" and that "the real heroes in this I think are the coaches. . . . They're probably like academic bartenders in some respects. I probably shouldn't say that in a teetotaling institution like this, but they [students] bring in all kinds of problems . . . and by and large they do a remarkable job."

All of the coaches and students we interviewed emphasized the importance of the academic coach—not only in class but outside of class as well. In particular, many of the coaches stressed the close link between their classroom participation and their outside-of-class meetings with students. As one coach put it: "I had two really good UNST professors who really worked with me. . . . I tried to tailor my coaching sessions based on what the student needs [academic and personal] were, so I was constantly asking how can I help you or tracking to see where they were going and what they needed help with." From his perspective as well as those of the students we interviewed, outside-of-class academic coaching was an integral part of their learning and persistence during their first year at La Sierra.

First-Year Experience

Before the first-year experience was introduced at La Sierra, retention through the first year was 60 percent. Since the second year of the FYE program in 2007–2008, that figure has risen to more than 85 percent each year. In the last few years students in the FYE have also had higher grade point averages (GPAs) and markedly higher satisfaction with their experience at La Sierra. And disproportionate numbers of Asian and Hispanic students (many of the latter live at home) are persisting beyond their freshman year.

Through personal attention, especially through personal and academic coaching and the first-year seminar experience, the FYE is clearly having a major impact on the success of a very diverse group of students at La Sierra. As one of the coaches told us, "I'm saying you're going to sit in classes in which people come from such a dramatically different life experience than you have ever had, that you're going to hear them say things that you never thought about, and that's going to enrich your learning because the world you're going to enter is that kind of world."

Early successes notwithstanding, the La Sierra FYE continues to morph into new forms. Program staff members have discovered that the students most at risk for stopping out simply avoided optional components of the program and that some successful FYE "graduates" still needed support into their junior year. Staff continue to expand the program and are helping very diverse participants become successful college students—academically and personally—who, over time, become self-directed learners who take ownership over their own pathway through college. In the words of one student who has gone through the FYE: "When you get here you get this big help of how to choose your classes, how to stay on the right track, what works with you, what you have to take and all that. *It just gives you a trail.* It's kind of like they're just holding your hand the first two quarters and after that you should be ready to just walk by yourself." Representing the voices of many other students we interviewed, a student who was completing her FYE put it this way: "I'm not from here. I moved up last year, beginning of this school year. La Sierra is a wonderful place. It's changed me in so many ways, both academically, spiritually, and it's changed me as a person."

El Paso Community College: Getting a Region Ready for College

At the core of the collaborative action agenda is the belief that all children, regardless of race or ethnicity or the neighborhood in which they live, are entitled to a first-rate education and to effective educators who believe in them. Because we know that real educational change never occurs as a result of efforts on the fringes, but rather requires changing how schools and classrooms operate and ensuring highly skilled teachers and school leaders, our work has been direct, intensive and comprehensive.

—El Paso Collaborative for Academic Excellence

When you drive to El Paso Community College (EPCC), you come so close to the Texas-Mexico border that you can see the pollution hanging over the violent town of Juarez, Mexico, from your car window. Juarez is the site of gang violence, drug cartels, and mass murders. The town is covered in a light-brown haze that you can almost taste in the air. El Paso, the U.S. city across the border from Juarez, provides a sense of hope not only for its residents but also for many of the residents of Juarez who cross the border daily to seek higher education. El Paso Community College is at the center of the hope afforded to the city of El Paso.

Since it was established in 1969, the story of EPCC has been one of an unfolding commitment to serving a borderland community that is more than three-quarters Hispanic and also younger and more impoverished than the population of most of Texas and much of the nation. Originally established as a makeshift campus at Fort Bliss, and later moved to the downtown Rio Grande campus, the college began enrolling students in vocational and transfer programs. Two decades later, as it neared an enrollment of 20,000 students, EPCC joined with the University of Texas at El Paso (UTEP), all local school districts, and various civic organizations to begin a regional dialogue about the formidable educational challenge it faced: only one-third of high school students in the region were college-bound.[1] This dialogue, which was formalized as the El Paso Collaborative for Academic Excellence, early reached a consensus that blaming others for students' low academic aspirations and achievement was an exercise in futility. Since its founding, the collaborative has worked to ensure that every citizen in the region has the opportunity to be challenged by teachers who believe that they can learn. Like the other members in the collaborative, EPCC has adopted a set of shared commitments: universal access, high expectations, caring staff, alignment across educational levels, and outreach to the region.

Today, EPCC is among the most productive public community colleges in the country. Over 30,000 students are now enrolled at five college campuses spread across the county, and more than 1,500 students are enrolled in the five Early College High Schools affiliated with EPCC. By 2011 the college was ranked in the top twenty in the nation for overall associate degree production and ranked first on the *Community College Weekly* list of associate degree producers for both minority students and Hispanic students.

The growth of the college is closely linked to an institutional commitment to empowering Texas borderland students to move toward their educational goals. In 2004, EPCC conducted a review of the educational outcomes of students who had started their college careers at EPCC and identified the most formidable challenge it faced. Placement and retention data showed that relatively few EPCC students were beginning college ready to take college-level courses. The majority of students who followed a traditional path into college—earning a high school diploma or GED, taking a placement test, beginning college courses—were prepared neither academically nor culturally. And only a relatively small percentage of students were making the transition from developmental education into college-level courses.

During our visit to EPCC, we learned why college readiness has been such a formidable challenge. Staff and faculty told us that many students come to college believing that a college degree is a ticket to a better life but with woefully little understanding about what it takes to get that degree—including what it means to be ready to take college-level courses. In short, many students arrive on campus at EPCC with little understanding of what college will demand of them. One counselor described many students' approach to college as almost a vicarious experience in which they are living out the aspirations of a family with little understanding of higher education. Not surprisingly, students often apply to programs that are linked to someone else's aspirations and take classes for which they have neither the background nor the commitment to succeed.

The challenges that many EPCC students (over 80 percent of whom are Hispanic) face in getting ready for college are often complicated by the fact that they come to college as English-language learners from neighborhoods that are culturally and economically distant from mainstream higher education. Many EPCC students come from families that are blending and reconciling two cultures; many students literally move back and forth between Juarez,

Mexico, and El Paso. For these students, the process of getting ready for college—from applying for admission, to securing financial aid, to making sense of a course schedule—is intimidating. As a staff member told us, "For a lot of them it's kind of holding on to their heritage in that they still want to keep their roots, but it keeps them from actually going full blown into . . . the American education system." In many instances bilingual, EPCC students told us that they had to become ready for a largely monolingual curriculum in a bilingual institution while, more often than not, contributing to sustaining their family in "another world." As one student put it, the challenge was understanding "how to work [her] way through college as a bilingual adult who had every intention of continuing to contribute to her home community."

As we came to understand it at EPCC and the other MSIs in the study, the concept of college readiness means not only that students are academically prepared for college but also that they have access to information about the activities that matter in college, strategies for managing tension between the demands of college and the demands of their everyday lives, and an understanding as to why college matters in their lives. To ensure that students are both academically and culturally prepared for college, EPCC has reengineered traditional pathways for students into college through a multilayered approach. The EPCC College Readiness Initiative—which emphasizes secondary education, placement, developmental education (if necessary), and college-level courses—at once enriches and accelerates the traditional path to becoming college-ready. The Dual Credit Program and the Early College High Schools initiative offer a nontraditional route not only to college readiness but to college credits as well.

The College Readiness Initiative organizes students' entry into college on a six-step path that provides students with opportunities to become college-ready before they start their college career.[2] In the first two steps, students still in high school, and also those who arrive at EPCC with a diploma or GED, have an opportunity to learn about placement, admissions, and financial aid in a comprehensive orientation, and then to take the college placement exam. In these initial steps, students begin to interact with staff in the Pretesting Retesting Educational Program (PREP), a case management approach through which students develop an individualized preparation program and use computer-assisted modules to refresh their academic skills. Following their initial placement, students have a conversation with a counselor who helps them interpret their placement scores and decide their next step. For many students the next step is accessing a campus lab or a web interface to work with tutors and intelligent software to refresh their mathematics, reading, and writing skills. Often upon retaking the placement test, a fifth step, they place out of one or more levels of developmental education or test into college-level classes. Some students take a sixth step and enroll in a five-week intensive Summer Bridge program that helps them build the basic skills they need to be ready for college while also learning strategies for managing time, finances, and the academic demands of college courses, along with developing a comprehensive plan for their college education and their life after college. We learned that this systematic approach to guiding students into college has increased the percentage of entering EPCC students who are culturally and academically ready to begin their classes and, at the same time, reduced the developmental education needs of EPCC students.

The Early College High Schools expand a traditional dual credit program. Across Texas, dual credit serves to jump-start high school students' college careers by giving them a chance to show they are college-ready and to discover that they can do college-level work while they are still in high school. The ECHSs bypass the limitations of the Dual Credit Program—high schools can offer dual credit classes only to the extent that college-credentialed high school faculty are available. Each ECHS, which is linked with an EPCC campus and staffed primarily by college-credentialed teachers, recruits motivated students with a cross section of experiences and academic preparation into a school with a college-going culture and supportive and proactive counselors. Once they have shown they are college-ready, ECHS students gain access to dual credit classes on their own campuses and college classes at an EPCC campus that, in most cases, is but a short walk away. A cohort of ECHS students graduate from high school each year with an associate degree, with some already having been accepted as juniors in regional and national colleges and universities.

As we talked with students, staff, and faculty about the EPCC investment in college readiness, we early became aware of the shared belief across stakeholders that every EPCC student can be prepared to seize a higher education if provided with relevant opportunities. Most noteworthy, two initiatives are having a very significant impact on student success. First, EPCC has redesigned the traditional path to college through the College Readiness Initiative and

PREP. Second, EPCC is forging a nontraditional pathway to college through Early College High Schools.

EPCC College Readiness Initiative: Redesigning the Traditional Path to College

Charged with increasing the number of high school graduates who meet the Texas Success Initiative standards upon matriculating to a college or university, the College Readiness Implementation Committee—cochaired by EPCC and UTEP leaders—studied placement data, reviewed published literature, and conducted focus groups. They found that students often entered college with little understanding of the costs and benefits of a college education, the cognitive demands of college courses, and the time it takes to complete a college degree. Immediate improvements to levels of student readiness were possible, they hypothesized, if the college could help the students who arrived at its doors—both those still in high school and those arriving at the college with a high school diploma or GED—understand what it means to matriculate and also what resources can improve their odds of success.

This approach was anchored in the widely shared understanding that EPCC students getting ready on the traditional college path can succeed. They just need relevant information about college. One student who was successfully making the transition to college-level courses from a less than stellar high school experience described the challenge as staying on top of it. In EPCC college readiness programs, knowing what was expected and what she needed to be able to do before she started college was critical for her. Across our interviews students described the importance of knowing how much they would have to read and what would be expected of them in terms of writing and math. The challenge to being ready for these students rested on knowing what to be ready for. Faculty and staff agreed. Many EPCC students, as one counselor put it, are "dusty" when it comes to academic work; they have to "retrieve" their own successful academic experiences from their past and remember what is involved with being a successful student or, in many cases, doing algebra. The need to refresh often incompletely developed academic skills, one PREP counselor explained, leads many students—especially nontraditional students—to lack confidence that they will be able to become ready or to balance being "a mom, a worker, a student, and all that stuff."

As we listened to students on the traditional path who successfully used EPCC college readiness programs and to the staff who supported them, we came to see that the initiative was both high-tech and "high-touch." All of these programs systematically gather for students the information and tools they need to get into the college program of their choice, and program staff and fellow students become an important network of support.

High-Tech Assessment and Learning Resources

EPCC leaders agree that the College Readiness Initiative has provided a relevant and efficient pathway into college for local students. In our interviews with students, staff, and faculty, two related strategies mattered: talking openly and specifically about what college readiness means, and establishing a resource-intensive matriculation process that leads to enrollment in college-level classes.

The College Readiness Initiative is foremost a conversation across stakeholders—staff, faculty, and administrators across institutions but also students and their families—about who EPCC students are, how well prepared they are for college, how they fare in college, and what can be done to improve their odds and speed them toward their educational goals. The leaders of the initiative recalled transformative conversations in the El Paso Collaborative for Academic Excellence about data EPCC collected as part of the Achieving the Dream Initiative. As one administrator told us, "In that room right there, in that boardroom right there, we had a round table and at that round table we had the presentation similar to what we showcased today: the data."

An administrator charged with implementing part of the initiative described layers of engagement with information about student outcomes. Administrators pass data along to frontline staff and use them to create and revise policies that govern the transition between high school and college. Frontline staff members help to interpret and collect data and use them to redesign the curriculum and programs. A dean described hiring faculty to use placement data to develop a precollege curriculum that prospective students could use to assess their own readiness.

This information does not remain at the college. In advising appointments and in revamped orientations, prospective students hear about what the college is learning about college readiness. This same information makes it into local school districts. "When we started," an administrator recalled, "we wanted to have information given to the high schools and the high school students and their parents but also the high school faculty." EPCC wanted, she went on to explain, to ensure that the El Paso community understood both "what college readiness meant" and what students and their communities could do to be college-ready before the first day of a student's first college class. Counselors described providing entire families with guided, bilingual opportunities to learn to read placement test results and degree plans and to access resources—financial aid and tutoring as well as transportation and child care—that would make college possible. Sometimes those conversations, one counselor noted, come to the agreement that "maybe this isn't the best semester . . . to come to school. . . . Maybe next semester would be the better time." These conversations are grounded in "the data."

The use of student outcomes data is bounded by the six-step protocol that structures students' entry into college. For students trying college for the first time, the process begins with an orientation that one student described as a workshop. The goal of that experience is to limit student choices based on what the college has learned about EPCC overcoming the challenges facing students. Students who are not yet ready for college, an administrator explained, often find themselves in classes that do not match their academic readiness and may not lead them toward their goals, two outcomes that work against student success. By limiting choices and thereby lessening the confusion students face, they have a chance to decide "what they want to do and the direction they want to take. In the meantime, they haven't wasted any time."

Facilitated by PREP staff, the orientation is a sophisticated kind of triage in which PREP counselors help students determine how ready they are for college, academically and culturally, and in turn what they need to do to meet their goals. To a large extent, the counselors we interviewed used the orientation as a means of providing students with an operational definition of academic readiness. The workshop script includes what the placement test covers, how scores are used, and what students can do to prepare. An administrator emphasized the importance of introducing students to how an adaptive placement test works. Students need to understand that on an adaptive test, mistakes on questions about mixed fractions—a relatively low-level mathematical construct that students likely mastered years earlier—may mean that the test taker never gets to make use of what she learned more recently in a precalculus class. A counselor confirmed the importance of being knowledgeable about the test. In her orientation sessions, she talked about the test as a tool that opens doors to college and in some instances to degree programs. Understanding what is tested and what scores mean, she emphasized, is critical for students.

This counselor added that the orientation goes beyond discussions of placement tests to link academic readiness with having a plan. In the orientation, EPCC staff members differentiate among degree programs and classes and clarify what kinds of opportunities are linked to different kinds of degrees, in El Paso and beyond, and how students can and cannot move between different kinds of degrees. Filling out the joint EPCC/UTEP application—the next step in the protocol—makes the definition of readiness "real" as students grasp whether they have a plan and what courses will be part of that plan. One counselor noted that it is not unusual for students who are completing the first steps in the protocol of the EPCC College Readiness Initiative to be referred to Career Services when they realize they do not have a plan.

This protocol guides students from an orientation to their first attempt at placement—the second step in the protocol. PREP staff members we interviewed were quick to emphasize the importance of retesting. Two College Readiness leaders said the first placement scores were not accurate for most students. PREP was developed for students to learn from their first test and test again. Between testing and retesting are two interventions that not only improve the accuracy of student placement but also provide students with the opportunity to be ready for college before they start.

After students take their first placement test, they have an appointment with a PREP counselor who helps them make sense of their scores. The counselors we interviewed saw this appointment as central to the College Readiness Initiative. One, for example, described talking an anxious student out of taking a class one level below his placement and encouraging another student dismayed by her placement deep in developmental education to believe in her abilities and make use of PREP labs to refresh her skills. As this counselor put it, "It's just a matter of going back and retrieving it, dusting it off; you'll be in a good place." Postplacement counseling, she explained, ensures that students start college with an appropriate experience—even if that experience is in developmental education. Students we interviewed confirmed the importance of the interaction with counselors following their first attempt at the placement test. In effect, counselors become their anchor at EPCC. One student who entered EPCC by way of the College Readiness Initiative described her matriculation process this way: "When I first came in they give you a placement test. They said, 'You did pretty bad. So we're going to put you in the beginning classes and then you need to go to one of our helpers,' so that's how I ended up with my counselor. Ever since then anytime I need help or anything I always go in and say can you please help me?" She went on to explain that her interaction with the counselor helped her understand how to access college—and bypass a number of remedial courses—and what program matched her interests. PREP counselors become indispensable helpers to many students as they prepare for college course work.

Referrals in postplacement counseling connect many students with what one counselor called "tools." PREP interventions—the fourth step in the protocol—include, in the words of a PREP administrator, a variety of techniques that help students refresh the math, reading, and writing skills assessed by the placement test. Pursuing the explicit goal of college readiness, students use PREP labs—spaces where new students have access to tutors and technology—to get college-ready. Because the placement tests used in Texas do not provide formative feedback, EPCC adopted a computerized math learning system that provides detailed feedback on what students need to learn and a set of aligned learning materials and additional diagnostics that help students know when they are ready. The goal, the PREP administrator explained, was an intervention for each student that was "very specific. It should be individualized and then they should be able to enroll."

From the point of view of a counselor, these interventions have led to precise and accurate assessment of challenges and competencies. Plato, the math learning system adopted at EPCC, "tells us exactly what it is that they need to go back to. . . . The way I look at it is kind of fill in the blanks because they've been exposed to this information. It's just a matter of going in and filling in the blanks." Students affirmed the value of this tool. We heard several stories of students skipping multiple levels of developmental education after working with Plato. One student said that the software along with the PREP lab worked because she was able to focus on a narrow set of skills and become ready through a set of explicit steps without being judged. A PREP lab manager noted that because the software is integrated with the college student record system, counselors can keep track of student progress and, when necessary, intervene in the progress of each student and help him or her

determine when it is time for the final step in the protocol: retesting that results in accurate placement.

"High-Touch" Networks of Support

The EPCC College Readiness programs are systematic, comprehensive, and
computer-assisted. While the high-tech matriculation process has helped
many El Paso students get academically ready for college, it is the human
connections with EPCC staff that enable many students to make use of their
preparation. The key factor in the success of the EPCCs is, in the words of one
leader, "personal connection": "The more I'm in this business . . . I think
we've forgotten that the key factor in helping people be successful is the connections that they make with others—could be with their faculty, could be
with peers, could be with a counselor. I think that's what the PREP program
does. It allows them to make a connection with a person."

Personal connections often begin when an EPCC staff member brings the
college to the places where El Paso students live. For one College Readiness
program administrator, this not only includes presenting information at local
high schools—from descriptions of financial aid, to opportunities to take a
placement exam, to recollections of her own experience as a college student
from El Paso. It also means representing a slice of college-going culture for
prospective students as EPCC staff members make college come alive for prospective students. Staff variously described their interactions with students
in terms of stand-up comedy, counseling, advice, talk about shared experience, and guidance. Staff members take up these multiple modes of communication to draw students into reflective two-way conversations about what
students wish to make of college and then to forge relationships.

As we listened to recollections of conversations between prospective EPCC
students and EPCC staff, we were struck by how students and staff members
described their roles. One student told us that her PREP adviser, who was also
from Mexico, talked about her own experience as a bilingual student and professional and "inspired me to give my best effort because she also had trouble
with the language and everything." Students who sustain interactions with
College Readiness staff, one staff member explained, begin to do things that
they themselves admit they wouldn't have done without those interactions.
She described students who, with her support, managed to make academic
progress despite losing a place to live or a way to get to school. They became

college students who were able to stick it out, in large part because they connect through personal bonds to EPCC resources that help them become college ready.

More than just drawing students into college-ready practices, College Readiness programs encourage students to carve out pathways that match their goals. One administrator who does outreach in local schools described an interaction with a high school student who wanted to become a diesel mechanic:

> His mom was very adamant about him going and earning a four-year degree, but that's not what he wanted to do, so he probably would have dropped out had he not found this other program. She was like, "No, no, no, the money is not as good." That was her thing. The money is not as good as if he earns an engineering degree, but it's like that's not what he wants to do. His passion is working on cars.

Reflecting on this interaction, she described her job as using information about programs and outcomes to draw this student into conversations about what he was ready to do in college and, as importantly, what he was not ready to do. "You be what you want to be," she told him. "At the end of the day it's you living in your skin, so it's what makes you happy."

As part of the process of validating prospective students as eligible members of a college-going culture, EPCC staff members invite students to reflect on their own college readiness and what it means for them to go to college. An adviser described how she used conversation about placement scores to ask questions such as "How do you feel about the test? Do you understand everything? What would you like to do at this point? . . . The last word is the student's." Students confirmed that their interactions with College Readiness staff often led them to think differently about college and ultimately to work harder than they had expected to and also to progress faster.

As we listened to these stories about engaging students, we were struck by a shared belief in the importance of accompanying students on their journey to become college-ready. An adviser, for instance, described walking through each step of the enrollment process with a recently divorced woman. She worked with the student to apply for aid, find money to pay for a placement exam before her student aid came through, locate a new place to live, retake the placement exam to raise her scores and qualify for a program, and use PREP course software to refresh her math skills. "It's getting them there," she explained. "They want to do it. . . . They've got so many other responsibilities." As a PREP adviser, she keeps checking in with students and building them up: "It's doable," she tells them. An outreach coordinator recounted meeting a student who saw the military as the only way out of his small rural community: "Nobody had ever really talked to him about going to college." E-mails and texts led to a scholarship. "He's now at Texas Tech," she noted in passing, and he had just texted her to ask if he could use her as a job reference.

Students confirmed the critical role of a contact inside college who stayed with them. For one student who was using the College Readiness Initiative to finish high school and prepare for college, a College Readiness instructor is the person she would go to for information, advice, and motivation. A returning adult student said her ongoing connection with her PREP adviser convinced her to "tough out" a developmental writing class. Another student seemed to sum up the presence of College Readiness staff: they help "map us into college."

Early College High School

If the EPCC College Readiness Initiative redesigns the traditional path to college, the ECHSs reconfigure public education altogether. These small, experimental high schools emerged as EPCC and the El Paso Collaborative for Academic Excellence responded to the data EPCC analyzed as part of the Achieving the Dream Initiative. The major finding was straightforward: many prospective college students—people, whatever their age, who wanted to make use of college—were not ready for college. An EPCC leader who has been instrumental in the development of the ECHSs recalled a meeting at which college presidents and district superintendents mulled over "what our data showed us" and decided, "We need to do something." One thing EPCC did was to redesign the pathway into college for high school graduates through the College Readiness Initiative. As that initiative was under way, a funder introduced the early college high school model to college leaders, and EPCC developed a plan for that as well.

Launching ECHSs involved giving a cross section of motivated El Paso high school students access to college classes as early as their first year in high school. Several challenges were associated with providing such access. First and foremost was the situation of borderland students. An assistant principal at an ECHS told the story of a student with a father in the United States and a mother in Mexico "working on getting her visa." With her father, this ECHS student crossed the border on weekends to see her mother; during the week she was the "housekeeper." The point of the story was not lost on this school leader: "So the obstacles that she had to overcome . . . and her dad . . . chances are he probably had limited schooling in Mexico, and here she is 4.0."

The situations of students notwithstanding, ECHS takes on the challenge of accelerating students' progress while establishing a college-going culture for students who come to high school with little understanding of higher education and, more often than not, significant financial and cultural barriers to becoming college students. Accelerating progress requires collaboration with multiple school districts and transfer universities so that ECHS students can move fluidly between institutions. With respect to policies and jurisdictions, the ECHSs are something of a miracle: these hybrid institutions coordinate academic calendars, curricula, books, credits, student roles, and faculty credentials and contracts across levels of education.

In spite of the challenges, these institutions are improving the odds for El Paso students. In a region that has struggled to ensure that high school graduates are ready for college, ECHSs are routinely graduating college juniors. As of this writing, the region continues to lag behind Texas and the nation in educational attainment: 70 percent of people in the region twenty-five years of age or older have attained a high school diploma or higher level of education, compared with 79 percent in Texas as a whole and 85 percent in the nation. But consider the case of Mission Early High School, the first of the EPCC ECHSs. Students at Mission are more likely to be Hispanic, economically disadvantaged, and first-generation college-goers than students in the average Texas school district. Yet these students have continued to outperform state averages on the state mathematics and reading assessments, and the most recent data showed that 87 percent of these students made an immediate transition to college compared with 57 percent in the state of Texas.[3] On average, Mission students have started college already having earned twenty-four college credits.

To learn more about the Early College High Schools, we talked with leaders across EPCC and interviewed key stakeholders (students, staff, faculty, and administrators) in a single ECHS. Two key strategies kept surfacing in these conversations. First, ECHSs define—through their policies, curriculum, extracurricular activities—a clear and coherent academic pathway that is relevant to El Paso students. Second, ECHSs enrich that pathway through what we came to understand as practice spaces with diverse resources for building college-level skills and a network of staff and faculty.

Student-Owned Pathways

When we asked students, staff, and faculty why students choose an ECHS, we early identified a key challenge faced by many El Paso high school students and shared by the high school graduates served by the College Readiness Initiative: going to high school is disconnected from going to college. Some El Paso students, one ECHS student explained, "just come to school and get their grade: 'Oh, I got a C. That's okay. That passes.'" Another observed that he and many of his peers come to school either to get away from the life they have seen their parents live or to satisfy their parents' expectations. Both of these students observed that many El Paso high school students are looking for the high school experience: sports, proms, and fun. ECHS staff and leaders noted all of these motives. They acknowledged that for most El Paso students, education needs to lead to a job in the region that enables them to provide for themselves. But they also worried that students who saw education purely as a way out or as someone else's aspiration or as a traditional rite of passage might find it hard to invest enough academic effort in school to become college-ready. For these students, education remains an abstraction that, an ECHS counselor explained, promotes fear rather than the steady pursuit of realistic goals. A student confirmed this challenge to getting ready for college: "You understand that I'm not going to be given special treatment. I'm going to be here to learn. And I'm going to do this. . . . You're placed in a situation where you have to work. You're not going to be given special treatment just because you're younger than everybody else." ECHS students are expected to invest significant amounts of effort in their own development. In support, ECHSs clarify the situations that college-bound El Paso high school students are in by providing opportunities early and often for each student to talk through what it means to be ready to complete a college degree.

The path to college that comes out of these conversations is grounded in a vision that is embraced by staff and students. At the root of the ECHS vision is open access to college preparatory education for all El Paso students. The leaders we interviewed emphasized that ECHSs do not go into districts to recruit students based on their GPAs. Teachers talked about going out to middle schools and talking to students to see what their interests are. As an assistant principal explained, his school seeks to "recruit that student that has the drive and the ambition. You don't need the straight A student. You need the student that has the will to do it." That will, he added, has to include a commitment to completing degrees. Faculty and staff explain to middle school recruits, and continually remind high school students, that ECHS students simultaneously complete high school diplomas and an associate degree. The message clearly gets through to students. Two ECHS students we interviewed considered finishing and completing an associate degree as almost automatic. Both were already envisioning careers in fields that they had researched and chosen through high school assignments, and they also had begun to pursue these careers in classes at UTEP.

Underlying this vision is, we came to understand, a deeper mission. An ECHS principal reflected that beyond completing credentials, her school staff seek to empower students who "are ready to begin and transition as juniors in a four-year institution and be able to be competitive with other people that are probably not their age but still be able to feel confident and comfortable that they can compete with the others in other institutions." The schools, one teacher explained, "instill the philosophy that if you want to get [into an ECHS], you've got to work hard. You want to succeed, you've got to work hard." Parents as well as students are challenged to meet those expectations and dream big. ECHSs cultivate students who are not just academically ready for college but also able to take their place on a college campus. They graduate having determined for themselves the point of their own education, and ready to continue their studies. The students we interviewed subscribed to the mission. One explained the opportunity as "a gateway to college" that had empowered him to take advantage of college. In the spring of his senior year, he recalled being "pushed" and asked frequently, "What do you want to be?" The child of recent migrant workers, he was ready to begin his junior year in electrical engineering at a regional university. Another student—who came from a similar background and would be a junior in criminal justice the next fall—described a similar experience. Her ECHS required her and her peers to think like college students. Recalling her anxiety about taking UTEP classes two years earlier, she laughed and said, "You get the hang of it, and . . . it's possible." An ECHS education has led her "to get through a big campus" but also, and more importantly, to find a path she loves: "I found that criminal justice . . . I love the field."

Educating graduates who are academically and culturally prepared to succeed in school and life has led to a set of strategies for providing students and faculty with the information they need to make sure that students have a plan for college. Staff put a premium on talking with students and their families about what going to college involves and how ready each student is. An assistant principal explained why this talk matters:

> I am first generation. The word "college" was never spoken in my house. I feel I have the responsibility to talk and educate the parents about overcoming that fear of what we're trying to do with the students. So I make it mandatory for me to have a parent conference. I need to meet with the parent and the student and discuss the whole process and where they are.

Other ECHS staff and faculty described similar motives for talking with students about college. The goal is not simply passing along information. In order to face the demands of the ECHS curriculum, students are expected to envision a goal beyond what one student called "high school stuff." They need, this student went on to explain, to see what they will do with math and science and even how poetry matters to their futures. Talking to other students in classes, clubs, and activities helped him "find what you really want to do . . . and what you really want to be later on."

Conversations about students' paths to college are reciprocal, ongoing, and ambitious. Foremost, the path to college is co-created—not prescribed. Teachers also work out pathways with their students. An ECHS science teacher described positioning her biology students as future health-care workers and researchers. As they work in a lab or prepare for a test, she tells them about "professionals, the importance of education, of a career," so they are acquiring the skills and habits of mind that will take them where they want to go next, in school and beyond. Teachers also work collaboratively, as two ECHS teachers emphasized, continually recreating their curriculum with EPCC and UTEP and also middle school colleagues.

An ECHS history teacher explained how she linked the high school classroom to the EPCC curriculum and college teaching practices. In her history classes, students talk about how to engage in group work and what it takes to gain appropriate college placement scores in reading and writing. She structures her classes so that her high school students ask questions not just about content but also about points of view—their own and those of their teachers. She asks them to think about how well they are reading school texts and whether they are willing to question their own and others' points of view. Many of her students, she reflected, come to understand high school as an opportunity to be responsible and to get themselves ready for the rigors of college classrooms. One student explained taking up this challenge in part because his teachers seem to love what they teach and who they teach and invited him to be passionate too.

Academic talk about students' paths to college is matched by practical talk. Staff and faculty draw information about college into routine contact with students. A counselor, for example, pointed to college banners on the walls of his office and a bookcase full of SAT preparation books, and told us, "Even from the beginning you can show them the pictures, you can show them the banners." These images and the possibilities they represent are made more real as students take placement tests and go on field trips to regional four-year campuses. College-going becomes more personal as students trace their progress on a chart on his wall, recording whether they had visited a campus or signed up for a field trip. This counselor explained that his students are accustomed to talking not only about how they are doing in their current courses but how what they are doing in those courses relates to what they will do next: "We are constantly asking them, What's your major, have you been registered, did you already fill out your college registration?"

This consistent focus on the path is not lost on students. One student described being an ECHS student as "being dropped into the college environment" with continuous support. "Initially you're terrified. And when you first get into your first speech class, and it's you, maybe three or four other students from the early college high school. But the rest of the students are twenty-year-olds. They're college students that have already graduated years ago. And the teacher, he may or may not know that you're from early college, but he treats everybody the same." Another student described the effect of being immersed in the college environment where everyone is treated the same: in that everyday practice she gained respect as a college student and "began to understand what actually an early college was."

While ECHS students own their pathways to college, faculty members take responsibility for "warming up" their ambitions. During an interview with a group of administrators, an ECHS assistant principal reminded us that many of his students come to school from communities that have few academic and financial resources and low expectations. Parents think that if their son or daughter gets an associate degree "that would be wonderful." In a high school that explicitly links being successful in high school with being successful in college, these students begin to build a pattern of success and "the incentive and the motivation to say, 'I'm going to continue with my bachelor's degree and maybe get my master's and my Ph.D.'" A counselor in this interview said, "Once the students are in here they're part of this sort of machine that just does not stop." They come to see new possibilities. The assistant principal nodded in agreement and added that an ECHS provides "hope that will lead these students to go on to the next stop." "And a pathway," a principal in the interview added.

Space to Practice

Along with inviting ECHS students and staff to co-create pathways to college, students need practice spaces in high schools that have diverse resources for building college-level skills. An ECHS administrator described the experience at the one ECHS that was not co-located with a college campus. Students, she explained, "were just having a hard time thinking of themselves as college students because they weren't going to a college, and their early college is an old elementary school." The principal responded by transforming the school culture, getting EPCC "professors" on the high school campus, and refocusing students on achieving Accuplacer scores that would enable them to take classes on an EPCC campus. The ECHS designers, she went on to explain, have had to be conscious in arranging educational spaces in which high school students feel like college students and thus have an obligation to do what college students do. When we talked with ECHS students, staff, faculty, and leaders about what mattered in the design of an ECHS, three strategies kept coming up: supporting educational space, establishing routines, and sustaining a network of guides and learners.

The ECHS we visited is a physical and cultural space that anchors in many ways the process of getting students college-ready. An EPCC campus dean recalled sitting in the room on the co-located EPCC campus and planning the ECHS with a superintendent. During the meeting, staff would point to where ECHS buildings would be and how students would move between the high school and college facilities, and then off in the distance to the homes and communities from which the students would come to the new educational space. The students in those communities were not abstract customers:

> When we're putting it together we knew that the students we were going to draw from were going to probably come to us less prepared than they would be at other districts. We also knew that they were going to [go] back to [their] homes [and] have different pressures there, sometimes even pressure to work while they're in school because the family needed that income.

Knowing the places from which students came and the campuses to which they would go had direct implications for the educational spaces that were designed. A campus dean told us that a library shared by the two campuses was designed to facilitate access to technology and support group projects and also to bring the local community onto the college campus, showing families that students could start getting ready for college early. She spoke with pride about having spaces that provide educational programs for local two-year-olds and connect faculty and students with sophisticated learning tools.

An ECHS education means establishing physical spaces for high school students to move between high school and college, but the link is stronger than physical proximity. ECHS classes and field trips and advising connect high school with college so that from the outset students begin to understand how to perform across them. At their high school, an ECHS history teacher explained, students enroll in traditional high school classes, AP classes, and dual credit classes. This teacher and two leaders described students and their teachers as talking frequently about the ways that student performance—especially placement tests—and their particular interests lead to multiple opportunities. Most ECHS students know that one of those opportunities is when they gain a placement test score that allows them to move between campuses. For these students, part of high school is walking up a sidewalk or across a parking lot or taking a bus to college. This part of high school, an EPCC ECHS liaison noted, includes informal interactions with staff members who often "make the walk" with students.

On their EPCC campus, ECHS students encounter more spaces of interaction that are designed to get them ready. Two ECHS administrators described the care that goes into sustaining a college-going culture—down to determining the mix of ECHS students and EPCC students in each class and establishing policies for Internet use. The overarching goal is to create a college environment, one administrator observed. The faculty members we interviewed at an ECHS and at a district office were convinced that the hybrid environment contributed to students' readiness. An ECHS science teacher noted, for instance, that faculty and students appreciated that ECHS and EPCC classrooms were defined by different but aligned policies and practices. An EPCC English faculty member described her college classes that included ECHS students as opportunities to teach all of her students how to interact in college.

The ECHS we visited maintains its coherence in two ways: through a set of academic routines and through a network of staff and faculty who challenge and guide students. The academic routines in these high schools constitute a system of activities that organizes the hybrid educational space. This system of activities begins with recruitment. College and high school staff and faculty spend time in local communities and middle schools, talking about opportunities and expectations and building buy-in through sharing stories of success. An EPCC dean explained this process. It begins with cultivating interest. As ECHSs have developed the reputation of a conduit to college, recruiting middle school students has gotten easier. Teachers and staff now "work with them to see what they are interested in . . . whether this is truly for them or they just want to go next door to the high school." When interested students arrive at this ECHS, they find their everyday academic lives structured by what the principal called "the College First Philosophy":

> So essentially what we're doing is that every decision that we're making, everything that we're thinking about, the way that we construct our master schedule, the way that we talk to students, we interact with them, the way that we recruit them, everything has a college feel to it. We're constantly reminding them of what the goal is and we're trying to up the level of maturity some so that they can feel confident.

This philosophy seems to run deep at the school and its co-located EPCC campus. Faculty and leaders we interviewed at both institutions made frequent references to ongoing inter-institutional meetings where curricula were compared and aligned. One leader described providing teachers at both institutions with professional development aimed at bringing to EPCC and ECHS students the technologies that are used in regional four-year colleges and universities.

The College First Philosophy guides academic routines. Most important, ECHS learning opportunities are college-level learning opportunities. Two ECHS faculty from different disciplines explained how they went about selecting assignments and activities that engage students with the same strategies that are used in the classes of their EPCC/UTEP colleagues. Being at an ECHS, they said, prompted them to ensure that students get more time in science labs, work more often in teams, identify points of view, and, one of them emphasized, "speak up." A humanities teacher explained that her mostly bilingual students worry about their accents, about how they'll sound among college students. She creates secure scenarios for them to practice speaking up where nobody's going to laugh so that they learn to ask and respond to questions and then begin to take classes over at the college. Across our interviews, we met students who were comfortable speaking up in school. One described becoming the kind of student who loves asking questions and asks them "over and over and over until I understand."

This college-level high school experience seems also to have a direct effect on the ways in which ECHS students assess their progress. As a counselor explained, these students, as a cohort, expect to be college-bound. As they move toward that goal, many begin to push each other to higher levels of performance. Since talk about getting ready is ubiquitous, students notice that "so and so did this. Okay, well, I've got to do that one better. So and so did and you announce how they did and okay if they scored that I want to do better. They took a college class and made a B? I'm going to make an A. It's that internal motivation that keeps them going to keep going further." This counselor, along with a science teacher and an administrator, told us that as students come to understand what is involved in being college-ready, many begin to want better educational opportunities for themselves and their peers. They may want a visit to a more prestigious university. They want to attain GPAs or test scores or take classes that lead to new opportunities, including scholarships that will fund those opportunities. In the words of an ECHS administrator who also teaches English at EPCC, they "get very mature . . . they're learning."

It is important to emphasize that the network of teachers and counselors guides students toward the goals that students seize for themselves. A student told us that ECHS faculty and staff supported her not only as she learned to be a college student but also as she discovered what she wanted to do: "They supported you. . . . They never shut the doors at you, and they never neglected to help you." Put simply, faculty and staff members believe that college readiness grows out of conversation. ECHSs, an administrator emphasized, hire faculty and staff who "are not just their teachers." They find qualified high school teachers who are prepared to interact regularly with college faculty and teach dual credit courses; they act formally and informally as tutors, counselors, and curriculum designers. Teachers and staff together serve as "students' mentors, their advisers. They stay on top of them. . . . They're the ones that really launch the students the most."

Beyond serving as guides, ECHS faculty and staff are for students a college-educated extended family. In many ways, these teachers and counselors share their students' worlds. For instance, an assistant principal explained that his own unlikely decision to go to college grew out of conversations with his family members:

> Neither of my parents went to college. I think one of them finished high school and that was it. You could get by at that time. . . . My father would say, "You have to go to college. That's nonnegotiable; you're going to college." So that was already instilled within me, and then having older brothers and sisters, they were going to college, so I went to college. I have a very good friend who has told me, "You know what, had it not been for you and your brothers, I would have never gone to college."

He went on to emphasize that he and his colleagues often sought out these conversations with ECHS students. They "know the names of all the students," he explained, and they listen: "What's wrong? What do you need? 'Well, I need this. I need that.' Okay, this is what you're going to have to do. Guide them through the process." We watched him pause as he guided us between campuses and talked with a student he had not seen for a while, setting up an appointment with her before he walked us to our next interview.

New Designs for Pathways for Student Success

Challenged to develop strategies to improve regional educational outcomes, EPCC has developed a culture that is anchored in the educational success of local students and, to that end, open to transforming the organization by understanding the needs of students and then building and implementing innovative ideas for advancing student success. Throughout our campus visit, we found participants consistently drawing on three shared beliefs about education.

First, the staff, faculty, and administrators believe in the potential of every student. They assume that although their students are not equally prepared— far from it—they are all capable of succeeding. This assumption has prompted leaders and frontline staff to develop multiple paths and strands of support for their students such that whatever their prior experience, students could find a way into college.

Second, EPCC staff members collaborate across levels and institutions as a routine part of their job, part of the way higher education works in El Paso. A senior leader explained a widely shared institutional belief in looking at data and improving rather than blaming students or other institutions. The college has created "this team environment where everybody is on the same page and working for the same goal, rather than feeling defensive." Convening cross-institutional groups is part of organizational life at the college. For example, several staff members recalled meetings attended by two college presidents and a handful of school superintendents. This commitment to inter-institutional collaboration leads ECHS leaders, teachers, and staff to look systematically for opportunities to manage and align policies and practices across levels. Finally, across the programs we studied, staff are reallocating resources as needed and thinking differently about traditional educational tools such as standardized tests, remedial education, and high school. Faculty are experimenting and adapting teaching styles, curricula, and tests in response to their students and their collaborators at other institutions.

Toward the end of an interview, an Early College High School principal summed up the impact of these strategies:

> You're asking what does a student look like. A student looks confident, feels confident, is not intimidated to talk to adults in a mature setting,

is able to ask questions and find solutions. That's what a student looks like. It's a student that when you get them in eighth grade or that when they finish eighth grade and come into ninth grade they're not really sure about what they want to do, what a major is, what a career is, what the differences are. When they leave they know exactly what they want to do, what the differences are. They can counsel, advise a traditional student in ways that a traditional student never even dreamed. A student that is successful, a student that sort of is enveloped by everything we have here, understands the process through and through and can probably help us advise the younger generations.

Simply put, EPCC is empowering students to be ready. While the college is still the point of access to higher education for students who need some remediation, fewer students in 2008 needed remediation than in 2003, when the College Readiness Initiative was instituted, and those who needed remediation spent less time in remedial classes.

San Diego City College: A First-Year Experience

When you think of San Diego it is likely to be about the beautiful parks and the beaches, or perhaps the Gaslamp Quarter with its restaurants featuring outdoor seating. Many of us may well link San Diego with that part of the American Dream that is California. The area of the city in which San Diego City College (SDCC) is located has patches of beauty, and people on the campus are very welcoming. But the buildings are low to the ground, and classrooms are tightly packed together. Students in one classroom can hear the activity coming from the rooms next to them. The thinness of the walls even caught our attention as we interviewed students, staff, and faculty. We wondered if it might be difficult for students to stay focused. Such noise distractions didn't seem to matter in the least to the students we interviewed. Every student we spoke with was highly appreciative of the opportunities they had to pursue their education at SDCC. The college is, we came to realize, a "borderland" college that is serving students who have come to California from all over the world in search of new opportunities.

In 1914, the San Diego school district established San Diego Junior College, the city's first and California's third two-year college. Over the next few decades the college expanded to better serve the needs of the city, first with an evening college and subsequently with three branches: San Diego Vocational High School, San Diego College–Arts and Sciences, and San Diego Evening Junior College. In 1972, the city of San Diego voted to create a separate community college district that would serve the urban core and surrounding communities. A multicultural institution that serves about 18,000 students and reflects the diversity of San Diego, SDCC enrolls a student body that is nearly two-thirds students of color—a majority of whom are Hispanic.

In 2004, the college received federal funding as a Hispanic-Serving Institution to centralize academic opportunities and expand support services for its many at-risk students. In that five-year project, SDCC received funding under Title V of the Higher Education Act to centralize academic support services. In turn, SDCC administrators and faculty developed a widely shared understanding of the challenge of the mismatch between what most colleges have offered first-year students and what a significant proportion of students need in their first year of college. Faculty and administrators we interviewed summed up this mismatch with the phrase "basic skills." California community colleges are part of a hierarchical system that is designed to provide access to degrees, not to provide opportunities to learn basic skills. These institutions are not and do not wish to be "basic skills colleges," in the words of an SDCC administrator. This administrator went on to say that the primary commitment to providing a rigorous college education puts these institutions in a bind: "As an open-access institution, we don't have the legal authority and most of us here don't have the philosophical bent towards saying, 'You're academically underprepared. Go somewhere else.' There is no somewhere else in California." His response to this bind was blunt: "We already are a basic skills college based on who our students are. So let's wake up and do something about it!" At San Diego City College, he went on, "we're trying to wake up."

"Waking up" is connected to three major challenges regarding entering students at SDCC. First, college faculty and staff need to respect the students who come to the college not only with limited preparation but also with an uncertain commitment to college and distractions from completing an education—often including having limited financial and academic resources. Every one of the faculty members we interviewed said that they have come to admire their students as people who choose to be in college in spite of challenges in their lives that often work against their being successful college students or even knowing what a successful college student does.

Second, SDCC has to ensure that there is space—not only classrooms but also staff time and institutional resources—for strengthening the basic skills of students. Committing substantial resources to basic education is very challenging. Academic support services—counseling, tutoring, support staff, and so on—make considerable demands on shrinking budgets. No less important, making space for basic skills education means offering the classes—including remedial courses and student success courses—students need when they need to take these courses. These below-college-level courses compete with upper-division classes for space and resources. "Everything," a leader explained, "is coming out of a shrunken, fixed box." Setting aside space to develop basic skills or meet with a peer mentor or develop an educational plan is equally difficult for students who have little time and few resources to spare. Beyond building new skills, SDCC is confronted with rethinking what it is that colleges and college students do.

Finally, "waking up" means talking openly about students' educational trajectories. While SDCC seeks to increase the number of college graduates and transfers to four-year schools in the region, statewide policies and SDCC resources strongly encourage students to take an efficient path toward an explicit goal without wandering. Students, an administrator explained, have to stay focused: "You've got to stay on track and it's narrow, narrow, narrow." And the track they pick has to be realistic. "It used to be all encouragement. . . . Yes, go to San Diego State University. They have financial aid; they have an Extended Opportunity Program. But now . . . as faculty and staff and first-year programs help students become academically prepared, they have to help students think critically about the value of different degrees and the realities of student loan debt." SDCC students need space to learn to be college students, but their college career has to have a clear end point almost before it begins.

An upper-level administrator summed up this challenge by calling our attention to what transpired four years earlier when all of the colleges in the district initiated pilot first-year experience programs. The triggers were "data and . . . experience" that pointed to "[cohorts of] first-year students that were unprepared to be successful in college-level courses." These students, he explained, needed additional support at the moment when the state was reducing budgets for higher education. SDCC was challenged with efficiently moving toward uplifting students who know little about college and are not quite prepared for college-level work. These data, he went on, "certainly caught our attention." Between 2004 and 2009, the college increased its total enrollment by over 3,000 students, but too many of these new admissions did not move forward. Data for 2004 show students of color and students in remedial education lagging behind White students in course success rates and GPA. First-time freshman GPAs were half a point below those for returning and transfer students; 40 percent of first-time freshmen did not return in the spring. The term-to-term persistence of students who did not self-identify as transfer students was fifteen points lower than that of those who self-identified as transfer students.

In response, Student Services at SDCC launched the college's First-Year Experience (FYE) program. As we interviewed students, staff, and administrators directly involved in the FYE as well as the faculty who taught first-year courses, we found that San Diego City College has successfully redesigned what students, staff, and faculty expect the first year of college to be. In what follows we sketch a portrait of the FYE program and then describe approaches to teaching and learning used by faculty who teach FYE courses.

The FYE: Redesigning College Entry for Students

Providing integrated support for underprepared first-year students is not new at SDCC. The Extended Opportunity Program—a statewide program—has been in operation for decades. In 2004, having received Title V funds to develop student learning communities, SDCC began developing a first-year experience for students who tested into remedial education. Leveraging what it had learned about improving the experience of entering students, in 2010 the college acquired a second Title V grant. As an administrator explained to us, the purpose of the grant was to focus on "incoming students with certain kinds of needs and [to] pay a lot of attention and give a lot of guidance." Along with providing a suite of first-year services—a comprehensive orientation, placement assessments, advising, tutoring, and counseling—to all students, the First-Year Experience would structure those services into a series of experiences that gave students a great start to college.

The basic structure of the FYE is straightforward. Students who qualify for the program enter the college the same way as all students at SDCC: after applying for admission, and often for financial aid, they complete English and math placement, attend a mandatory new student orientation and first-semester course planning, register for courses, and begin college. Students in the FYE receive early-priority class registration in their first year, are connected with a peer mentor and a personal career counselor, and sign a Mutual Responsibilities Contract that commits them to meeting with their peer mentor and counselor. In addition, they draft a personal education plan, participate in a series of campus events, and enroll in twelve credits each semester in a prescribed course schedule that includes courses in English and math as well as personal growth classes.

The FYE is a highly circumscribed path for students that leads them to begin their second year in a program with a clear purpose. We identified three core strategies that are at the heart of the FYE: (1) use information about students' characteristics and goals to customize their first year; (2) connect students to a reciprocal network of peers and staff who guide them to and through college; and (3) facilitate for each student the development and implementation of an efficient and realistic educational plan.

Getting relevant information about college is vitally important to SDCC students. The students we interviewed recalled arriving at college being confused about and even afraid of an education that "I wanted to do and I knew I needed to do." For example, one student remembered wondering, "How am I going to do this?" Another said that she initially made choices about her major based solely on what she had seen around her while growing up and struggled with whether those choices would take her where she really wanted to go and with how her classes related to her initial goals.

Another student told us why information about college-going mattered. Many of his peers held a narrow, largely instrumental view of college that neither motivated them nor helped them make choices about what to do when course work became demanding or when even making time to go to class was difficult. For students who come to SDCC focused on how their education will pay off, he said, starting school is "a little blurry." As they juggle their lives and academic work, they do not know how to approach thinking about "what you want for the next ten years, what you want to work on, or what major you want to do." Many stop out because they do not have information that helps them decide what to do for now.

In our visit to SDCC, we took note of the way the FYE program gathers and circulates information: FYE staff members listen to students. Interactions are at the center of the FYE—five formal appointments, monthly meetings with a peer mentor, and four events over the course of the year—and are designed to invite students to voice their interests and needs. When she was asked about what we came to understand as listening proactively, a staff member exclaimed, "But that's my job." In so doing, she draws on her interactions with other students and anticipates what new students might need to ask, "even if they're not aware they need to ask for that." As student interests and needs emerge, frontline staff members make referrals, often introducing students to a tutor, a career adviser, or a center director so that students are not only aware of new services but also comfortable with them. These kinds of interactions are backed up by a set of data systems: progress reports, FYE attendance databases, and an early alert system. An institutional researcher described sitting with faculty and staff to explore ways to know what's really going on with students. Beyond crunching numbers about student retention, the FYE program is, in the words of this staff member, building a "culture of inquiry" around student interests and needs.

This culture of inquiry extends to students themselves. One of the students we interviewed said that the FYE served as a kind of stepping-stone to his future by helping him discover who he wanted to be. He started school thinking "I'm not ready. I don't have the money. I probably don't even have the speech to even go to university. I just felt like I wasn't ready." Initially with his FYE counselors and then in personal growth classes, he figured out that college is intimidating for a lot of SDCC students who have to decide not just what they wish to do but also whether their education makes financial sense for them and their families. He and his first-year peers, he told us, face a critical decision: "You're kind of like 'Oh! Do I really want to do this for the rest of my life?' You're thinking about it financially. You're trying to help out your family." The FYE program provided him with the opportunity to talk through his decision making with his peers, a peer mentor, and a counselor. These conversations, he added, were enriched by information provided in FYE counseling sessions and through "personality tests and stuff like that." As he became more "aware of . . . what's going on," he and his peers became more willing to "try your first step and see what you like."

SDCC has used what it has discovered about FYE students to structure their pathways. Based on SDCC's decade-long study of students' first-year progress, the FYE has reassembled a suite of individual programs, many of which were already available, into a pathway. As an administrator described this:

I think you start building a student expectation that goes out more than two or three days from where they're standing right now. They can begin to see what a semester looks like and that helps them picture an academic year and then a goal and a conclusion coming into view, be it graduation or transfer. I just don't think that having a student come across raw, even to a wealth of opportunities and services, is sufficient. I think you have to put them together in a package, you have to introduce the student to the package and then you walk them through at least their first semester, if not the entire first year, so they get used to that new pathway.

A highly structured path, a staff person added, is critically important for two reasons. First, students on the FYE path with no prior college experience learn the things new students need to do to be successful in college. Second, and even more important, program staff guide them into activities that have been structured for FYE students and in many instances are facilitated by a peer mentor—a successful SDCC student who shares his or her strategies. The pathway culminates in an educational plan that is "based on their assessment results and their career goals and helps them decide on their major, helps them in their first steps on the college campus."

The FYE uses information about FYE students' interests and needs to narrow their first-year path. The staff members who interact with FYE students routinely described determining where students should go next and pushing them toward relevant support. Program benefits—priority enrollment and support—come with a trade-off. In the words of an administrator, "You do what we say": "When you assess into certain levels of English and math that's what you take your first semester. You don't put it off, you don't delay, you don't start wandering through the curriculum taking what your friends like or what you heard about. You start on the pathway to what we know to be a successful pattern. . . . Start with what you need to build up to and then move into the college-level curriculum."

Networks of Learners and Teachers

When asked what matters most about the FYE, a student answered "Connection." The FYE helped him understand that his academic success is the result of interdependence and networking. Contact with others—from peers to advisers and faculty members—led him to secure the keys for getting started in college, managing an intimidating environment, and establishing "future references." Many of the SDCC students, staff, and faculty we interviewed described various ways in which the FYE network of staff and students draws students into deeper involvement in their own education. In the words of an FYE administrator: "We're noticing students are taking advantage of the activities, seeing their counselor. They're returning and their GPA is a little bit higher than students that were less involved. We're seeing a difference in the students."

This network puts FYE staff and students in two-way relationships. A lead counselor explained to us that counselors and mentors—who are as diverse as the students they serve but who all "pretty much grew up in the neighborhood"—guide FYE students by building a relationship: "They share their own experience with them and kind of build a rapport with a student. They are there to listen as well as maybe guide them. We don't want them to say, 'Okay this is what you do.'" Peer mentors, an FYE staff member—herself a community college graduate—reminded us, are critical in this process. As experienced and successful students, peer mentors share their strategies, and first-year students can bond with them to help integrate themselves into the campus community.

We came to think of the contact between the members of the network as reciprocal, both contractual and voluntary. An FYE program administrator told us that the program is successful to the extent that students show up. A frontline staff member and former SDCC student described the importance of inviting her mentees to come to events with her. They get involved when they realize, "Oh, okay. I know somebody who is going to be at that event." An administrator added that the FYE network turns out students and staff for program activities because the network gives each student the opportunity to be on a team, one that includes a peer mentor and a counselor but also other students in FYE personal growth classes. Being part of an FYE team, a staff member told us, involves students in activities that keep them moving toward their educational goals. The FYE team often includes supplemental instructors, experienced peers who provide academic support in their classes. Many FYE students take classes as part of a cohort or walk together to meet with academic support staff when they feel they are struggling academically. It is just as common for teammates to accompany a student's team on a visit to career counseling, mental health services, or other campus resources. The team, an FYE leader told us, supports students as they engage in service learning.[4] Peer mentors coach students as they explain who they are and what they need at service-learning sites off campus. Team members who have walked in students' shoes facilitate students' first steps around campus and ensure that they get involved early in their own education.

A Personal Educational Plan

The structures of the FYE and the FYE network share an overarching purpose for each student: the development of a realistic and efficient educational plan that provides them with a map of college—a pathway to and through college. The FYE facilitates both the development and the usage of the map throughout the first year.

The contractual nature of this process, one leader emphasized, is critical. For most SDCC students, and especially those eligible for the FYE program, going to college is not simply the next step in growing up; it is a choice. Academically and often financially underprepared for college, and with few of the habits of successful students, FYE students are likely to make delayed decisions about filling out financial aid applications, picking classes, or arranging transportation or child care. Too often, students get caught starting their education without books, without fees, and without transportation. The FYE rearranges the process of student choice by requiring students to make decisions early so that, as a leader recalled, there is "no more scrambling. . . . They're ready to go."

The benefits of the FYE program—early enrollment, comprehensive academic support, a ready-made social network—come with requirements. A plan is one of the requirements. The program arranges a student's first year through what we came to see as a planning process: deciding to enroll, picking classes, reflecting on one's interests, selecting a major, gathering information about requirements, and even preparing to transfer. From one student's point of view, the program "put [her] out there," so she could not be shy or "put [herself] in a box." "There," for her, meant having regular appointments with her peer mentor and career counselors and then with tutors and other staff who know where all the resources are. "There" also required visits to the college to which she was preparing to transfer and interactions at a service-learning site for which she developed a résumé and wrote thank-you notes. She and her peers were, from the point of view of a counselor who supported her cohort, required to make an educational plan within a program designed to "help them prepare throughout the rest of their time at SDCC . . . what they need to do to be successful in reaching that [goal]."

As they talked about the process of developing an educational plan, both staff and students emphasized the importance of the planning process as much as the outcome. For many, the requirement to submit an educational plan by the end of the second semester as part of their FYE contract was essential because it triggered ongoing self-reflection on their journey to and through college. The completion of required courses, regular contact with the network, and the submission of a plan are mandatory: failing to meet program requirements triggers alerts and can result in probation. But the plan also plays a different role. A leader who argued that the requirements are what make the program work told us: "We don't force students to choose a major. We encourage them because it helps them with their own thinking. It helps them latch on to something they're interested in." In inviting and supporting academically underprepared students to seize ownership over their education, the FYE educational plan supports decision making rather than a decision. The process promotes thinking about and latching on to an educational path for students who are, one student told us, often still making sense of their futures and balancing what they want with what their family wants, with what will pay off, and with what seems academically and financially feasible. Students are often, to use a counselor's words, "undecided or torn between a few different options."

Reflecting on journal assignments in her personal growth class, an FYE student described how this planning process unfolded for her:

> I flipped the pages in the book, and I was going through them. . . . I remember one of the questions was . . . How is that going to benefit me in the future? So is this career going to benefit me? Is this what I want? . . . Those journals got us thinking. Well, at least for me. . . . I felt like even though it was a drag having to write it down, it truly did get me thinking about what it is that I want to become in the future, if I'm on the right path, if I should turn left or turn right or wherever I was.

Journals and other tools—personality-based inventories, group discussions, reflective writing, individual and collaborative research on educational options, campus tours, service learning, job shadowing—were brought up by a counselor, a peer mentor, and an administrator as they described the process of crafting an educational plan. These tools, a peer mentor emphasized, are used to show students how to plan, not what to decide. Counselors build on conversations initiated by peer mentors. They start by exploring the educational and career goals that students bring to college and then invite students to reflect further on those goals by providing them with relevant information. One counselor explained introducing students to a series of inventories at a first meeting and reviewing the results—a list of "top five careers"—and providing more detailed information at a second meeting. Step by step, she explained, students move toward plans for a career and a college education.

From college classes to meetings with advisers and mentors, the FYE plan is an opportunity for students to wrestle with their expectations of/for college, including potential majors. Most of the FYE students, staff, and administrators we spoke with had a spatial metaphor for college. College is represented as path, pathway, course, route, pattern, trajectory; college is a series of steps within boundaries from where students are standing to their future. The FYE provides a map of college. We noted three major features of this map.

First, the map includes well-marked routes that students and staff have found to contribute to student success. While formal program assessment and action research on how students are moving along FYE routes is important, routes are successful because—as a counselor explained to us—they are often different trajectories than the student might otherwise have traveled, and they are paths rooted in students' growing understanding of what they can do and what might make them happy. "They end up seeing the opportunities," she observed, "that they didn't know were available or that are even more suitable. . . . I stress to my students in meetings and in our classes . . . every time I see them that they have to do what will make them happy." Finding a path starts with finding personal purpose.

Reflecting on her participation in a personal growth course, a student explained that the FYE empowered her "to reflect on myself and . . . on the things I prefer, my preferences, my interests and things that I didn't even know because I never took the time to think about and actually write down." The FYE changed her from being an underprepared student to one who "knows what's going on" and what to expect and what she needs to do to be successful.

Second, the FYE map of college helps students get somewhere by mapping out both the next step in an education and the possible ends of that education. A student who found the idea of getting a college degree intimidating explained that the FYE helped him know what to do step by step and also to develop a clear vision and a long-term pathway:

> I'm trying to study the whole, you know, how neural synapses just go on, and how to fix your brain. I was just really interested in the brain, so psychology was kind of a broad major for me. So, I was . . . maybe I'll just study neuroscience. And, you know, I really like how the lab and research work, so I've gotten into . . . biology and chemistry. And I kind of like how this goes. So, I've just started getting more into it, and hopefully I'll start studying a little bit more. I'm really excited. I want to go to the university. . . . I want to just get into it.

His experience seems to coincide with the map that a senior leader said SDCC helps FYE students develop. Students begin to have expectations "that go out more than two or three days from where they're standing right now"; they develop a "picture" of a semester, an academic year, a degree.

Finally, the map defines the first year of college, in the words of one leader, as "a kind of experience that [students] see as valuable and self-ennobling, if I can go that far out on a limb, something that is attractive to them and something that for many of our students is very different from what their lives have been up until now." The FYE maps "a way of working with new students that is successful and tested and understood and widely implemented." Systematically collecting and sharing information, FYE staff use what they described a case management approach. By way of elaboration, one program administrator described her job in terms of facilitating staff meetings in which front-line staff talk about student progress one case at a time and figure out what mode of communication to launch next—from texting students to a growing presence on Facebook and other social media—in order to maintain contact and provide support. Students clearly see in the FYE a map of their own education. The program, one student explained, "pretty much opened the doors, and they opened opportunities for us to go ahead and find what it is that we like or what it is that we find ourselves fitting into best. . . . I don't know where, I don't know how I would have gotten through." As a peer mentor put it:

It's amazing to see students realize for themselves for the first time in their life they're an adult, and they're able to make their own life decisions, and no one else can dictate that for them. And a lot of them will make a whole 180-degree change from what their parents had wanted them to do to what they are actually going to pursue after we've talked more and really identified what their personal interests and abilities are. . . . After we meet a few times, they'll say, "I'm really wanting to follow through with being an accountant because that's where my interest is and my abilities are."

They arrive, she accented, at an "agenda that they really want themselves." In short, the FYE provides a map for students who on their own would otherwise be likely to wander out of higher education altogether.

First-Year Teaching: Relevant and Collaborative Learning

The route into college charted by the FYE passes through a set of math and English classes that students are required to complete in their first year. As we interviewed faculty who teach these courses in the FYE, we came to understand that they share a set of teaching strategies that are at once relevant and collaborative. Most faculty members make substantial use of the SDCC Supplemental Instruction (SI) tutoring program, an initiative that incorporates trained, near-peer facilitators in classes. Teaching strategies, in concert with the presence of SI tutors, shapes the first-year experience by building a network of students and campus staff along with facilitating students' development of an educational plan. Based on our discussions with mathematics and English faculty, we now turn to four strategies that drive teaching in the FYE: taking students by the hand; challenging students to pursue their academic goals; creating spaces for talk about college-going and learning; and extending the social networks into first-year classes.

Taking Students by the Hand

The metaphor "take students by the hand" was used again and again in our conversations with faculty and staff at SDCC. Faculty saw taking students by the hand not as enabling students but rather as reaching out from their role as faculty member to connect with students through instruction, the curriculum, and opportunities to learn about college-going.

As they responded to our questions about student challenges and successes, faculty members rarely lumped their students; they teach individual students who have unique stories and aspirations. One instructor, for example, explained that in the first week of a developmental math class packed with content he teaches no math:

> I want to know who these students are as individuals. Why are you here and what can I do in this class for you? . . . Then I start lecturing. I would ask you [pointing to the interviewers present] who you are, who you are, who you are, and who you are. And now I start thinking, "Okay, how is my class going to work knowing that I know his limitations, I know her limitations, I know her limitations, and your limitations?" How can I then bargain that. . . . But you also have a lot of strengths. Because I figure, well, if you've been adding, subtracting, multiplying, and dividing junior high, elementary, and high school, you must have something in your brain. Let's just see where you're at.

SDCC faculty members listen to students' stories and come to understand their habits—two faculty members described talking with other faculty and with staff to learn more about their students and what worked for them. As they understand where each student is at, they engage in what a math faculty member called "a long-term process of patience, persistence, and simply not giving up" and teaching new habits and academic content "in the way I think that they understand it." This process unfolds before, during, and after classes, in office hours that are often held in tutoring labs, and through e-mails as well as through study groups with peers. It continues until students have mastered subject matter—passing classes matters—and have developed the behavioral patterns and skills to cope in college.

A math teacher we interviewed described teaching at SDCC in terms of flexibility. Her department keeps textbooks as long as possible to limit costs to students, and she makes course content available online and through student-generated summaries of textbook chapters so that students have multiple opportunities "to get the work done or demonstrate, even if they missed two or three weeks of class at the end, . . . that they got it done." Perhaps more important, though, are the lengths to which she goes to provide individualized support. Her classes include "time where we just chat" so that she understands how her students are managing the course and what additional adjustments she might need to make. Through a supplemental instructor and her own teaching practice, she makes individualized support available before, during, and after class in office hours she holds in the tutoring center.

Other interviews revealed similar strategies and a commitment to teaching students how to be college students as they learned math and English through what an English faculty member referred to as the case management approach to teaching:

> We know what they're doing. We track them. We see where they are in the classroom. We offer them help along the way. We teach them how to receive help. A lot of our students don't know how to take help. So I think those are some of the core values of success . . . that students need not just help on getting good grades but college readiness skills.

The SDCC faculty, another English teacher explained, "focus on . . . things to help students get where they needed to go." They develop learning communities that enable students to complete credit-bearing courses at the same time that they complete remedial courses, and also offer accelerated classes in which students can move through as much content as they can manage—with many students receiving credit for two courses in a single semester.

Faculty members incorporate a case management approach into their personal teaching practice as well. They become adept, as a math teacher told us, at managing the pace of learning, allowing students to engage problems at their own speed and revise their work as needed. All of the faculty members we interviewed described strategies for drawing individual students more deeply into academic activities—whether by getting students to add a one-credit Writing Center course or requiring as part of their courses meetings with an SI tutor or a study group hosted by an SI tutor. Two faculty members we interviewed—one teaching math and one teaching English—described integrating "stuff" from the FYE personal growth classes into their courses. Their students, in their estimation, need to have college "deconstructed for them," as one put it. They need "soft skills . . . things that they're supposed to have when they come to school, which they don't. They don't know what office hours are about. They don't know any of that stuff. They don't know their learning style. They don't understand who they are really."

Across our interviews, faculty members were clear that teaching the way they did took considerable effort—for they want students to own their learning.

The purpose of taking students by the hand in first-year courses at SDCC is to show them that they are ready to start college. To this end, an English faculty member described using collaborative learning and portfolio assessment so that students become aware of their strengths. Another faculty member explained positioning first-year students in writing classes and in tutorials as agents in their own education: they have to define what they want to learn and what accomplishment will mean to them. His classes, he added, provide them with "different ways for students with different learning styles to address how they gain skill. It's not just seeing a tutor. It's practice, practice, practice." As he reflected on how his teaching differed from how he was taught, a math faculty member explained that he invited FYE students—many of whom have been told they cannot do math—to determine what they need:

> You need to go forward and . . . you can do it. This [difficult math problem] is just a stick in the road. You bumped on it, you tripped, let's get back up. Every time you fall get right back up. Every time you fall you just get right back up. That's my theory . . . "you can do it." If you're willing to learn, you can do anything. This is not supposed to stop you from getting where you need to go.

A Challenging First Year

For SDCC faculty, taking students by the hand is bound up in challenging them to seize their own education. A faculty member stressed that the very first classes for underprepared college students must be meaningful: "I think that once they're in, what I try to do in my classes is challenge them and make it meaningful so that it doesn't feel like a waste of time. It doesn't feel like high school. It has to be a different tone and a different level of kind of demand, I think, and challenge." Making college meaningful and demanding for SDCC students requires—to draw on a math faculty member's explanation— gentleness and wisdom and compassion for lives that make it "hard for [students] to concentrate sometimes in my class." As he elaborated:

> I want to get them to be scholars. I want to push them like I was pushed, but it has to be done gently. I have to play almost like the good cop, bad cop kind of thing sometimes. Sometimes I have to be firm and sometimes I have to be soft. I have to carry the big stick. Sometimes I wave it, and sometimes I just show mercy and say, "Oh, it's not the time."

Challenging first-year students begins with faculty clearly expressing to students SDCC's expectations of a college education. Three of the faculty we interviewed described their methods for making academic expectations explicit for students. They talk with students about why faculty members hold office hours and what students might do to learn how to ask questions. One of them, a member of the English faculty, described this same approach to "deconstructing" textbooks, writing assignments, and grading criteria.

All of the faculty members we interviewed talked about strategies for teaching FYE students how to engage college-level material and assignments. The most basic strategy was their willingness to talk openly with students about what each assignment will involve, why they are assigning it, how the assignment can be approached, and what challenges it will entail. In short, faculty and their SI tutors model the doing of college-level work. In our visit we came to appreciate the positive impact of faculty and SI tutors serving as role models. With a full measure of candor, a math faculty member observed that he is "not everybody's cup of tea." He gently forewarns students that he will challenge them and expects them "to learn to challenge themselves."

Faculty members draw on a range of other strategies for making academic expectations clear to students. One faculty member described using a college-level text in a remedial writing course. Her goal is to ensure that students have a chance to work with the kinds of materials they will encounter beyond the first year by providing feedback and opportunities to revise their work so that they can go from shocked to ready by the finish of the term. A math faculty member described a similar approach, posing math problems that require students to think conceptually rather than simply to do calculations.

Beyond having clear expectations for students, FYE faculty members challenge students to become active in their own learning. Two English faculty members described inviting students to frame their own questions and pursue them in their own voices. A math faculty member told us that he positions his students as learners who must "keep at it until you actually understand this, not just regurgitate it, but actually understand what you're doing." For him, the classroom is "not a one-way thing." In his classrooms, he communicates to students that "I believe they can do it," and concurrently pushes them and encourages them to "tell me off" when they need to because, "Well, I think you've got to. You're going to have tensions. You can't have . . . this kind of change, you can't have change without tension."

Spaces for Talking

In order to teach the way they do, SDCC first-year faculty members establish spaces for talking with their students and among themselves about student success in college—both persistence and learning. As she thought about how she managed to differentiate instruction for her math students, a faculty member described volunteering in the Math Tutoring Center both before and after her class. She wants her students to be able to approach her routinely in "a little more open environment" than a faculty office. We came to see this practice as typical: first-year classes routinely open up safe and convenient environments for conversations that are mutually determined by participants. Faculty make time to "talk about stuff" in one-on-one conferences, in an array of organized peer learning activities, and even in assignments that invite students to choose their own topics. The faculty members we interviewed distinguish these spaces from office hours and formal instruction and use them to encourage talk with students about their progress, their learning, and their lives.

All of the faculty members we interviewed described interrupting instruction to talk with students, individually and in groups, about their progress and learning. They did this despite having to guide as many as fifty students through a packed syllabus in a single semester. At the beginning of their classes, for instance, three faculty members described talking about what it means to be in class and why it might be meaningful to students' educational goals. As an English faculty member explained it, "We just put it on the table . . . and we ask them to kind of get out their feelings initially about how do you feel about being in this class." Such conversations are in some cases supported by what a math faculty member called "kind of a pre-assessment . . . a quick little thing to see where they're at" with the relevant math and also basic academic behaviors like attending class and completing assignments. These initial chats, she added, help students make sense of how they are moving through college. In other cases, another math faculty member suggested, this initial talk about progress is a "hard sell" in which she provides students with detailed feedback on their skill level and what it may mean for their progress at SDCC. She helps first-year students see "why you want to be in this class" and to "make a decision" about how they will participate.

It was clear in our interviews that stopping instruction to talk about progress was not limited to an initial assessment. In one faculty member's practice, talk about students' progress and their learning takes place not only in classroom conversations about statistics but also before and after every class when an SI tutor hangs out with students "doing problems as just a student." For a writing teacher, conversations both in class and outside of class are written into a sequence of journal assignments and writing group activities that provide first-year students with "time and space to kind of grow as writers in writing that they chose as well as assignments . . . kind of blurring that line of personal writing with academic writing." Talk about progress and learning also occurs informally. A math faculty member, for instance, described his approach to creating space for conversation by pointing to a room of seminar tables and white boards where his students engaged problems that, he admitted, are difficult: "So I have this idea: . . . I want them to understand what they're doing. How do I get at that? Well, that's tough. . . . I have a conversation with them. We talk, and we interact so I can get some kind of an idea if they actually know what are they doing here."

We learned that talk about progress and learning happens among faculty as well as between faculty and their students. As faculty members described the leading edge of their teaching practice, they frequently pointed to robust conversations with colleagues along with hallway conversations. As one put it, faculty members have "a lot of freedom and a lot of respect for one another, vibrant community, very idea-driven, so a lot of ideas happen and people actually want to do stuff."

Making space for talk about progress and learning has two purposes: documenting success and reflecting on what led students to that success. An English faculty member, for instance, made space for conversations around writing portfolios in order to provide opportunities for her and each of her students to "see a student who has demonstrated understanding" as well as the strategies that had led to that success. A math faculty member described scaffolding conversations about whether students are ready to "treat this [class] as a job" and show up for work. These conversations about being and supporting "scholars"—about learning and becoming ready to learn more—were, we came to see, part of the job of first-year instructors and students at SDCC.

No less important is faculty members' choosing to stop teaching in order to talk with their students about their lives. They do so, one faculty member emphasized, because they cannot teach their students without doing so. As a math instructor recounted:

My first semester here my Math 46 student was doing quite well and midway through the semester he was mistaken for a gang member and shot four times. And it just seems like every semester I have these kinds of events happening in my class. . . . You cannot ignore them. I mean they're just catastrophic for the climate within the class. . . . I ask them how are you today, and the first thing out of their mouth is "I lost my job," or "My apartment burned down," and . . . you can't ignore that in the classroom.

Reflecting on the ways in which an incident in one student's life affected the climate of his class, another math faculty member elaborated further what it means not to ignore students' lives in the classroom. "I slow down and we talk about it." Students, he continued, listen when they believe that faculty "back them up." When his students' lives interrupt his syllabus, he reviews material they have already covered and restructures his curriculum, looking for ways to meet course learning goals in light of the constraints of his students' lives. Just covering content, we realized, does not work for SDCC faculty. For them, in this faculty member's words, "teaching basic skills . . . is different. It's so different. It's rewarding and frustrating all in one. It's agonizing, it's annoying, it takes a lot of energy." It takes creating spaces for talk.

Supplemental Instruction

Early in our interviewing at SDCC we asked a math faculty member to talk about what it is like to teach first-year students at the college. Comparing the college to other institutions at which she has taught, she recalled being dumbfounded by the diversity of her students: "I had no idea . . . how that diversity would change my teaching." She went on to reflect at length on the ways in which she balanced teaching each student with getting her class—"I've got a class of fifty students in there"—through the curriculum. As we listened to her and her colleagues, we realized that at SDCC taking first-year students by the hand in the classroom not only means making space for talk about college-going and learning but also establishing collaborative networks of learners and teachers who know each student and customize support for each student. The faculty we interviewed described teaching, in the words of an English faculty member, as "making community." That is, they see their courses—and they teach across levels, from remedial courses to sophomore transfer courses—as a collaboration among their students, their students' families, academic support staff who include experienced SDCC students and graduate students from local universities, and Student Services staff. "You put everyone together," as one faculty member put it.

The SDCC approach to Supplemental Instruction seems to exemplify the systematic implementation of a network of learners and teachers. SI at SDCC, as we learned from an English faculty member who was instrumental in developing the program, grew out of a conversation among Student Support Center directors and other administrators who had the freedom to talk about what the model might mean for "our campus." In his words: "What would it look like to you, Professor So-and-so, to have a tutor in your class? Do you just want a grader? Do you actually want to build a community? What does that mean if you hear that?" With a shared understanding of what SI could contribute, staff adopted a model developed at the University of Missouri–Kansas City so that SDCC could "do [SI] our way" to support "basic skills development" in the FYE program—and this despite being told that "this program will not work with basic skills or it has not worked yet with basic skills students." Central to the model—and the novel SDCC adaptation of it—is the emphasis on sustaining a community of learners and teachers. The basic SI model is built around limited faculty involvement, but SDCC faculty have discovered that SI works at the college to the extent that faculty and tutors develop a relationship. SI tutors become colleagues who draw faculty more deeply into learning how to teach SDCC students.

SI tutors are experienced SDCC students and graduate students from nearby universities who learn a method of tutoring focused on asking the question "What are we working on today?" and then listening for what the student is struggling with. Within the SDCC tutoring cycle, the students decide what the session will be about and what will be accomplished; each interaction aims at helping students to seize their own voice. SI tutors work from this framework, but they get to do more, as one faculty member elaborated:

So they're talking about what happened in the class and letting the students answer. They might get up on the board and show how to write a sentence fragment, how to correct a sentence fragment, but they're not reteaching the material. They're not teaching assistants. That's not the goal. The goal is to be tutors and provide, again, scaffolding for a discussion that may not have occurred without them.

The presence of a trained facilitator, he added, changes the culture of a class-room. Faculty members become more alert and begin to collaborate—faculty and SI tutor are never pitted against each other—to understand how students are experiencing classroom teaching. Simply put, SIs provide faculty members with valuable feedback. As a faculty member told us: "Students feel more comfortable often with them, so they'll talk to them and let them kind of know how they're doing. Even if they wouldn't tell us some things, they'll talk to their tutors."

At best, as a math faculty member who has worked with SI tutors explained, SI tutors get students to show up for class and even call them out in class. They are, she added, an inspiration for students—not a grader or another lec-turer. As experienced peers who students know by name, SI tutors sit next to them and help them get their first-year academic work done while their class marches through the syllabus. The SI tutor serves as another point of contact, another node in the network, working with individuals or groups for a few minutes or a whole class period—whatever students need.

FYE as Participation in a College-Going Culture

A senior leader in Student Services described the FYE as "organic," and that word helps to capture much of what we learned in our visit to SDCC. The FYE has emerged from a shared belief that a college education is relevant to the lives of SDCC students and in turn that these students deserve a place in col-lege. Guided by this belief, SDCC staff and faculty seek to know their students. SDCC, as faculty and staff members repeatedly emphasized to us, gave them the freedom to do things that work. In six different interviews, SDCC staff and faculty members called our attention to ways that they were using data to un-derstand each student's experience as an individual case. Their understanding of students' experience of college drives both purposeful experimentation with program structures and a deepening commitment to SDCC students.

The final dynamic that defines this story of success—commitment to SDCC students—is harder to name. As his interview wrapped up, one math faculty member gave us a gentle hug and offered this: "Do you know why I give hugs? . . . My wife taught me this. She says, 'If you don't love them, how do you expect to get information into them? You've got to love them.' You have to love your students, and that's very hard for us. It's hard." The work of the

FYI is "hard work" that means facilitating a robust first-year experience for students who are not yet ready for college. It's hard work because it entails everyone believing in college students who have been defined as unprepared to be in college and, in turn, accepting the responsibility for providing and seizing "opportunities to keep at it until [students] get it right, which goes against the grain of traditional education." For its underprepared students, SDCC has created a first year of college that goes against the grain of traditional education and makes students ready for college by accepting, with and for students, responsibility for their education. A 2013 survey of FYE students found that a larger proportion of them believed they had fewer challenges to their academic success and a positive experience with instructors than did students surveyed in 2011. Perhaps more importantly, institutional research shows that FYE students return for their second semester at higher rates than their non-FYE peers; those FYE students who work with supplemental instructors or engage in service learning persist at even higher rates and earn higher grades.

Stories of Success in HSIS

Each in its own way, the three HSIS we visited are defining a locally relevant college education and, to that end, building communities of students, staff, and faculty that guide and engage first-year students—in English, Spanish, and other languages—in their pursuit of a postsecondary education. Each of these institutions is redesigning the first year of college as a laboratory in which students not only master the first-year curriculum but also discover what college might mean for them and how they can take ownership of their college education.

La Sierra University has heavily invested in personal attention to all students—including personal and academic coaching—in their First-Year Experience program. Through its College Readiness Initiative, El Paso Community College slows down the matriculation process in order to ensure that each student is prepared academically and culturally to pursue his or her education; the EPCC Early College High Schools begin the process of getting students college-ready in ninth grade so that, upon graduating from high school, students not only have charted out an educational trajectory but in many cases completed the first two years of college. San Diego City College narrows the path into college for underprepared students to a route the college can support inside and outside the classroom, a route that guides students to make their own educational plans.

In these distinctive and carefully carved out first-year experiences, all three HSIS are expanding educational opportunities for students who often have little sense for what college means. By embedding the process of entering college in a sequence of purposeful dialogues between first-year students and more experienced campus stakeholders, these colleges are inviting students to become college-educated individuals who are preparing to pursue fuller lives for themselves, their families, and their communities. In short, these three institutions have reimagined—and redesigned—the first year of college as a place in which every student can become ready for what comes next.

5 | Historically Black Colleges and Universities

It's All in the Family

Families come in all shapes and sizes. They are filled with joy, frustration, support, betrayal, and love. Family members can be close to you at some points in your life and the people you are least likely to talk to at others. Family members provide support during your struggles and your happiness. While some family members hold you accountable for your actions, others overlook your mistakes and make excuses for them. Historically Black Colleges and Universities (HBCUs) operate much like families. Their faculty, staff, students, and alumni are deeply loyal and often tell stories of the unprecedented support that takes place on campuses. They also protect their institution from outsiders much as family members protect each other and their family's name. This is one of the reasons HBCUs have persisted for so long, but is simultaneously one of the reasons they often struggle to survive.

We begin this chapter with the story of the Peer-Led Team Learning (PLTL) in science and math at Morehouse College. We also examine the Minority Biomedical Research Support–Research Initiative for Scientific Enhancement (MBRS-RISE) program, which provides rich learning opportunities for minorities in the fields of science, technology, engineering, and mathematics (STEM). We then move to Norfolk State University, where we explore the Summer Bridge program, which draws upon role modeling and peer mentoring. Both of these institutional initiatives foster increased student success. And lastly, we consider the all-campus retention program at Paul Quinn College, which engulfs its students in a family-like environment in order to promote success.

Morehouse College: The College of Brotherly Love

Morehouse College was born out of a church basement just two years after the Civil War. Like many Black colleges birthed around the same time (including nearby Spelman College), the small Atlanta-based college's mission focused on producing future teachers and ministers. However, Morehouse was distinctive in that its dedication was to African American men. Other Black colleges were equally open to women, a fact that sets them apart from the majority of mainstream colleges and universities at the time. Originally called the Augusta Theological Institute, Morehouse College began in Augusta, Georgia, under the leadership of Reverend William Jefferson White. In 1879, the school moved to Atlanta, Georgia, seeking refuge in the Atlanta Friendship Baptist Church basement. In this new location, Morehouse College was known as the Atlanta Baptist Seminary. In 1885, the college moved to its current location in southwest Atlanta. Finally, in 1913, it became Morehouse College, named for Henry L. Morehouse, the secretary of the Northern Home Mission Society. Since 1913 the institution has been situated in the Atlanta University Center (AUC), a loosely affiliated consortium of Black colleges including Spelman College, Morris Brown College, Clark Atlanta University, and the Interdenominational Theological Center. The surrounding neighborhood is low-income, and the institution has had a conflicted relationship with the locals for decades. Morehouse students have been mugged near the campus border and, at the same time, Morehouse students have been accused of looking down on the local neighborhood from the relative privilege of a campus that often draws from a group of men who hail from middle-class and upper-income households.

Morehouse College is a selective, private, four-year college. Ranked the second-best HBCU in the nation by *U.S. News and World Report* in 2013, Morehouse has an endowment of $105 million and a total enrollment of 2,553 students.[1] The institution is considered one of the strongest HBCUs in the nation, boasting a six-year graduation rate of 53 percent, which is well above the 37 percent average for African Americans in all colleges and the 30 percent average for HBCU students.[2] Morehouse students are diverse in terms of ethnicity, religion, region of the country / world, and socioeconomic status. This selective campus enrolls a large percentage of students who qualify for Pell grants. Morehouse students range from sixteen to twenty-three years of age, and the college has a larger percentage of students who come from high-end households than the average HBCU.

The institution has a well-documented track record for empowering young Black men and sending them to graduate and professional programs. Of the top twenty institutions that produce the most undergraduate Black men who pursue doctoral degrees, Morehouse ranks seventh. The institution is one of only three small liberal arts colleges performing this well among a slew of large universities.[3] Morehouse has continued to have significant success in STEM fields. For example, out of the top twenty institutions producing the most African American science degrees, Morehouse ranks fifteenth; in contrast to all but two of the other institutions in this group, Morehouse is a small liberal arts college rather than a large public institution.[4]

Morehouse College's success in the STEM area is particularly noteworthy given our nation's competitive needs as well as the lack of Blacks, especially Black men, in the STEM fields. While there is interest on the part of many Black men in STEM fields, many are discouraged from pursuing STEM majors once in college or make the decision to switch majors after taking so-called weed-out courses, which focus on culling out of science classes those students who have difficulty with science concepts.[5] Roughly 20 percent of Blacks who enter four-year colleges intend to major in STEM, but only 6.4 percent of STEM bachelor's degrees in 2011 were awarded to Blacks.[6] And across the fields that make up STEM, Blacks continue to be underrepresented in the physical sciences (6 percent), engineering (4 percent), and mathematics (5 percent), despite evidence showing that Black students are more likely than their counterparts to believe they would achieve a degree in STEM.[7] At the graduate level in science and engineering, Blacks account for only 3.8 percent of master's degrees and 4.7 percent of doctorates. Even more jarring are the disproportionately low numbers of Black males in STEM. Males earn only 34 percent of bachelor's degrees awarded to all Blacks in STEM, and they are least represented in agricultural sciences (41 percent), biological sciences (30 percent), and physical sciences (42 percent).[8]

There are many reasons why African American males are less likely to succeed in STEM programs. First, choosing a STEM career simply never occurs to many Black males who grow up in neighborhoods where they are unlikely to meet a Black scientist or engineer and are likely to receive inadequate STEM training and preparation at the primary and secondary levels due to lack of access to college preparatory classes in science.[9] Some Black males who develop an early interest in STEM are dissuaded from science careers, in the same way many women are, because their teachers lack confidence in their potential or ability as scientists, sometimes due to racial bias. On arriving at college, many Black males find it difficult to believe that they belong in STEM majors in which they see few faculty with similar backgrounds.[10] All of these dynamics can be compounded by poor study skills or a disinclination to seek help due to the stigma attached to it.[11] In the words of one Morehouse administrator, "In the minds of many Black men, if you acknowledge or seek tutoring services, the implication is that you can't hack it, you can't cut it." Morehouse College has disproportionate success in STEM compared to most mainstream colleges and universities because it uses a unique approach that sees Black men as scholars.

The Morehouse Mystique

Morehouse engenders a certain mystique among its students and graduates, one that leads these young men to understand and believe in their potential and ability to act and lead. This mystique is a purposeful part of the college's ethos that permeates the curriculum, cocurricular activities, spaces on campus, and the expectations of the men. If you talk to an alumnus of Morehouse College or a current student, you often quickly hear the words "Morehouse Mystique." Although every Morehouse man will give you a slightly different answer, the college's official stance can be described as "We call that something the 'Morehouse Mystique.'" The phrase is not easily defined or understood, but it's also more than just a clever slogan. The mystique is joining a brotherhood like none other. And after being ignored, stereotyped, or marginalized, it's about finally finding that "home that, deep inside, you always knew existed, where you are the heart, soul and hope of the community. And where you are not alone."[12] The students at Morehouse described the mystique for us. One senior smiled while saying:

> When I came to Morehouse, seeing so many Black males achieving, it really hit home. It hits home for a lot of people because they don't really have those male role models. When you come to Morehouse, not only do you have famous alumni, you have teachers right in front of you, you have older students. I think Morehouse really serves its purpose in producing male leaders. I know I have grown as a student, person, and as a leader. I thank Morehouse for that.

Another student described the mystique as follows: "If you are here and something deep within you doesn't want to long to be a better you—to have your brick in Morehouse itself—then you did something terribly wrong coming here. I am maturing here and growing here and going through the experiences that will make me a man."

Unlike most African American men at majority institutions, the students at Morehouse have official and unofficial mentors. In the words of one student, "I have many mentors—an MBRS-RISE mentor, an academic adviser, and then you have some professors who you kind of build a close relationship with, and they help you along the way and you can call them your de facto mentors." These mentors role model professional behavior, and more than that, they role model being a "Renaissance man"—the phrase used by the institution to describe a Morehouse man: a man who is well spoken, well dressed, well balanced, well traveled. Morehouse College also promotes the ethos of brotherhood. One student described it thus: "I believe because this is an all-male school there needs to be some kind of foundation of brotherhood. When I got here my freshman year, this idea was promoted through orientation. I thought, 'This is for real.' I'm my brother's keeper, got my brother's back."

Peer-Led Team Learning

Peer-Led Team Learning is an innovative alternative to conventional peer learning. PLTL uses a facilitated learning approach in which individual faculty members develop and provide content and problems that are tied directly to relevant course content for peer-led workshops to address. PLTL sessions are completely student-led and student-driven, with a peer leader assigned to work with a group of six to eight students. The groups are small enough to be manageable and large enough to have a nice cross section of ideas. Within their small groups, students work on a packet that contains challenge problems that are fairly complex. These questions are aimed at forcing students to think conceptually through science problems. Students are encouraged by their leader to have a dialogue around the challenge problems to get a sense as to what students understand and what they still need to learn. A typical group works on complex problems for 60 to 120 minutes. During the PLTL meeting, the peer leader's job is to facilitate, to ask questions, and to summarize at the end of class but never to answer direct questions. The students find the answers. This strategy is what separates PLTL from tutoring. According to the PLTL faculty leader:

> When we go through the PLTL training, I talk about the experience of learning how to drive a car. If somebody else tries to tell you how to drive

a car then that doesn't give you mastery. You can watch somebody drive for years and years, but you'll crash if you go out the first time and try to drive on your own.

Before becoming a PLTL leader, students go through intensive training. This training lasts for two days, and the leaders spend about four hours each day working on various scenarios and digesting diverse learning styles. They learn that teaching has to be approached in multiple ways and from multiple perspectives. One PLTL leader told us, "As a professor you can't necessarily teach one way because everyone doesn't learn the same way." Explaining how he leads the PLTL group, a student offered this description: "In training, we learned how to involve students so they are actively participating in doing things themselves." The leaders are taught not to tutor but instead to work with the group to find the answer as a group.

The PLTL leaders also learn how to manage their peers to maintain a learning environment in the group. In the words of one leader: "Sometimes people slip. They want to wear their headphones or use their cell phone. At times it is hard, but I think that it can be dealt with [by] being a strong leader. If you start off lax and you don't care about the headphones and cell phones, you run into problems when the material gets harder." The peer leaders are aware that they are not in the role of professor and as such have less control or authority over the group, but they can work with professors to hold student members of PLTL accountable. Another student described the leader role in a slightly different manner:

Being a peer leader just involves having a very good understanding of the material that you're leading. I don't want to say teach because we're not teachers or instructors. We facilitate recitation sections, so we have to know what we're taking about when we do these sections in order to help the students grasp the material because that's ultimately what we're paid to do. And as a leader I sometimes have to refresh certain topics that I have forgotten, but I think it's really refreshing because I ultimately want to be a professor.

According to the faculty leader of the PLTL program: "B students actually are better, at least from my experience. B students are better at doing this because they've done well in the course but struggled. They are cognizant of how students might stumble."

The Benefits of PLTL

One of the student leaders explained the benefits of PLTL to us in great detail. First, he noted that PLTL allows students to further digest the material they learn in class lectures—to "take a step back" from the material. Next, PLTL involves having peer leaders help students learn how to study for exams in addition to learning subject matter content. Lastly, peer leaders demonstrate strategy and show students how to succeed.

Learning with the assistance of peers who are also friends breaks down apprehension about making mistakes. One junior described this for us, stating:

> You can be embarrassed about getting something wrong in PLTL, but that's a waste of time. It completely defeats the purpose. I tell all my students, look, we know you're going to get these things wrong, the objective is for you to get it wrong here with me so you don't get it wrong on the test. I tell them, your pride doesn't take the test, so leave it at the door.

Not Your Mother's Tutoring

Morehouse faculty members emphasized to us that PLTL is fundamentally different than tutoring. We wondered how it was different. Students told us that PLTL is a form of facilitation rather than being authoritarian in nature. Being a part of PLTL doesn't carry a stigma; the assumption is that everyone needs and participates in PLTL. Another aspect of PLTL that differs from tutoring is that it is peer-led and team-led—meaning that at any time the peer leader or a member of the team can be leading. One student described it this way: "As a peer leader you provide academic help to a student. But if another student knows the answer, he can provide help as well. So it's basically the whole team coming together to fix those links [students] that don't understand the concept as well. You gain respect from your peers. The dynamic works really well." Another student informed us that PLTL helps with much more than lectures because the program is focused on questioning and inquiry: "It provides alternative ways of seeing problems."

Peer leaders have strong, nearly collegial, relationships with the faculty members involved in PLTL and are comfortable advising them on the progress of other students. One student expressed to us:

I've always felt as though I could go up to any one of them and ask for help, and I feel like those relationships or ties have only been strengthened now that I'm on the other side and I'm a leader. I feel like I can now express to a professor that other students don't seem to understand and perhaps we need to look at the problem from another angle.

In many ways the PLTL program acts as a safety net for students. If they don't understand something in class, they know they can work it out in PLTL small groups. Overall, both the student perspectives and the data collected by program administrators show that PLTL is having a significant impact on student learning. According to institutional data, before PLTL, completion rates in classes such as chemistry hovered around 48 percent, with this percentage passing the class with a C or better. Since instituting PLTL, Morehouse boasts a completion rate of 70 percent for students as well as higher individual grades. Institutional data also show that the PLTL leaders do significantly better on standardized tests, scoring higher on the MCAT, the medical school entrance exam. PLTL empowers both students needing help and those providing the help.

Minority Biological Research Support–Research Initiative for Scientific Enhancement Program

Morehouse developed the MBRS-RISE program as part of National Institutes of Health initiatives. This long-standing program was created to counter the dearth of minority participation in biomedical research. At Morehouse College, students are admitted in the fall of their first year. Through the program they receive academic advising, peer mentoring, training in research, and research opportunities. They also participate in a research seminar series and graduate school tours. In their junior year, MBRS-RISE students are exposed to a variety of careers and educational options that are available to them as a result of earning a degree in science. During their senior year, the leaders of the program concentrate on analyzing data and writing papers for publication. Students are also coached on their graduate and medical school applications. Although the program has formal aspects, faculty members also spend ample time catching up with students. According to one faculty member: "About half of our meetings are dedicated to finding out how students are doing in classes, what's going on with them personally, how they are doing on their research, and how their graduate or medical school applications are coming along. We hear from each student and find out where they stand."

Students often come to Morehouse unprepared for the rigor even though they graduated at the top of their class. Depending on the caliber of a student's high school, he can struggle somewhat during the first semester of science courses. Programs such as MBRS-RISE provide cocurricular support to buttress what is learned in the classroom and reinforced by PLTL. Specifically, one faculty member told us:

> One of our students who was at the top of his class in high school came to Morehouse underprepared for college science. He struggled a bit his first semester. We placed him in several summer programs to prepare him to join MBRS-RISE. Eventually we saw his grades increase, and he is going to be a competitive applicant for graduate school. You can see his confidence building as he's moving along through the RISE program.

Another professor described his approach to teaching in the MBRS-RISE program as follows: "The idea is that the student who is in my lab will get experience in developing a research question and designing experiments, actually carrying out those experiments, analyzing data, and presenting data." He also told us that the various components of the MBRS-RISE program are implemented sequentially and with the guidance of the mentoring professor. In this faculty member's case, he noted: "When I take a freshman, he's usually involved in just shadowing, working alongside someone. It will not be until the later part of his sophomore year, junior year that he gets his own project." The faculty member offered us a rationale for this approach, noting that students in their early years are not always aware of what is required for serious research. Of importance, the faculty member also expressed concern with having students work too many hours in the lab, noting that ten hours is about the maximum for undergraduates given their other classes and commitments.

The men at Morehouse greatly value the impact of the MBRS-RISE program on their professional and personal lives, telling us that "through the RISE program you learn to start applying to graduate school, you start developing your personal statement, your four-year plan. RISE guides you to your goal, and it makes you a lot more prepared and competitive." And being a part of RISE leads to an excitement about learning and doing science research. One student told us enthusiastically: "When we talk about our research, you can tell others like it or that they are excited about it. They ask what you are working on and what you did this summer." And students keep other students accountable as well. One student relayed to us the following sentiment: "It's very competitive here. You have to always be on top of your game. A lot of guys don't want to be the dumb person in room, so we have to study more than we ever have before."

Across the board, students communicated that they have extraordinary and close relationships with faculty members. These relationships result in mentoring across personal and professional boundaries and are essential to the success of the men of Morehouse. One college junior said: "My mentor tells me more about life lessons and pushes me. I feel that all of my teachers kind of push me. They have some kind of influence on me to basically be better than I am and to go to the next level." Students told us that the MBRS-RISE program helps to acclimate them to both science and Morehouse overall. It gives them a home on campus and validates their interest in learning and scientific research.

Introduction to Research

Many of the young men who choose Morehouse College come with the intention of being a doctor. Within various Black communities across the nation, being a doctor earns significant respect and admiration. These young men have rarely been exposed to scientific research in the area of medicine, and the MBRS-RISE program serves as an entry point for them. A biology faculty member at Morehouse told us that he often asks his general biology class, which is made up of freshmen, how many of them want to be doctors or dentists. "About 99 percent of the students raise their hands. However, out of one hundred people in my biology class, we send about twenty to medical school. What happens to the rest of the students?" This professor credits the MBRS-RISE program with helping students to understand what it means to be a scientist and to pursue research.

One Morehouse junior told us: "I initially came to Morehouse as a pre-med major. Through RISE, I am getting to see everything that's out there in terms of science. Through RISE you're required to do research throughout the school year and also do research throughout the summer." The RISE program also helps students see connections across the curriculum and avoid too much focus on subject matter expertise only. Combined with Morehouse College's strong liberal arts curriculum, RISE encourages depth and breadth. Students told us stories about connections they made between classes that many might think are disconnected. A biology major told us about his experience taking visual arts: "When I took a visual arts class, I thought, 'Oh, it's just visual art, do a little drawing and I'm through.' But it was actually different. We learned about Egyptian art. The professor was an excavator. She goes to Egypt and she finds these tombs. I learned about tombs, the process of mummification."

Students and faculty alike called attention to the importance of linking every part of students' college education to their developing scientific identities and skills. What is essential for students is seeing themselves as scientists early in their academic career. In the words of another biology professor:

I think early exposure to the sciences is really important. A lot of students who don't participate in these programs assume that they are going to medical school, and then they look up their junior year and they haven't done anything to prepare for medical school admission. They realize that there are some deficiencies in their grades or that they haven't done summer research.

In contrast, the average MBRS-RISE student graduates with multiple research internships under his belt, several summer research experiences, and focus on his future.

Attitudes and Perspectives of Faculty

Morehouse is a place that takes pride in ensuring that every student has access to faculty. Morehouse faculty members, and especially those in the sciences, graduate from leading research institutions. However, the college seeks out individuals who are interested not only in pursuing a rigorous research agenda, but also in creative teaching as well as opportunities to mentor undergraduates. Speaking about faculty mentoring in STEM and through the MBRS-RISE program, one professor said:

I think that mentoring means that they see us outside the classroom. They learn a lot about our paths to where we are now. We create an environment where they can ask open questions that lead to fruitful discussion and inquiry about subtle cultural aspects of being an academic, about research—things that you just don't get in the curriculum.

The faculty members also refer to the students as scholars, addressing them in e-mails and during interactions as such so that they immediately see themselves as intelligent and in the role of scientists. According to a biology professor: "It's inspiring to work with these students. This is a population that society said does not achieve at all levels of the population, and then you come here and see 2,500 students who are trying to better themselves—African American men trying to improve their lives and the lives of their families. It's really inspiring."

Faculty members at Morehouse College are willing to share their mistakes and failures with students because they feel that this vulnerability leads to learning and helps students to see the capabilities and accomplishments of faculty as the product of hard work. One faculty member mentioned:

> My favorite thing to do is talk to students about how I failed or how I've been rejected, because I think it's part of the process. Students sometimes have the perception that you are a success story because you have a PhD or a tenure track job and you have to remind them of how you got to where you are. I often tell them about failing my first linear algebra test, especially if they are struggling, and it leads to a discussion of what it looks like to understand.

Most of the faculty members, especially the younger ones, want students to have the experience of conversing with peers while in the classroom. One faculty member explained: "My lectures become more of a discussion. It's not Socratic where you get up there and ask unending questions. I think it's really important that you have dialogue; you have that back and forth." Although faculty and students are not true peers, the course discussions are fashioned to feel like peer-to-peer interactions. Faculty members want students to feel comfortable expressing different points of view and respectfully challenging their professors.

The men at Morehouse College excel in part because faculty members present them with diverse learning opportunities. They promote summer internships and research opportunities and believe in the students' ability to do them. Over and over students told us of opportunities they were offered and how faculty members pushed and prodded them until they followed up on those opportunities. Those who attend Morehouse College not only gain through the MBRS-RISE program; they also continue to benefit from the relationships and connections they made there when they go on to graduate school. One professor of psychology told us:

> I tell them that their biggest resource when they leave Morehouse will be each other. Here, you'll have somebody who's come from your background in so many ways, and they'll be off at some other school going through the same thing. I tell them to keep in touch as these men are going to be your support system before you find a mentor in graduate school.

Although PLTL and MBRS-RISE operate as separate and independent programs, they cannot help but intersect on the campus of Morehouse College. According to one faculty member: "At this point, PLTL has penetrated every discipline in the Division of Science and Mathematics. In just about every gatekeeper course in chemistry, physics, biology, psychology, computer science, and math, there is PLTL in at least one course. And when I say course, I mean the entire course. All students have some experience with PLTL." These students then apply to the MBRS-RISE program. Faculty in the PLTL program told us that this program prepares Morehouse men to participate in MBRS-RISE and to be better investigators because they are more adept at working in groups and better at problem solving having gone through PLTL. The programs and practices at Morehouse College come together to bolster the success of the Black male students, pushing them to collaborate and serve as their brothers' keepers as it pertains to success in the STEM fields. The proof is in the performance of Morehouse College over the past ten years. During this time, the Atlanta-based college has been the top producer of Black male baccalaureates in the biological sciences, math and statistics, physics, and psychology, and the number two producer in chemistry. And 52 percent of the students who participate in MBRS-RISE pursue graduate degrees in science, with another 10 percent obtaining postbaccalaureate degrees.[13]

Norfolk State University: "Ride or Die"

Norfolk State University (NSU) is a public, historically Black university located in Norfolk, Virginia. It was founded in 1935 as an offshoot of Virginia
Union University, a nearby HBCU. The campus looks like many regional public
universities—a bit sterile. The university encompasses a great deal of land but
doesn't seem to have a central gathering place for students. When we arrived
on campus, we parked in a large industrial-style parking lot and started our
search for our meeting place. Most of the campus buildings look alike, and
it took us some time to figure out where we were going. Once we were inside,
however, our hosts greeted us with a great deal of warmth. This same sense
of warmth is evident in the relationships that faculty and staff have with students at NSU. We quickly realized that NSU offered much more than its bland
architecture and sparse campus; it provided a sense of family to students. One
student told us that the university was family-oriented and felt small, offering
the right fit. He didn't feel like a number. Another student described the family-
like atmosphere, noting that everyone from faculty to janitors to lunch servers
treats students like family: "I started seeing the close-knit family relations
that you can gain with people and professors and your friends on campus.
When you walk past some of the janitors and say hello, they know your name,
and people in the cafeteria know your first name. It's like a family bond that
you can't find everywhere."

The students at NSU have a solid commitment to the institution, even to
the point of defending it against some of the local community's misconcep-
tions. They are acutely aware of the stigmas against HBCUs, especially public
HBCUs, even among some of their friends as well as among residents of the
Norfolk area. One student aimed to persuade us: "Some people downplay the
institution and consider Norfolk State as somewhat of a community college.
We tell them 'no.' Norfolk State is a four-year institution just like Hampton
and Old Dominion Universities." Over and over students told us that despite
a lack of resources (for example, state-of-the-art buildings, or residence halls
with all the creature comforts), NSU offers them a great education. They understand that a lack of resources means that they don't have access to many
of the things that students have at better-resourced institutions, but also seem
to have a sense that the material resources are not as important as the human
resources that NSU has. In the words of one student, "I've learned that the

only difference between the 'bigger' colleges and Norfolk State is that opportunities are handed to you at those schools; here you have to work a little bit harder to get them, but we get them."

Even though NSU is a university with an enrollment of roughly 7,000, the students we visited with sense a strong commitment from faculty and feel that the professors are personable and push them to do their best work. One sophomore student explained: "I had a professor and she's kind of a mentor. She saw something in me and convinced me to change my major and saw something in my future that was better than I had planned. She did outreach for me. I can call her anytime." Other students spoke of these close personal relationships with professors, mentioning that the NSU professors "understand when you stress out and can help relieve the stress in your life because they've been through it."

A Link between Student Affairs and Academic Affairs

For decades there has been a profound disconnect between student affairs and academic affairs on most college campuses. Instead of acting as two divisions united in their education of students, these two sides of college campuses too often know little about each other and lack respect for the work that is generated by the other. Successful colleges and universities, especially those trying to empower low-income students of color, have found that it is essential for student affairs and academic affairs to work hand in hand. According to an administrator at NSU: "Student affairs and academic affairs have always been involved with one another. We treat the whole student." Part of the reason NSU operates in this manner is that they have a commitment to nurturing students; administrators we talked to told us that it's not appropriate to refuse to help students because their issues fall under academic rather than student affairs.

Norfolk State houses a "student success hub," which brings together personal support with academic support. On any given day, this large hub offers tutoring services, peer mentors, academic advisers, and a math learning lab. In this setting students can get help, including anything from selecting a major, to getting off of academic probation, to understanding their semester performance. The advisers who work with Summer Bridge are trained to understand diverse learning styles and to recognize when students learn differently than they do. They acknowledge various ways of approaching problems and don't make the assumption that all students learn the same way.

In addition to these predominantly academic services, staff members are trained and prepared to talk about personal issues as well. One adviser shared a story about a young woman who was a model student. In the midst of her struggle with her sexuality, her grades plummeted. But with the help of academic support and personal counseling, the young woman was able to turn her grades around, come to terms with her sexuality, smooth out her relationship with her family, and become a highly successful student.

Summer Bridge Program

With Summer Bridge you come into the university with friends or at least acquaintances. We all still know each other, and we still talk to each other and study together.
—Summer Bridge student, NSU

The Summer Bridge program is a four-week, nonresidential academic success program for new students that acclimates them to college life in an attempt to prepare them for college and ensure their academic and social success. All Summer Bridge students are offered six or seven credit hours, which jump-starts their college education, making them feel secure in their pursuit of a degree and giving them a peer support system that lasts into their college experience. As described by one of the program's directors: "The purpose of Summer Bridge is to boost academic skills. Students become very familiar with each other and act as a cohort. When they return to the university in the fall, they are ready to go and have already built up a rapport with our faculty, staff, and other students." In the words of one student, "We are like brothers with the other guys in Summer Bridge; we have each other's back." When we were interviewing the students, a group of men this time, they exemplified this closeness, even talking in unison sometimes. Initially a bit unclear about the nature and impact of this closeness, we asked them about it. With a full measure of enthusiasm, they told us: "Everyone on campus knows us and know[s] that we are friends. It's so bad that if we walked in the student union right now and I was by myself, someone would ask me, 'Are you sick?' 'What's wrong?' 'Where's your crew?'"

These men described themselves as "ride or die," and when asked to elaborate on this saying, one young man said, with a deep passion in his voice,

"Ride or die means that no matter what happens, no matter what arguments we have, no matter what we go through in our life or in any situation, if I call him, he's there." The dedication to each other extends well beyond personal commitment into academics. When we asked one group of young men how they support each other academically, they said, "We do not play. We are 3.0 or better." Two of the young men shared a story with us about how they hold each other accountable, explaining that "a couple of us were going to the International House of Pancakes for dinner and we had to tell one of our brothers, 'If you don't get your grades right, you can't go.'" The young men described situations in which they check on each other's grades and explained how they refuse to get Cs in their classes, even resorting to friendly competition. To these men, "failure is not an option," as none of them feel that they can afford to fail. They are committed to themselves, each other, their families, and the communities where they grew up.

The positive peer pressure that exists among the Summer Bridge students leads to an increase in overall grade point average (GPA). For too long, many researchers, policy makers, and citizens have held onto the notion that African American males do not do well academically because it is seen as not cool or as "acting White." This is not what we found at Norfolk State University. We found the opposite. One of the men explained it to us this way: "I started hanging out with these brothers. They were getting 3.5, 3.6, 3.0 GPAs and above, and I'm hanging around with my 2.3. I couldn't brag about my academics around them. So I worked a lot harder and got my GPA up to a 2.8 and then a 3.0." For these young men, learning is more than the grade. They want to make sure that their peers are "getting something out of their classes," noting that they give each other feedback and informally tutor each other. These students spend time reflecting on the value of what they have together. One young man explained: "I think what makes our group work so well is that we are honest and open. We have heart-to-heart talks where we sit down together. We tell each other everything, including about our problems—life, home, my mom is doing this, and his dad is doing this. We talk about everything."

If one of the members of the group starts to slip, the men stage interventions, find out the cause of the problem, and offer support. When we asked questions about a member of the group slipping or faltering, the men responded with "It ain't one of us, it's all of us," demonstrating the unity and bond that exists among the men who participate in Summer Bridge at NSU.

Although the program began a few years ago with only thirty-eight students, it now has one hundred. Students are invited into the program. The students fit a specific profile in terms of academic preparation. They just barely meet the institution's SAT or GPA standards, which are a 2.75 GPA, an 18 on the ACT, and an 850 combined math and verbal score on the SAT. Sometimes students don't want to attend Summer Bridge, as they would rather work during the summer before college. NSU uses parents as advocates for participation in Summer Bridge, urging them to help their children understand that having extra preparation is necessary for success in college. Program administrators use an interesting approach to making sure that most students accept their invitation. Instead of addressing the invitation to each student, they address it to "The Parents of" each student. Parents typically share the invitations with their children and apply encouragement and slight pressure to attend.

According to students in Summer Bridge, the program instills the self-discipline that is essential to performing well in college. Self-discipline is essential for being attentive in the classroom, attending class regularly, and managing a semester-long schedule. Students have an especially difficult time juggling assignment deadlines, and the Summer Bridge program teaches them how to be accountable to professors with regard to this work. In the words of one student: "You have to get the work done. Summer Bridge made me realize that I can't watch TV, I can't play on the computer, I can't call my friends until my work is done. While other students had to learn these lessons during the first weeks of school, I learned them during the summer." Summer Bridge helps students to navigate the institution. Unlike at many colleges, NSU's student body is made up of mostly first-generation students who often don't have parents who are familiar with college and the nuances of the system. The lack of a parental safety net can be frustrating to students, and Summer Bridge mitigates this frustration.

In addition to the preparation for their college experience, the students we interviewed also appreciated the course credits they earned over the summer, which jump-started their college careers and made them feel as if they were already on a safe foundation. Summer Bridge can provide more than just a foundation for sound academic performance. Academic advisers working with the program told us countless stories of how the program changed the lives of students; those same students confirmed these stories. We were particularly struck by the story of a young man grew up in a troubled atmosphere and felt that he needed to fight beginning at a young age in order to solve his problems. He fought at home, in school, and with his father. Fighting was a way of life, and while in high school he often exchanged blows with his father. He played high school football and was good enough to earn a football scholarship at Norfolk State. He enrolled in Summer Bridge, and for the very first time he had positive male role models and didn't have to fight to defend his territory. In many ways, this young man is now fighting for others' success in college. He is involved in all aspects of the institution's student success work and is making a difference in his family as well.

Summer Bridge leads to significant gains in retention at the university. For example, in comparison to the overall retention rate at NSU of 70 percent, Summer Bridge students have a 90 percent retention rate. The same students are tracked throughout the academic year; the men have an average GPA of 2.6 and the women an average of 2.8 compared to the overall freshman GPA of 2.3. At first glance, these GPAs might appear to be less than desirable, but it is important to remember that these students were all marginal in their academics when they entered the institution, having low SAT scores and very low GPAs in high school. Like many HBCUs, Norfolk State is adding value to the students' lives. These numbers are essential to the program's continued existence, as the NSU board of trustees is often looking for inefficient programs to cut. Summer Bridge's leaders know that if they have data to back up the success of the program, it will continue. In fact, when the board of trustees found out that the Summer Bridge program was producing disproportionately successful results, it asked to increase the funding for the program to support 300 students rather than the current 100.

In addition to academic empowerment, these young men and women have been empowered to be a force for change the world along with reflecting on their own responsibilities in life. During our interviews, both men and women discussed their goals and dreams, with many wanting to be teachers to uplift children in communities similar to the ones from which they came. One student told us:

I just want to make the world a better place because the message that we have out there today is just crazy. I'm not a bad person. My mother raised me well. She was a single parent, and I just feel like she taught me that I could go and teach others and hopefully touch them so they can pass it on. Everything starts with the youth of today.

This young man also confided in us as to how he avoided getting in trouble or involved in gangs. His story provoked one of his peers to say: "I'm going to be honest. I took the other side of his life. I was a gangbanger. You can't choose who your family members are." For both of these students, a college education is a way out of a life that is "messed up."

That way out is complicated. When the former gang member started to think about college and sports scholarships, he came to realize that no one wants a gangbanger in their classes or on their team. Through the Summer Bridge program, NSU offered both these students—a former gang member and a young man who had to avoid gangs—an opportunity to pursue a different life. This former gang member told us with a deep sense of humility and passion: "Summer Bridge changed me forever, period, for the rest of my God-given life. If it were not for this program, I would not be in school. I would not. I wouldn't make it." These students have woven together their own safety net and hold each other accountable.

Students are also held accountable by teachers and mentors who participate in the program, with one student telling us, "They check your grades, they know if we are doing well, and they don't let us come into their office with lies about our progress." The student added, "They love us." The students see their teachers, advisers, and mentors as role models and family and seem to be willing to accommodate any request from these individuals. And they enjoy the tough love and straight talk offered by the leaders of Summer Bridge. Some of the students refer to the advisers in Summer Bridge as "mom" or "mama." They see Summer Bridge as a family and have familial relationships with the staff, explaining that the staff members look out for them and hold them accountable. The students credit their retention—or, as they call it, "coming back"—each year to these parents away from home who provide opportunity and inspiration. One student referred to Summer Bridge as a birthing: "It's kind of like a birthing in the education system. You feed somebody knowledge, you feed them different good things to help them along the way, and then you birth them."

The faculty at Norfolk State and especially those teaching in Summer Bridge also see their relationships with students as familial. One faculty member described the NSU faculty as caring. She explained that because many of the faculty members also went to NSU or other HBCUs, they have a personal stake in the students' future. They care about the whole student, and the students trust them. Several faculty members told us that it is completely normal to see students and faculty hugging and laughing as if they are family members. Perhaps because of the familial relationships, there is a great deal of respect within these relationships and among the students and faculty. Much like at Morehouse College, the faculty members refer to the students as scholars, making being intellectually astute and smart something that is desired, and implanting the idea of being a scholar and doing scholarship or being intellectually curious in the heads of the students. One faculty member told us that she calls the students scholars because it communicates to them that they are capable of doing great things. When this faculty member gives an assignment, she often asks the students, "Why are you going to do the assignment and do it well?" and they answer, "Because we are scholars." At first the students were stunned to be called scholars, but now it is in their heads, and it is how they see themselves. Having students view themselves as scholars is deeply important to the faculty members at NSU because in many ways these students represent the faculty's past. Many of the students are from the same towns and grew up with the same challenges. Faculty members realize that their very presence in the classroom and in the lives of these students makes a difference. According to one professor: "To see people who actually look like you and tell you 'You can do this' makes you feel good. We see something in the students that they didn't even know was there."

The Breakfast Club

The Summer Bridge students also participate in a program called the Breakfast Club, which meets once a month at 7:00 a.m. Many of the students bellyached about 7:00 a.m. meetings, telling the Breakfast Club leaders, "You're killing me." The leaders explained how important it is to get up early in the morning: "While you're sleeping people are making important decisions, and then you come after the fact and the decisions are already made." The Breakfast Club is a student-focused program that features motivational speakers, ranging from the president to successful alumni, and provides students with ample networking opportunities. Due to its exclusivity (based on membership in Summer Bridge), membership in the Breakfast Club has become somewhat high status. People often ask, "How can I become a part of the Breakfast Club?" The high status and the diversity of the speakers and opportunities keep students attending monthly.

The students involved in the Breakfast Club are also eligible to participate in an annual retreat; however, they must attend every 7:00 a.m. Breakfast Club meeting throughout the year, complete a college student inventory to assess their performance throughout the semester, and meet regularly with an adviser. For many of the students this is the very first time they have ever stayed in a hotel, seen fine linen and china, and been asked to dress more formally. According to one administrator of the Breakfast Club: "The students behave incredibly well. Let me tell you—at the same hotel where our students stayed—a few weekends later the law students from the College of William and Mary had a gathering, and they got kicked out. When you grow up with everything, you often take it for granted and don't care." Much of the success in terms of the students' behavior is linked to work that is done with them throughout the year and prior to the retreat. According to one administrator: "We have etiquette dinners where we train the students. By the time they get to the retreat, they are prepared to eat and socialize in a more formal and professional manner."

Members of the Breakfast Club are assigned mentors according to gender; there are both male and female mentoring programs affiliated with it. At first glance, separate male and female mentoring programs might seem sexist or antiquated, but administrators explained their rationale for separating the groups. As shared by one program leader: "We had a retreat, and I had this epiphany. I decided that night that I was going to separate the group by males and females after our meeting that evening. I wanted to be able to have straight talk with them." During the "straight talk" sessions, group leaders asked students to write down any questions they had on a piece of paper. These questions could be academic, personal, or social. The first session of straight talk was supposed to last an hour, but it lasted five and a half hours—until 1:30 a.m. Students were highly engaged and had many, many questions. One of the mentors involved in the retreat shared his delight with us. "We were kind of amazed that students really need someone to talk to. When we separated students by gender, their questions were much more real and honest. We were shocked by some of the questions, the things these men didn't know because no one ever sat down and had straight talk with them." Students asked questions about women, dealing with professors, how to navigate financial aid, how to manage their parents' expectations, poverty, and homelessness. According to the male students who participated in the straight talk groups, it is less difficult for them to talk when there aren't women are in the room because they can let their guard down and refrain from trying to impress the women. What happened in the room when these men were alone is remarkable and runs counter to the way most researchers have depicted African American men.

One of the young men explained the beauty of their conversations to us in detail. In his words:

> They put us in a room, and so many emotions came out in that one day. I'll never forget it. None of us knew each other before we started talking. There were forty to fifty men in the room, and everyone was in tears. Grown men were talking about their fathers, relationships, their moms, everything. Before the retreat the men in the room didn't talk to each other, but after the retreat we all speak to each other. Guys started meeting up, calling each other.

When asked what served as the motivation for their openness, they told us that it was the openness of the faculty members involved in the retreat.

In most cases, the facilitator of a straight talk conversation might feel compelled to answer all of the questions, especially in this case, where the facilitator was a professor. However, according to the professor, when he was asked the questions, students would randomly say, "Hey, listen, I can answer that and talk about what happened to me." The male and female groups were committed to each other and rallied around the idea of straight talk by creating names for their groups—the men are the Spartan Men of Optimism, Valor, and Excellence, and the women are the Leaders in Academics Dedicated to Impacting and Empowering Self. Rather than a mere academic or professional experience, the retreats have become a time for young men and women to explore manhood and womanhood. Young men were asked raw questions pertaining to their past and upbringing. One student told us that he was asked, "Would you forgive your father for not being there for you? Do you hold a grudge?" The students described the sessions as providing them with a starting point, and then with the "basic knowledge that the professor gave us, we just took off." The young men explained to us that these types of conversations have led them to think about the type of father they want to be. One student stated boldly, "I'll be the best father in the universe to my child." These men also discuss the meaning of manhood, noting, "A man is someone who takes responsibility." They have become "brothers, soul mates, and best friends for life."

Many of these men told us that they were just waiting to talk, that they wanted to talk about their experiences and their past. The gathering of the men gave them the opportunity to trust each other. In the words of one young man: "I almost cried. My throat—you know how your emotions . . ." When speaking about his willingness to trust the other men, he divulged to us that he told them, "Whatever you all do with the information it's on you, but I trust you enough that you will keep this in confidence." This young man sees himself as the "protector of the group" because he is older and because protecting them is in his character.

We were struck by the extent to which these young men desired to make sure that women had similar experiences. They valued their experiences, trust, and communication with other men so much that they were concerned that the women didn't have the same experience. But the women were having similar experiences. One of the young men shared with a great amount of sincerity: "This year, the girls are really coming together. I am happy to see this because many times girls don't mesh well, but these girls are trusting and coming together. At this year's retreat, they are really tight rather than competing with one another." The young men protect the women and see them as sisters. In fact, if another young man on campus is interested in one of the Breakfast Club women, the men will ask, "What's your GPA, what are your goals?" They feel strongly about these women and want them to be respected and treated well. They also see them in a positive light, as "strong, intelligent, and worthy of respect." These young men and women want to be friends for life and plan on supporting each other even after college. We were surprised that they were so open and honest and willing to talk to us, especially given the age and racial differences between us. When we asked them why they were so honest, they told us, "We're just honest . . . and comfortable with what is in our heads."

One mentor offered us a vignette to explain the impact of the Breakfast Club. He told this story:

I gave a lecture to a group of students and suddenly students were following me around campus, and a few male students followed me to my office. I looked at them and said, "Okay, guys, what do you want to talk about?" and one of the guys says, "I want you to show me how you tie your tie." I said, "Didn't your daddy teach you? That's a double knot Windsor." They all said, "No, I don't have a daddy." My assumptions were completely different. So I said, "No problem, I'll show you." And I'm showing them and I'm thinking to myself, "The impact that I have here is tremendous compared to other places."

Other faculty told us that they make themselves available to students after 5:00 p.m. and often plan activities for them on the weekend. These activities involve learning how to do "typical" things around the house, such as landscaping, managing household finances, or washing the car. Although these activities are commonplace for many middle-class students, they are not for low-income inner-city children in the areas around Norfolk. Faculty members try to provide male role models for the young men and female role models for the young women, teaching them with skills that reach far beyond the classroom. Although all of the mentoring that faculty members do outside the classroom seems unrealistic or too much to bear for some, those we talked with found pleasure in being mentors and considered it part of their role as a faculty member. In addition to faculty members using their off hours to mentor students, we also came across staff members working with the program who personally "adopt" students each year. Some staff members help pay students' tuition, buy their books, and offer them a home-cooked meal on the weekends. The reach of those working at NSU is admirable and quite remarkable, and in essence the work of a family. Anchored in these efforts, the Breakfast Club has some impressive outcomes. In 2011, the program had 107 students; this number has been consistent or higher since the club's establishment in 2009. Although the program lasts only one year, by the end of that year students have formed friendships that continue into their future years at NSU. They have a foundation on which to learn and manage their personal development while also having faculty and staff relationships that continue to bolster their success. No less significant, they mentor the next cohort of students.

Mentoring Each Other

One of the essential aspects of the Summer Bridge program is that it includes peer mentoring, much like that at Morehouse College. Students come into the program in the summer and then go through the entire year gaining support from their advisers, mentors, and the Breakfast Club. Then they are expected to mentor the next cohort of young men and women. One young woman described her relationship with another male student in Summer Bridge, detailing the incredible support system that she experiences due to the foundation established during the summer. Describing her peer mentor, she said: "He supports me a lot. He pushes me. He pushed me a lot more, so last semester . . . I kind of slacked off a bit, but with his help, I ended up getting a 3.0."

One of the peer mentors described his experience helping other students as having its ups and downs, as one has to listen to students' problems and calm their anxiety and frustration. The peer mentor also acts as a campus guide and one-stop resource, not only guiding new students throughout campus but also providing information on how to connect with advisers, financial aid counselors, and professors. In addition, peer mentors encourage new students to be active and to get involved with organizations and social activities on campus, reinforcing the notion that engaged students are more likely to be retained in college. Although peer mentors are likely not aware of the research on college retention, they are nonetheless aware that they are an important link at Norfolk State, and they seem to enjoy their role in helping others. They value the trust that other students have in them and are impressed with those students who are willing to admit that they have a problem. They realize that the best and most effective way for students to move forward and do well in college is to admit that they have a problem and seek help. The peer mentors also find a certain sense of satisfaction in working to solve students' problems. One student told us, "If a student's grades turn around or if the problem turns around for the better, then it's rewarding to know that you did help them to get to a better position than they were in." Another peer mentor explained: "Having the skills to be a peer mentor is a gift. You have to be able to listen and read people." More specifically, he told us:

If you see a student walking around, always walking around by themselves with their head down, not interacting with anyone, there might be something wrong. So you have to learn how to read that person's attitude, and if you feel like you need to approach that person, approach them. The student might be afraid to go to counseling, but they will talk to us, as we are peer mentors.

As we were talking with the students who participated in Summer Bridge and are now serving as peer mentors, we were surprised by their empathy for other students' situations in life—they seemed to understand the fear that some students faced with regard to failure, homesickness, fitting in. They draw upon their own experiences in life in order to connect with other students. One peer mentor, sounding like a seasoned student affairs professional, told us: "If the student doesn't have support for his family, if they are the first person in their family to go to school, they don't know what to expect from college because their parents didn't go or their grandparents didn't go. We have to point them in the right direction." The peer mentors are particularly good at counseling students who are being pressured by their families to come home and help support the family rather than stay in school. Although this is not the norm for African American students (compared to their Latino counterparts), some students feel an overwhelming sense of responsibility to support their families. The peer mentors understand this guilt and are prepared to help students manage it. They teach students to "stand up on their own" and say, "I'm doing this for me."

The students we talked with at NSU understand the need for multiple mentors in their lives. They seek out academic mentors as well as mentors to help with their social skills. These students realize the impact that they can have on one another, even noticing the reaction to their positive examples: "People see you as a respected man, and when they see you do something positive, they want to do something positive. I tell new students that if they don't respect themselves no one else will." These students are entering their second year of college with a new outlook on their lives and their futures.

Paul Quinn College

It would be unrealistic and even damaging for us to ignore the things that they've been through, and are still going through, and just expect them to do the academic part of it and act as if those other things are just forgotten because they walked into a classroom.

—Michael Sorrell, President, Paul Quinn College

Paul Quinn College (PQC) is located in South Dallas, Texas, in the middle of a food desert. The land is dry, and you won't see a grocery store anywhere in sight. What you will see are fast-food restaurants and convenience stores. You also see quite a few people walking along the edges of the dusty, litter-filled road—there aren't any sidewalks—on their way to catch buses into downtown Dallas. As you drive onto campus, past the security guard, you immediately notice the pristine cleanliness of the grounds. The institution's president is insistent that the campus always be clean and that the students treat it with respect.

Founded in 1872 by the African Methodist Episcopal (AME) Church, Paul Quinn College is the oldest Black college west of the Mississippi. The ministers of the AME Church set up the small school in Austin, Texas, to educate former slaves and their children under the name Connectional High School. In 1877, the college moved to Waco, Texas, and was renamed Waco College. It was really a college in name only at this point, as it offered only industrial courses such as carpentry, sewing, blacksmithing, and leather tanning. By 1881, the college had a name change as a result of the good work of Bishop Paul Quinn. It also expanded its curriculum—still focusing mainly on manual labor—to include more courses for women, including cooking and kitchen management. The administration also added courses in Latin, math, English, and music. The college moved to Dallas in 1990 and acquired the campus of the former Bishop College, a defunct Black college.

Although Paul Quinn College boasted a robust enrollment during its initial years—over 1,200 students—enrollments fell off in the early years of the twenty-first century, and today the campus is home to just over 300 students. Many people had given up on the small college, thinking that it would go the way of other AME Church colleges such as Barber Scotia in North Carolina or the struggling Morris Brown College in Atlanta, Georgia. But under the leadership of Michael J. Sorrell (since 2007), the college has grown at an admirable rate. While it is still struggling, Sorrell's innovative and entrepreneurial approach has breathed life into the small college and bolstered the retention of its students. Sorrell is willing to ask just about anyone for financial support, tapping local and state foundations and local corporations, and using his connections from his days as a securities attorney.

PQC does noble work in terms of educating students. Its students, typically from low-income families, are often underprepared and shortchanged by the primary and secondary educational system. Most are first-generation college students and cannot rely on their families to help them navigate through the system that is college. One staff member described the students to us:

> These students lacked exposure, and when they were growing up they stayed in their neighborhoods. They didn't venture out and do things outside of their neighborhoods, so when you bring them to an educational institution, you are trying to broaden their horizon and expose them to things that they are not used to, they stray away. Their guards are up because they are not sure if they can trust us.

In order to support these students, PQC has instituted a comprehensive, all-campus approach to retention. Although most retention plans are effective at engaging students, PQC's plan goes beyond the traditional plan and attempts to uplift, love, and surround the student with support. The retention plan is equal to that of the "love of a family."

The unique approach to retention at PQC stems from its leader, President Sorrell. He is a dynamic person, filled with energy and a spirit that makes you feel that you aren't doing enough to make the world better for all of its citizens. Upon our arrival on campus, Sorrell embraced us and had a look of excitement on his face, as if he could not wait to show us the campus and to tell us the PQC story. When we asked him to talk about why he came to Paul Quinn (he was a successful securities attorney in Dallas), he said: "I believe that there are times in your life where your particular training and your skill set and your gifts line up with the task at hand. And if you are willing to put in the work to a certain degree, you get lucky." Sorrell has some valuable gifts for being successful as a college president. In his own words, he is "particularly gifted at motivating people to higher levels of performance and for the common good." He believes in the possibilities of every individual, telling us, "I have always believed that if you teach people and you tell them you believe in them, they will outperform whatever the normal predictors of their success will be."

We over Me: The Secret to Retention

Paul Quinn College has "We over Me" as its institutional slogan, and the idea permeates the entire culture of the college; it begins with the president. Instead of working on Wall Street as a new college graduate, Sorrell decided to get a degree in civil rights law at Duke. When asked why he didn't pursue Wall Street, he explained to us, "When I was twenty years old, I sat there and thought to myself, 'If I go to Wall Street, I will make an unbelievable amount of money, and I'm not sure I won't become an asshole. I had a very honest conversation with myself." Sorrell's interest in Paul Quinn College stemmed from hearing about the institution and feeling that he had something to give to its mission. In 2001, he expressed interest in the job of president. He was thirty-five years old, and although he couldn't secure an interview, he had a conversation with the bishop who chaired the board of trustees. Sorrell was immediately dismissed; the bishop told him he was too young and wasn't an academician. To which Sorrell replied:

> No disrespect sir, this ain't Harvard. I don't think you need an acade-
> mician. Plus my undergrad degree is from Oberlin, I was a graduate
> fellow at Harvard, I have two Duke degrees, and my high school is the
> best high school in the city of Chicago. I can hire people to do the aca-
> demic work. You need someone with a vision.

Paul Quinn didn't hire Michael Sorrell the first time, and instead hired a series of unsuccessful presidents who put the institution in dire straits. However, Sorrell was offered a seat on the board of trustees. After watching Sorrell's work on the board, the chair asked him to be president.

When President Sorrell walked onto the Paul Quinn campus, it was desolate, the grass wasn't cut, and the administrative offices had padlocks and chains on them. He immediately realized that he had to give everyone who was left at PQC something: "I had to identify something to give them—and that something was hope—and I had to send them a message that we are going to be a different place." During Sorrell's first week on campus, a fight broke out, with kids pulling out guns and knives. It was then that he realized that he didn't know where he was and didn't have experience with these kinds of students. When the students came for their appeals hearing, they were late, didn't wear ties, didn't comb their hair. As Sorrell recalled: "I said, 'Do you know we're about to kick you out of school?' So they give me their appeal statements, there are misspelled words, they're written by hand. I thought to myself, 'What planet is this?'"

Sorrell believes in second chances, so he made the fighting students an offer. He told them: "You can't go to school here anymore. You're done. But I will make you a deal. I will consider letting you back in if you go to a community college, take twelve credit hours, maintain a 3.3 [GPA] or better, and take a remedial writing class. If you do that, you can come back." Unfortunately, none of the students took Sorrell up on his offer. After talking with several groups of students who were in his office for disciplinary issues, Sorrell was overwhelmed and looked at the students, saying:

> You know, we owe you an apology. If we have somehow made you think that you are what a college junior looks like and that the level of preparation that you have is going to afford you a shot at a quality life, then we have lied to you and we have failed you. I wasn't the president that admitted you to this college, but you are my responsibility now. I apologize to you, but you will not go to school here anymore.

According to Sorrell, this approach sent a message to the students that "we're not playing anymore." Interestingly, some students who had been at the institution in 2003 and left for various reasons but came back told us that Sorrell is a completely different type of president than the person who was running the college in 2003. These students had never met the past president and didn't even know his name. In contrast, these students now feel that they can come to Sorrell with any issue, whether it is personal or professional: "He makes himself known and open and available to his students."

Sorrell also met with the faculty and staff and said, "Everyone has ninety days to prove that they will work as hard as I will work and that they love this school." He told the employees that he would never ask them to do anything that he wasn't willing to do. According to Sorrell, there are three sets of people you encounter when interviewing potential staff: "One set you'd love to have, another set you could make work, and then another set . . . under no circumstances would you hire. Eighty percent of the people at Paul Quinn fit the third category when I arrived. Seventeen percent were in the middle category, and 3 percent were in the first category." Ninety-five percent of those on the faculty and staff at PQC are new. Sorrell's philosophy about hiring and retaining faculty and staff is simple: "They have to be about the students. If not, they don't belong at Paul Quinn."

In order to make a change in the student mind-set on campus, Sorrell instituted a dress code. He began to require students to dress business casual on campus. He wanted students to respect each other and for those visiting campus to respect the students. In Sorrell's words: "When I visited classes, I was humiliated. How could I bring supporters of the institution to campus and have my students look like this?" People (including parents) fought Sorrell on the dress code, saying, "You are trying to turn this school into an elite institution." And Sorrell responded: "You are absolutely right. I'm not going to apologize for that. We are going to be one of America's great small colleges, and great colleges graduate their students."

In addition to the dress code, President Sorrell implemented his personal value statement as part of the ethos of the institution—a value statement that serves as the foundation for the student success strategies used by the college. He calls these values the Four L's of Quinnite Leadership. They are:

1. Leave places better than you found them.
2. Lead from wherever you are.
3. Live a life that matters.
4. Love something greater than yourself.

President Sorrell also communicated his disdain for selfishness. He did this by introducing the idea of "we over me." And in many ways, his leadership and style exemplify "we over me." During orientation, Sorrell gives out his cell phone number, asks students to friend him on Facebook and add him on Twitter, and lets all of them know that they are welcome to visit him in his office. Whereas many college presidents—even small liberal arts college presidents—would not make themselves so accessible, Sorrell's accessibility seems to be the key to Paul Quinn College's success. Sorrell takes his role seriously and takes accessibility to a new level. One student told us that the president will do almost anything to support students and recalled two incidents in which the president did extraordinary things to make sure that he succeeded at PQC. He recalled: "One time I wasn't having a good time, and my freshman year I was thinking about leaving the school. He came to Houston and had dinner with me and my mom to convince me to stay. Another time, when my grandma died, he came to Houston to attend the funeral. He is my mentor."

Sorrell is a servant leader, and his expectations are high. He leads by example and has an intensely strong moral compass. In his words:

I lead by bleeding, and what I mean by that is that when this campus and these students need something, I'll do it. I shovel snow when it needs to be shoveled. I pick up kids when kids need to be picked up. I believe at my core that we are going to redefine the way in which underresourced communities are treated. I mean that this is that time, this is that place, this is that moment.

During our visit, we teased Sorrell about being charismatic and charming, and he responded, "I work very hard to actually tone it down because I think people will have a tendency to want to dismiss what we're doing."

There are many people who might look at the revitalization of Paul Quinn College as a bit of a savior story: Michael Sorrell saved the institution. However, he is quick to let them know that the survival of PQC was and is a group effort. He told us:

I didn't save this college. We saved this college. I make sure everyone here understands that I appreciate them, that they all had a role to play in what we have done and retaining our students. I don't want this to look like some ego-driven exercise. I am a strong-willed person and I recognize that I have a big personality, but I also try very hard to make sure people understand—it's we over me.

In listening to Sorrell, we were curious about people who don't subscribe to the "we over me" philosophy. What happens to them at a place like PQC? He let us know that there is no room for them at the institution. They don't last. As we discussed the "we over me" philosophy with those we spoke to, they all understood it and respected it. One faculty member told us: "The philosophy is just something that attracts you to the school. It's about working for the greater good." Faculty and staff think that the campus ethos of doing for others comes from the top down. Others told us the ethos is part of the individuals who want to work at a place like PQC. They are willing to work for lower salaries because they believe in the higher purpose of education for the underserved. Over and over we were told that faculty and staff wanted to stay at PQC because it is like a family—it's "their family." One of the student leaders said it this way: "We are one family that just so happens to be a college. That's the way we are. I always think of this as my Paul Quinn family, and its members are my brothers and sisters. I even call President Sorrell's little boy my nephew. We just have that mentality here."

The "we over me" philosophy also permeates the conversations of students and often leads to a change in their own personal goals and outlook on life. One Latina student told us that she was a business major and was set on making money for herself. After a few years at PQC, she realizes that it is important for her to be financially successful while at the same time reaching out and supporting the Latino community and other low-income communities that do not have access to resources. Students were also quick to let us know that those students who didn't buy into the "we over me" culture were no longer at the college. Although retention is important at Paul Quinn, the institution wants to retain students who care about one another and the institution as a whole.

A young Black man told us that he believes in being a servant leader and believes in "we over me." He told us that being at Paul Quinn has helped him to think about the needs of others in addition to his personal goals. He has learned to be selfless. The lessons taught at PQC run counter to the current ethos of the nation, which is fixated on self-promotion and individualism. Much like the Latina student above, this man also told us that those who don't buy into the "we over me" philosophy end up leaving PQC: "It never works out for them. You see them come and you know that they are not going to last. You can tell. I've seen some students stumble and eventually get on track; other students don't last here."

Staff and faculty at PQC care genuinely for students. According to one of the faculty members, "We tell the students, 'You absolutely are leaders, you're being cultivated to lead, you don't have a choice, it's not negotiable, if you're going to stay here we expect, we demand, that you lead.'" She reiterated that at PQC they don't give up on people, because students deserve to have someone believe in them, and noted that the faculty and staff "fundamentally reject the notion that underresourced communities can't perform at a high level." Paul Quinn is attempting to make leaders out of the students that many colleges overlook. In the words of a retention staff member: "Any institution can say that their prototype is a kid with a 3.5 GPA and high test score[s]; that's not us. Our prototype is a kid with a 2.7 and a 17, 18, 19 ACT score, who comes from a low-income family and is funding his or her education entirely with financial aid. We have to convince that student that he or she can be a leader and that success is inevitable." The provost told us that the students at PQC possess everything they need to be successful, but what they don't possess is what they couldn't control. They couldn't control the environment in which they grew up—an environment that didn't have the resources to fulfill all of their intellectual and social needs.

"We over me" also translates into being very busy students. Because Paul Quinn College is very poor, students are encouraged to volunteer and lead in areas across the campus. They gain many and varied experiences while on campus and gain an understanding that taking care of and nurturing their institution is part of their duty as PQC students. One student described her role in taking care of PQC to us. She said: "Being here as a student is a full-time job. There is so much to do in a positive way. I stay busy, and it's all for the betterment of Paul Quinn College." Another student explained her relationship as one filled with love for the institution and her peers: "I care about people because they care about me. They teach you to love something larger than yourself. We can't say we're a Quinnite Nation if we don't care about our fellow Quinnites. We have to display love all over."

"We over Me" Farm: The Practical Implementation of a Motto

When Michael Sorrell came to Paul Quinn College he noticed that the school had a failing football team in every sense. Not only did the team fail to win a game, but the sport failed to raise any income, and the students on the team were failing their classes. In a bold move, he eliminated the football team. He didn't gain many friends with this move, but he had a vision for the football field. As mentioned, PQC is located in a poor area of South Dallas, in a food desert. People in the community and students lacked access to fresh food and knowledge of good nutrition.

Sorrell turned the football field into an organic farm that feeds the community (the school tithes 10 percent of the food to the community) and the students. Moreover, the farm allows students to learn about entrepreneurship, nutrition, hard work, activism, and community politics. Unlike anything most people have seen on a college campus, the farm is buttressed by two goalposts and has become legendary in the community, garnering local and national media attention. On any given day, one sees several White granola-type people working the farm. Establishing an organic farm and ministering to the local community is just the start for Sorrell. His next move is to bring a grocery store to South Dallas so that the residents and the students are no longer chained to fast-food and convenience stores for nutrition.

While working with the farm, students learn about the money behind food, especially organic food. On the "We over Me" Farm there are no pesticides, which takes considerably more work on the part those staffing the farm. "We're out there every morning hoeing, pulling weeds, spraying nutrients. The worst thing to pick is peas because they grow so fast and you have to search for them and pick them right away. Watermelon, squash, and most of the other vegetables are easy." One student told us, "When you go out to the farm and you grow something and you see it go off with a family, it really touches your heart, and you start realizing that 'we over me' is a good idea and it helps the community."

Along with farming, students learn a solid work ethic and gain a sense of belonging on campus. They feel a type of ownership of the farm—sweat equity. They have to get up early and to work hard at the same time that they are taking corresponding courses in entrepreneurship and nutrition. Based on what she learned at Paul Quinn College and the "we over me" perspective, a Black female student shared that she planned on opening an automotive shop after graduating with the goal of rehabilitating formerly incarcerated individuals. She told us that her brother had been sent to jail for something he didn't do. She knows firsthand that those with a criminal record—guilty or not—are rarely given a second chance, and she wants to provide that chance to people. Although the young woman came to Paul Quinn with the idea of opening an automotive shop, taking the college's social entrepreneurship course pushed her to "want to do something for the world." PQC helped her to mold the idea into something bigger than she could have imagined on her own.

A business professor connected his class to the farm and issues of health and wellness, which included having his students take a detailed look at the food industry. In teaching this way, the professor told us that he has a larger vision:

I hope that they learned a greater appreciation for global problems and local issues and where they fit into these problems. I want to inculcate the idea in them that they are not isolated atoms but that they are part of a broader whole. I teach them that contributing to the broader whole can also aid in their own development.

Students at Paul Quinn College are solving real-world problems that have an impact on their local communities, and these experiences are keeping them in college as they feel a sense of purpose in the world.

Teaching Activism: "I Am Not Trash"

In 1968, roughly 1,300 sanitation workers in Memphis, Tennessee, marched in support of their civil rights and the right to organize. While they marched, they wore large, striking signs that said "I AM A MAN." The Memphis workers were the inspiration for a recent protest movement at Paul Quinn College. Upset with the city of Dallas's decision to expand a landfill in the Highland Hills / Paul Quinn College neighborhood, students pushed back and tried to educate the larger Dallas community. Students could not understand why the city was willing to expand the community landfill, yet no one would provide the same community with a grocery store.

In the activist tradition of HBCUs, over eighty students at Paul Quinn demonstrated outside city hall against the expansion of the landfill on September 21, 2011. And then on September 28, 2011, frustrated with the potential decision of the city council, the Paul Quinn students, faculty, and staff members protested once again. This time they marched outside city hall until the city council meeting began. The protesters stood up at the start of the meeting and remained standing for two hours until the meeting ended. While standing, the Paul Quinn students and staff wore "I AM NOT TRASH" t-shirts, harkening back to the historic "I AM A MAN" protest in Memphis. The Paul Quinn contingent came to the meeting to request that the city set up a citizen-led task force to consider the landfill issue. Despite their efforts, the city council voted 8–7 against the idea of a task force. Paul Quinn College's battle for access to fresh food and distance from trash continued until the protesters were able to garner enough outside support to block the landfill expansion. According to one faculty member: "We all took part in the march. And when the students came back to campus after the first protest, the faculty members went to the cafeteria and we waited for them to arrive. When they made it to campus we clapped for them and were so proud. Their faces were just beaming." Faculty members who worked with the students on the protest wanted to teach them that success is about "transcending certain barriers and obstacles and hopefully excelling."

The student government association president planned the event. He was inspired by the books on civil rights that he had read in one of his classes. From his perspective:

> As seniors, we showed the freshmen that this is what we do at Paul Quinn. We're a small school, but we fight for our community. The school can only get better if the community is better. If they want to bring all of the trash to South Dallas, it shows the way the city thinks about this area of town.

He added: "The city says a larger landfill will bring more money to our community, but we'd like a Walmart or a Kroger grocery store. These stores would also bring money and jobs to the community." Seeming wise beyond his years, he told us: "The march instilled in us 'If you don't like something, change it.' That's instilled in us. But if you're going to change it, make sure it benefits everyone, not just yourself. That's how it is here." The idea of activist leadership permeates the entire campus, and students see it as central to the "I Am Not Trash" movement. One student explained to us that every year he has been at the college, the students have been involved in something that had them out in the community and at call centers. In his words, "When someone is in need, we are there." Being responsible and accountable to others gives the Paul Quinn College students a sense that they are contributing to society in profound ways and reinforces their sense of belonging at the institution.

Faith as Retention Strategy

Paul Quinn College is a faith-based institution, affiliated with the AME Church. The religious traditions of the AME Church permeate the campus—from photos of bishops, to religious symbols on walls, to prayers at special events, to ministers on the board of trustees. Faith also spills out into the classrooms. Teachers pray with their students much as families do in their homes. One professor who has been with the institution for three years told us that she begins and ends all of her classes with a prayer. For two researchers from secular research institutions, this idea seems over the top, almost like proselytizing. But to a professor at PQC, it is part of the ethos of the campus and underscores her efforts to motivate and retain students. She wants to incorporate faith into learning. In her words:

> I want to see faith in action. I think it's important, and I ask the students if they have any special requests. Right now we have a student whose father is very ill. So we have been praying for him. I find that when I pray with the students they connect with me and they see that I care about their well-being.

This professor also thinks that praying with her students has led her to better understand them and to recognize difficult situations in their lives. Prayer also allows this professor to "touch each student individually." When we asked her if students object or feel forced, she told us that she never forces students to participate. She added that on the days when she doesn't start off with a prayer, the students remind her to do it.

Faith also manifests itself in other ways in faculty and student relationships at Paul Quinn. Faculty members have a genuine belief in students, communicating to them that they can succeed in college and following their words up with actions that ensure student success. One student shared that faculty members care about the students, and even when challenging them, they make students feel comfortable. When talking about her biology professor, she said: "He did everything that he could to help me be a success. He met with me over and over and made me feel comfortable. I was successful and came out of three of his classes with B's." Students believe that faculty members truly care about them, and they think that this care comes from the president of the institution and trickles down through the rest of the faculty and staff.

Faith can also encompass letting students experience a faculty member as a person—letting them experience the nonacademic side of the faculty member in order to develop a closeness. One of the business professors described to us how he stimulates thinking and sets a tone for his class by playing R&B music. He spends the first fifteen to twenty minutes playing music and educating students on the music and the history behind it. In his words: "We just listen to the music. We spent time listening to it and I have found that many of the students are into R&B. They give me suggestions. We are building a rapport together." Having faith in and instilling faith in students may seem like a nonconventional approach to strengthening student retention; however, in a family-like atmosphere, rooted in religious tradition, faith provides the support that students often need in order to maintain hope in their futures.

Taking Care of Family

As we sat on campus in a huge conference room filled with oversized, outdated chairs, mismatched oriental credenzas, and huge portraits of the college's founders, students came in and out of the nearby administrative offices. They were laughing, very much at home, and always coming to get something they needed or to share good news or accomplishments. Paul Quinn College is a family. And these students are taken care of as if they are family. During our visit, faculty, students, and administrators provided examples of how they take care of each other. At one point, for example, several faculty members realized that quite a few of the students couldn't see very well. Students complained about poor vision and that their heads ached. As a result the college made a collective decision to start a fund to secure eye exams and purchase glasses for the students. Once students could see, their grades improved substantially.

Faculty members also told us that they often give students money—up to $50 a month—to help them pay their bills. One faculty member mentioned buying a pay-as-you-go cell phone for a student who couldn't afford a cell phone and was the only person taking care of a sick mother. One of the staff members summarized the PQC atmosphere and family thus: "You probably can't even begin to imagine the spirit of kindness and compassion and generosity that is associated with most of the students as well as the faculty and administration. No one walks around keeping tabs. It's just the norm here."

In addition to caring, one finds structure and discipline at PQC. As mentioned earlier, President Sorrell instituted a dress code when he took over the leadership of the institution. Most students don't like it during their freshman year and tend to complain to the faculty and student affairs staff, but by their sophomore or junior year they start to understand the importance of the code and that it is preparing them for when they are no longer at PQC. Students realize that they are prepared for job interviews because they already have the proper clothes for a professional setting. In addition, because they feel part of the larger Paul Quinn family, they understand that care is the underlying value of the dress code.

To make sure that all students had access to professional clothing, PQC started a "community closet." They were able to do this by asking for donations from President Sorrell's professional contacts. When we asked Sorrell what he says to students when they push back about the dress code, he told us, "It's more expensive to buy designer jeans and tennis shoes than it is to go to a Walmart and buy a shirt and dress slacks." He also joked with us that he and his wife have donated so many things to the community closet that he often sees students walking the campus with his old clothes on and gets a chuckle. At first glance, it might seem that a dress code wouldn't matter, but the ethos of the PQC campus is remarkable. The lawns are immaculate, the students are all nicely dressed, and everyone greets you as you walk through campus. There is a certain level of respect that students pay to themselves, their campus, and others. Sorrell credits the dress code and the expectations that accompany it.

Because the school has roughly 300 students, the president knows them all and personally holds them accountable. According to staff and students, even though the president is concerned with fund-raising, finances, and the overall institution, he spends ample time with students, getting to know them and holding them accountable for learning. One student relayed the following story to us:

> Pretty much any time we would have an issue we would walk into the president's office and say, "Prez, this is going on," and he makes sure that everything was taken care of. I remember going into his office with a couple of classmates. We told him that we didn't like the first floor of our residence hall and that we wanted it to look different. He wrote us a check. We went to Home Depot, we bought all of the supplies, and everybody started painting.

Students realize that PQC is about more than traditional academics: "It's about opening doors of opportunity and making you realize that you have to give back to your community." The students told us about the mission of the institution—servant leadership—and how they want to embody that mission with their actions and lives.

Much like the president, other faculty members go beyond the call of duty to motivate students. Students told us countless stories of faculty members helping them and holding them accountable. Professors call students when they miss class, express concern when they are ill, and even knock on residence hall doors when they miss classes. It is clear that the president looks for faculty members who are willing to work beyond the confines of the classroom and for little pay. Students told us that the president "doesn't want teachers that were here for just one class. Students have to be able to communicate with faculty and to physically walk up to faculty and find them when they need them." Students are very aware that the president's first priority is students. He values faculty but reminds them that they are there for the students above all else.

The provost told us that at Paul Quinn the faculty and staff love the students. As she spoke, she was filled with emotion and even a bit cautious about using the term "love," telling us:

> I can't believe I'm about to say this, but we genuinely love our students. And when you genuinely love your students, then it allows you to be your truest best self because you can trust, you can ask them to trust you, and you can be transparent because you realize you don't have to hide anything because you're going to get stuff wrong. Our job is to educate them in all facets of life.

When we were visiting PQC, we also heard the president make a similar statement; he told us, "You can't lead people you don't love." All too often in higher education and education in general, we are afraid to express love for our students. At PQC, expressing and showing love for individuals and the surrounding community is the norm.

Paul Quinn College is also about possibilities. As we talked with students they told us many stories of their desires to create something new and to build upon their dreams, and how PQC allowed them to do this. One young man wanted to create a men's vocal choir and shared his idea with "Prez." Instead of being discouraged or told not to go ahead, he was told to do it. Being associated with a vocal choir empowered the young man to do better in his academics as well. Another student told us that she wanted to be a photographer for the school to gain professional experience. She asked "Prez," and he said yes immediately. She now serves as the main photographer on campus and, because she is committed to the institution's mission, her photos beautifully depict the soul of the students and the spirit of the campus. Still another student wanted to start a Latino/a organization on campus. She asked and was immediately given permission by "Prez." All of these students told us that PQC's faculty and staff believe in them and their potential. At the same time, they conveyed the very high expectations that everyone has of the students, especially President Sorrell.

Sorrell teaches a class on servant leadership that is a hallmark of the curricular experience at PQC. He has the students read widely—books such at *Outliers, The Alchemist,* and *The Art of War.* He shows them films they are not likely to see otherwise and pushes them to find the lessons hidden beneath the surface. Sorrell is fostering deep critical thinking among students who are often cheated by the education system in the United States. One student described the impact of the way Sorrell teaches and the books he assigns:

> All of these different poems, speeches, and individuals that he has us read or read about—in the end they are about people that went out and did things for others. They paid it forward. They might have had some of the best situations, best circumstances, and in some cases, they threw it all away for what they believed in.

Finding Your Voice and Meeting Your Goals

Since Sorrell came to PQC, he has encouraged all of the faculty members to push students, to have the highest expectations, and to accept nothing but the best grammar and writing. He knows the world outside PQC can be cruel to those who do not understand how to operate in a professional world, and he works to ensure that all of the students are ready. The core curriculum at PQC pushes writing and public speaking hard, as the president is convinced that these two skills are necessities to high performance after college. In his own course he concentrates on high-level writing, discipline, and public speaking skills, asking students to speak in front of the class about issues of importance to them and societal issues in general each week. Some of the students we spoke to didn't like the high expectations around writing, but they were also aware that being able to write and having to rise up to high expectations is a part of participating in the real world and will help them when they land a job. One of the staff members in the retention center explained the PQC approach to academics as follows: "The academics are extremely important, but beyond that we want to develop great human beings and students who know what to do, who know how to interview, who know how to speak to people, who know how to go into environments where other people may not look like them."

Through the intense reading, writing, and speaking, students are taught lessons to enable them to function at a high level in society. Students were particularly influenced by the Quinnite reading list, a list of "great books" put together by the president that all students have to read over the course of their time at Paul Quinn. One student told us, "In every course except for math, we use a book from the Quinnite reading list, and by the time you graduate you read every single book on the list." The reading of core books also spills out of the confines of the class and into the residence halls with students having deep conversations with each other. Students told us of one professor who uses Plato and Aristotle to teach about American government, drawing from these fathers of philosophy to push students to understand modern-day politics. The same professor also uses music and poetry in class to stimulate thinking. In the words of a male student: "We even listen to music. Every class period we start off with a different song, whether it be a hip-hop song, any song. He finds, randomly he finds a message within each one of those songs and compares it to our government and the way we live. It's phenomenal. I don't know how he does it."

Students are also expected to be current with national and international events, and this is no small feat, as gaining access to knowledge that many take for granted can be difficult in South Dallas. In one class, students were asked to read the *New York Times* each day and were held responsible for everything in it by the professor. It took the students nearly two weeks to find the *New York Times* because none of the stores in South Dallas sold it. According to one student, "We went everywhere. People told us, 'We're not in New York, why should we have the *New York Times*?' So we headed to the northern section of Dallas near Southern Methodist University, and everyone was sold out. We stopped at a doughnut shop and asked them if they had the *New York Times,* and they told us, 'It's 11:30 a.m. in New York.' It was a hassle to find the paper."

The Writer's Hub: Providing Focused Support

In order to augment its inclusive approach to retention and to reinforce the commitment to writing and proper grammar and usage, PQC instituted a Writer's Hub to assistant students with their classroom assignments. Faculty members use it extensively and hold students accountable for using the service. They provide extra credit for visiting with the writing specialist and incentivize students with this extra credit in an effort to get them to work ahead in their classes. One professor told us that she asks the students to turn in both a rough copy of assignments (one reviewed by the Writer's Hub) and the final copy. This strategy allows her to see progress over time and to identify weaknesses in students' writing. According to the manager of the Writer's Hub, having faculty members who allot extra credit to students who visit the Hub is a major incentive.

As mentioned, being able to write and speak well permeates the campus and is emphasized by faculty, staff, and the president in all aspects of the college experience. When we were on campus interviewing, we noticed the careful fixation on grammar—a fixation that is supported and demanded by President Sorrell. On one occasion, we were sharing some of the emotion we felt when interviewing Paul Quinn students with the president, and his first response was, "Did they use good grammar?" Sorrell is focused on making sure the students can communicate ideas in an effective way. The students at PQC seem to be fully aware of the institution's insistence on the use of good grammar and public speaking. Students told us that they are often told, "What's in your head is in your head, but you have to translate it onto paper." We found that students were working ahead of their deadlines in order to use the Writer's Hub to strengthen their papers.

The manager of the Writer's Hub has a very close relationship with the students and interacts with almost every student on campus. She told us that although many students come to work on papers with her, others come to talk, as they crave someone to listen to them. Because the Writer's Hub is located near most of the classrooms, students typically stop by before or after classes. According to the manager, when students come to Paul Quinn, many of them have problems with sentence structure and basic grammar. Students are encouraged to visit the Hub often instead of being a "one and done" student. One of the writing professors explained to us: "Writing is more than just writing. It's our representation of ourselves, of our thoughts, of our ability to think and to reason. Students have to learn that in order to be successful you have to be able to represent your ideas clearly. You must be able to speak in a way that you want to be heard."

On Being a Black College and the Connection to Retention

To those at PQC, there is something special about being a small, historically Black college. They see the institution as being vitally important to low-income African Americans as well as other students who are less fortunate. According to one professor: "Being at a Black college, with its rich history of uplift, affords students with opportunities to get the help they might need in other areas besides academics. They have a chance to be nourished, to be shown kindness and compassion, and to see that education is important for a career but also broadens you as a person." Another professor explained being at PQC, in particular stating: "I think this place is not for someone who does not believe that there are needles in haystacks. You have to dig a little. It's not for everyone, and it's definitely not for someone who doesn't believe there's a gem under all that messy veneer."

Being an HBCU is about a commitment to African American education, but it also encompasses a spirit that permeates the campus, and that spirit is dedicated to reaching out to all students desiring an education. While we were at PQC, we met non-Black students who told us about their rich experiences at the college. One young Latina told us of her journey to and through college. In 2002, her parents brought her to the United States from Mexico. Despite having a 3.5 GPA and having taken many Advanced Placement courses in high school, as an undocumented student she didn't have many options for college. Paul Quinn was willing to accept her. In this young woman's words:

> I can tell you every year that I've been here has definitely been better than the year before. I see a lot of improvement as a student. I thought it was going to feel a little bit weird because it's an HBCU, but everybody made me feel welcome from the beginning, and that's why I stayed. I believe in the mission of this institution. I feel like I am part of a big family.

Family is essential in Latino culture, and the family-like atmosphere at Paul Quinn is an immediate draw for Latino students.

A student from Detroit, Michigan, with a high school GPA of 1.8 who decided to come to PQC on the recommendation of his sister, told us that the college is his home away from home. He also conveyed a sense of family to us, noting that his adviser is his teacher and mentor. With her help, this young man is now a top student, boasting a 3.4 GPA. We asked how he was able to turn his academics around so drastically. While he credited his mentor, he also attributed his success to his own hard work, belief in himself, and a fear of disappointing the people who took a chance on him when no one else would. He told us, "I had to accomplish more and do more and really show that I am worthy of the opportunities I've been given and I'm worthy of the titles that I have."

As we sat with this young man, he told us about all of the opportunities that he has been given at PQC. In his words, "President Sorrell has given me more opportunities than I can count." As he talked to us his face lit up with a sense of surprise and awe, as if he could hardly believe what he had accomplished:

> It's just incredible the opportunities I've been given here and the leadership roles I'm in. I'm junior class president. I'm president of Alpha Phi Alpha fraternity. Sometimes I really don't believe that I'm living this life. I never imagined myself being in college for one, and two, being as successful as I am. It is humbling to realize that people believe in me when I didn't even believe in myself.

The young man went on to share how the faculty and administration at PQC supported him outside of the classroom as well, giving us example after example of people reaching out to him when he first came to the institution and struggled with academics and rallying around him when a family member passed away. Perhaps the greatest gift PQC has given this young man is a sense that he needs to "leave every place he visits better than he found it." This same student dreamed in front of us, sharing his desire to attend law school after graduation. His story was most powerful because he believed that those at PQC would continue to follow him and support him after graduation. He told us: "They definitely lay out a plan for you. They aren't going to send you out into the world without any guidance or help. They are behind their students 100 percent."

This young man from Detroit meets weekly with the president to discuss his law school admission strategy. The idea of mentoring permeates the entire campus, and mentors can be found anywhere—from nurses, to secretaries, to security officers, to professors, to the president. Mentoring also takes place among students, with the older students mentoring the younger ones and the stronger students mentoring the weaker ones. The idea of peer mentoring can be found in most classes and on the campus in both formal and informal ways.

As we talked with students they told us stories of deep care for students on the campus. They are able to discuss personal concerns as well as academic concerns. They feel safe, and they feel as if the members of the PQC family are just that—family. One student summed up the PQC approach and ethos thus: "Find me another college where you can walk up to the president and say, 'Hey Prez, I heard you are going to my hometown. Can I ride with you?' You can just hop in the car with no problem. You just won't hear a story like that. I guess that's what makes Paul Quinn so special and inspiring. It makes people want to stay here and come here."

The students at PQC can be a challenge in that they have not been socialized in the ways that many middle-class students have, not having had chances to attend summer camps and learn how to manage their schedules. The retention strategy at PQC takes these issues into consideration. It is aggressive. According to the provost, the retention plan includes "aggressive advising that pulls students in, flags them if they have attendance issues, exposes them to enrichment activities, teaches them financial literacy and servant leadership. The basic premise of the program is that we do not accept that any student will not be successful in four years." The provost also explained to us that many of the retention issues that PQC students face are vastly different from those of the average middle-class college student. Many of the students are being asked to come home and help their moms and dads pay the bills. The pressure is placed heavily on their shoulders to take care of their families by contributing through work. With low-income, first-generation students, colleges have to keep in mind that the retention challenges often have nothing to do with class readings or the academic work; instead, the out-of-classroom, home, and family challenges are big stressors. Faculty and staff try to acknowledge student stressors but to make sure that students don't use them as an excuse. One faculty member, who uses tough love to get through to students, told us: "It is important that the students move away from the mind-set of

'I'm poor, I was brought up here, my parents are divorced, and I don't know my dad.' They need a mind-set of 'I can change what happens in my life, and I will feel the repercussions of my actions and decisions.'" With the all-campus approach used at Paul Quinn, the institution has achieved an 86 percent retention rate.

Stories of Success at HBCUS

Each of the HBCUS we visited has a strong sense of family and peer support. At Morehouse College, family equates to brotherhood and taking care of one's peers. The young men at Morehouse hold each other accountable and consider their success to be contingent on the success of their brothers. At Norfolk State University, family includes student-to-student relationships—relationships that engender not only solid academic skills but also "real talk" conversations in which students can share the details—sometimes painful, sometimes joyous—of their lives and feel a sense of trust and support among other students, faculty, and staff. And at Paul Quinn College, family involves holding everyone accountable so that they help not only themselves and others but also the institution as a whole. PQC exemplifies a tough love approach that has resulted in a direct link to the college's increased enrollment and retention.

6 | Asian American and Native American Pacific Islander–Serving Institutions

Pathways to and through College

Asian American and Pacific Islander (AAPI) students arrive at college and often find themselves stereotyped as "model minorities." Whatever their ethnicity or personal experiences, they are treated as culturally and academically prepared overachievers and, at the same time, "perpetual foreigners" who will not or cannot assimilate into mainstream culture.[1] They often find themselves caught between parental and cultural expectations for their educational success and institutions that have historically seen little need to help them succeed as AAPI students. The model minority myth belies the fact that many AAPI students come to college from the margins of the global economy from communities with little experience with higher education.

For AAPI students, as for most students, college represents an opportunity to improve their lives. Not surprisingly, the academic outcomes of AAPI students are closely related to the educational resources in their local communities and their parents' income and education levels.[2] AAPI students represent dozens of countries and even more languages and cultures. They include students whose families have been in the United States for generations and others from families who are recent arrivals. Some AAPI students came to the United States and college as part of global migration patterns that draw people toward social and economic opportunities. Others arrived as political or economic refugees. All find themselves in a society that has used immigration as a means to recruit talent as well as to reunify families—a nation in which there is also a widely shared understanding that we are becoming an immigrant nation.

The complex educational needs of these diverse students led to the establishment of Asian American and Native American Pacific Islander–Serving Institutions (AANAPISIS). The 116 institutions eligible for AANAPISI status in 2009 are located in urban areas where AAPI communities are concentrated. These institutions enroll about three-quarters of low-income AAPI students.[3]

To provide these students with an equal opportunity to learn, AANAPISIS are taking on many of the major challenges taken up by Hispanic-Serving Institutions. AANAPISIS educate many first-generation college students from low-income families who struggle to afford college and those students who begin college with limited English proficiency.[4] These colleges are actively engaged in responding to the needs of these diverse students—especially AAPI students—by expanding and improving academic support, leadership, and mentorship opportunities for students, and by monitoring the progress of AAPI students.

In this chapter we explore programs and practices at three very different ANNAPISIS: a community college that is introducing students to college on an island in the Pacific Ocean; a research university that is making space for AAPI students; and a community college that is redesigning a college education for working students in a diverse American city. We begin the chapter with the narrative of the First-Year Residential Learning Community at the College of the Marshall Islands, a vibrant community in which students are learning free from the distractions of their everyday lives. At California State University–Sacramento (Sacramento State) we explore the Full Circle Project, a campus-wide collaboration uniting academic and student affairs that not only is improving the persistence of Asian American and Pacific Islander students but also providing them with an ethnic studies program that is educating a new generation of activists. Finally, we explore two initiatives at North Seattle Community College: the Navigators in the Opportunity Center for Employment and Education (OCE&E), who are transforming college education into a point of access for human resources; and the Workforce Development Council (WDC) Nursing Cohort program, a nontraditional pathway to certifications and skills that is preparing students for the workplace.

College of the Marshall Islands: A Demanding and Nurturing Residential Learning Community

Situated on the eastern edge of Micronesia and comprising 20 coral atolls and 1,200 islands spread out over 750,000 square miles, the Marshall Islands have long been widely known as a "paradise," home to a people known for their creative and delicately woven crafts and their navigation skills. Over the past 2,000 years the Marshall Islands have been colonized by many different settlers—including the Spanish, British, Russians, Germans, and Japanese. At the end of World War II, the Marshall Islands became part of the United Nations Trust Territory of the Pacific Islands, and then in 1986 signed a compact of free association with the United States, clearing the way for the dissolution of the trust in 1990.

It took thirty-three hours on four different flights before we finally arrived in the Marshall Islands—exhausted. Our plane landed on a tiny strip of rough terrain on the Majuro Atoll surrounded by ocean. The sea is everywhere and is the most visible thing to the eye on the Marshall Islands, a remote, self-sustaining place. The area surrounding the College of the Marshall Islands (CMI), both the main campus and the Arrak campus, is beautiful. There are coconut trees and coconuts everywhere. Although the ocean surrounds everything on the island, drinking water is a scarce commodity. Along the road that leads to the Arrak campus there are small houses made out of corrugated aluminum. While at first glance one might only see poverty on the Marshall Islands, we found the people to be rich in spirit and generosity during our five-day visit. When we arrived on the Arrak campus, we were greeted by a faculty member and several students along with a sign—names inscribed—welcoming us.

Originally established as an American community college, CMI was subsequently chartered by the Republic of the Marshall Islands as an independent institution in 1993. CMI is located on the Majuro Atoll, the capital of the Marshall Islands. The college is dedicated to advancing the well-being of the Marshallese people; its motto—"Seeking knowledge guarantees wisdom" (Jitdam kapeel)—honors the evolving Marshallese story through the honing not only of students' manual skills but the skills of the intellect and the heart. To that end, in 2007, CMI adopted a set of core values that includes stewardship, truth seeking, respect, high character, balance, and self-worth.

Far from the U.S. mainland, the college represents one strand of the AANAPISI mission. While the origins of the College of the Marshall Islands can be traced as far back as the mid-twentieth century, CMI became a separate institution from the College of Micronesia in 1993. Over the past decade, CMI has significantly expanded its main campus in Uliga on the Majuro Atoll. Located about twenty miles from the main campus near the tip of the atoll, the Arrak campus was established a few years ago to provide a multidisciplinary facility to support aquaculture and agriculture research as well as to house an extension center. Developed as a U.S.-style community college to serve students from the Micronesian region, this AANAPISI offers associate degrees in the liberal arts, elementary education, business administration, and nursing. While CMI is by conventional standards a small college, with fewer than 1,500 students, faculty, and staff, it is one of the largest employers in the Marshall Islands.

For the duration of its existence, the College of the Marshall Islands has been faced by one overarching challenge: most entering students are severely underprepared for college. As reflected in an in-house study completed several years ago, only 6 percent of first-year students in both 2007 and 2008 persisted to a degree within a traditional timetable. Why such a low persistence rate? Most significant, English—the language of instruction—is the second language for most students. Moreover, the majority of students have not developed the basic academic skills—including mathematics and reading—expected in an American community college. A majority of students who consider enrolling at CMI are at the elementary school level in terms of their basic academic skills: placement test scores routinely indicate that nearly one-half of Marshallese high school graduates who are interested in pursuing post-secondary education are not yet prepared to start college in the lowest developmental courses in English and math. Along with that, many students come to college with the basic challenges of poverty in the developing world: poor nutrition, inadequate housing, and the need to work in order to help support their families. And, as an administrator put it, "you dig a little deeper . . . and what you learn is you have people who are living with large numbers of family members. They don't have places to study and do work. They are not getting enough food, much less healthy food. . . . It's not encouraged nor is it part of their experience to know how to take care of themselves well." Also, there is a widespread absence of the discipline that students need to be successful in college. A majority of students enter CMI without the habits they need to succeed in college, such as showing up on time for class and having good study and nutrition habits. An administrator at CMI said that about "90 to 95 percent of CMI students are not ready for college." They need an "awakening" as to what college is and how to prepare for it.

In 2009, CMI established a residential English-language immersion program on the Arrak campus designed for at-risk, out-of-school youth to improve employability through vocational training and/or to prepare them for entry into the college. The ten-week ABC (Accelerated Boot Camp) Toolbox program was aimed at building students' basic college-going skills through a curriculum composed of courses in English, mathematics, and a vocational area (carpentry) and an extra curriculum that included field trips to reinforce English-speaking and reading skills. Along with ensuring that students acquire the most basic academic skills, at the heart of the program was a boot camp–like environment in which students were expected to acquire the personal discipline needed to be successful in college. In interviews with graduates of the program, we learned that the military approach used over the entire program was especially valuable for many students. As one student put it, the program teaches them to "work hard, don't cheat, lie, smoke. . . . Before Toolbox I was sloppy, I overslept. . . . Toolbox changed my life."

Modeled in part on the ABC Toolbox program, the First-Year Residential Learning Experience (FYRE) was established on the Arrak campus in the fall of 2011 to help students who are even less prepared for college than typical entry-level students at CMI. In the first year FYRE was a one-semester experience, but in the second year it was extended to two semesters. FYRE is anchored in providing a collaborative and supportive residential learning community that addresses the major challenges that undercut the achievement of CMI students. Along with taking developmental courses in English, mathematics, and computers, students develop the habits of mind to ensure that they have the discipline to be successful in college. While a range of practices are contributing to the success of students in the FYRE program, three strategies are at the center of what has made this program successful: (1) create an all-embracing residential community; (2) teach, train, and push and pull students to become self-disciplined; and (3) engage students in a college prep community.

An All-Embracing Residential Community

The Marshallese have survived on their islands and atolls with minimal resources for over 3,000 years. Survival has long depended on relationships, oral and participatory learning traditions, and the willingness to place cooperation with one another over individual success. This strong community orientation, a key feature of Marshallese culture, provides the foundation for the FYRE program. Breaking step with most college campuses, including even the main campus in Uliga, the FYRE program was designed to capitalize on the strong emphasis on community in Marshallese culture by incorporating familiar community-oriented practices into the fabric of the program while also engaging students in the often novel expectations of an American community college and, in turn, the practices they need to be successful.

As cohort members in the two-semester FYRE program, students live and study on the Arrak campus. Because it is located a considerable distance from the main campus and their homes, students emphasize how much they value the residential aspects of this community, which relieve them from normal everyday pressures. As one student described it, the Arrak campus is "like paradise. . . . It is a beautiful place. Another described it this way: "We are far away from all of the bad things, so we can do our study safely and quietly." Echoing this perspective, an administrator at CMI emphasizes that FYRE provides students with a "peaceful place to learn and study . . . free from distractions . . . and students feel connected, part of groups." This residential community provides a space for an "ethos of community" to develop and flourish across the major participants—students, faculty, and staff. In no small measure, in the words of a CMI administrator, "the success of some of the students is their having their secret space." For these students, the program works in large measure because it is residential, away from "lots of outside distractions."

The residential aspect of FYRE is closely tethered to the affinity for community that is all-encompassing: the FYRE community includes not only students but faculty and staff as well, with most of the faculty—including their families—housed on the campus. As a FYRE student put it, you get to know "everyone and so that's what I mean by reducing fear, because . . . you'll get to know everybody because you live with them every single day." Closely allied to this residential community, there are not major differences with respect to the roles of all members of the community. For example, the director for residential life and security not only supervises most aspects of the everyday schedules of students but also helps them with everything from completing their homework to teaching them the importance of nutrition in their everyday diet.

In addition to teaching classes, faculty members—some of whom are from as far away as the United States and the Philippines—are available to students throughout the day and often in the evening and on weekends. Faculty and staff routinely engage with students in a wide range of activities that include everything from cooking and eating healthy food, to exercising, to going fishing together on weekends, to participating in community service activities. And perhaps no less significant, faculty members interact with one another as colleagues—across the fields of English, mathematics, and computers—to discuss the challenges students are facing and what can be done to address them. A math instructor elaborated on this:

> We faculty work closely and we talk about our students. . . . One of the students in my class—his mathematics skills were really low. I shared with his English teacher and asked, How is this person doing in your class? The same thing, same story, from my side and her side. I shared with her the observation that . . . sometimes he will sit in class and maybe his mind is some other place. . . . She said he is doing the same thing in her class. . . . So I told her, okay, I'm trying to help this guy out. I'm trying to give him some extra help like tutoring.

FYRE students adopt this overall community orientation and collaborative ethos. As one student noted, "We share foods," and "We share mostly our love for each other . . . like the way we talk, we treat someone like's it's your brother and it's your sister, that's how we love each other." They also play a major role in taking care of the physical campus by participating in regular clean-ups. And they play a central role in the fall Academic Week. In this weeklong event—the most recent theme was "Celebrating a Learning Community"—students join with faculty and staff in a wide range of activities, from PowerPoint-making contests and math quizzes to essay writing and cultural games. For many of the people we talked with, the FYRE community is, as one student put it, like a "family on campus." In the words of a faculty member, "I am like a father and a parent." The participants in FYRE repeatedly use the family metaphor.

Teaching Self-Discipline

A major focus of FYRE is addressing the challenge that most students do not have the habits they need to be successful in college. Not only do most lack discipline with respect to their study habits, but many haven't been taught to take responsibility over their lives both in and outside of school—from developing healthy eating habits to not oversleeping in the morning.

FYRE faculty and staff address this challenge in three major ways. First, a major focus of a first-year seminar required of all FYRE students in the fall and spring terms is teaching effective study habits. These habits include time management strategies (such as using a calendar to map out long-range classroom projects and activities and creating a to-do list with prioritization); creating environments that foster concentration; taking and recording notes; using effective preparation and test-taking strategies; engaging in active listening; and communicating clearly. Students are exposed to a new set of academic habits at the moment they begin taking their first college classes.

Second, FYRE students must meet a demanding set of daily expectations that force them to practice the habits they need to be successful. These expectations are reflected in students' schedules, with their day beginning at 6:00 a.m. with forty-five to sixty minutes of exercise—including push-ups. After breakfast students begin a rigorous schedule that includes not only classes but study time, reading time, recreation, meeting with faculty and advisers, skill-building workshops, tutoring, meals with their respective cohort group, and various campus projects and activities including workshops on such topics as math anxiety, a healthy diet, or even basic dental hygiene. After a demanding and highly circumscribed daytime schedule, lights out is enforced at 10:00 p.m. To be sure, at first some students resist the rules, structure, and high expectations that suddenly inform their everyday lives. But FYRE students early begin to appreciate that learning self-discipline is extremely important if they are to succeed in college. Again and again FYRE students told us that they had learned to "manage their time" and become "disciplined to study hard" and "committed to self-improvement" and "become independent." As one student reflected on his first semester in the FYRE program: "Now I take an interest in study. . . . I start to like to study hard every day."

Third, faculty and staff regularly push and pull students on an individual basis to get them to seize ownership over their college journey. At the beginning of the fall semester, faculty and staff members embrace the dictum "Take FYRE students where they are and go from there." While that can involve handholding, especially as faculty and staff members get to know students on an individual basis, a push-and-pull ethos begins to take over during the first semester. A faculty member emphasized that straight talk and tough love become signature features of relationships with students, especially in outside-of-class advising and tutoring: "I'm trying to push them to study . . . even if

I have to go around and call them. 'Okay, we have to meet at this time. You have to come.'" As observed by a member of the FYRE staff, "Teachers know how to change students." They do not, this person went on, allow students to excuse themselves from taking responsibility for their learning. One of the ways faculty members invite such change is to ask students a simple question early in the fall term: "What do you wish to become?"

FYRE students look out at a difficult future. Estimates in 2006 put the unemployment rate in the Marshall Islands at 36 percent. Traditionally, the Marshallese depended on a subsistence economy centered on fishing, and despite the disruptions of European colonialism, small-scale agriculture continues. The nation has tried to develop industries around tuna and coconut processing, but the mainstay of the economy remains the nearby Kwajalein Atoll military base. Seventy percent of employed Marshallese work in the service industry, and nearly one-third work for a government that receives roughly 60 percent of its revenue from payments from the United States. Some Marshallese are now finding employment in a growing service sector that provides services for the U.S. military, tourists, and marine transportation.[5]

A faculty member spoke candidly in saying that FYRE students need a lot of shepherding:

> Always in the classroom I would say, "We're here to learn. This may look like a resort, it looks like you are living in a hotel, there's air conditioning and the place is really nice, but I would like to remind you that you're here to learn, not for a vacation. . . . My dear students, you are not any more in high school, you are in college. . . . I respect you as my students. Yes, I am friendly to you at times, but it doesn't mean to say that if you don't do your homework I would excuse you and I would ask you to do it and give it to me tomorrow. If it is due today, then you have to submit it today."

At the same time, this faculty member said:

> I'm like your mom, your second mom, in this classroom, and I ought to know what is happening to you, and you ought to tell me because I wouldn't know. If you need anything from me you can knock at my door if you need my help. Don't hesitate to call me if you ever need help. And yes, the students, we're like a family.

In short, students' relationships with teachers and staff—push-and-pull relationships in which students develop an appreciation of the positive results often associated with higher expectations—can go a long way in helping them to become more self-disciplined in their pursuit of a college education.

Engaging Students within a College Prep Community

Coupled with its community ethos and the training and push and pull of students to become self-directed, FYRE is above all a learning community. During the fall term, students take a mathematics course that meets daily, combining lectures, in-class tutoring, and computer-assisted instruction. And along with a computer course, students also take two English courses. In the spring, students take another mathematics course along with two additional English courses. By the year's end, most are on their way to completing the foundation of an associate degree.

As we learned in our visit, a culture of mutually reinforcing teaching and learning on the Arrak campus is visible both in courses and outside of the classroom. FYRE students—often tapped intentionally by staff and faculty—help peers who are struggling in their course work. As a staff member observed: "If I were to pick a strength of the students here, it is that they believe and feel that what they are doing is part of a responsibility to each other that is important to them. That clearly is important to them . . . leaning a little more toward kind of a responsibility to others over individual freedoms." FYRE students often meet outside of class to help their peers with their learning—what they refer to as peer tutoring.

For example, students in the FYRE program established a Fallout Club whose driving purpose is to get together and help each other out through everything from peer teaching to group learning. As a staff member who had worked closely with Fallout described it: "If one student doesn't understand the homework for that day, they would ask the other ones [who] would show them how . . . and they would ask each other questions." The Fallout Club subsequently became an official student organization on the main campus to support ongoing relationships among former FYRE students who attended the main campus and to support relationships with the new FYRE students on the Arrak campus.

The commitment of FYRE faculty and staff to student learning and progress is a story in and of itself. To begin with, faculty members work closely with one another in supporting the learning of all students. By way of example, the mathematics instructor and the computer instructor support each other's students. The computer teacher provides math support—what he refers to as "tutor support"—to students in math courses who need assistance. In his words: "We support the math faculty, and they support me, so it's interdisciplinary support for the student. And I can support the math faculty because we are using the same lab, and we are handling the same students all the time and most of that we do while I am teaching my class." This teacher and his colleagues are watching over a cohort of learners and providing the support each member needs when that support is needed.

The faculty members who teach the FYRE academic core—mathematics, English, and computer courses—also tutor students several hours each day outside of class. And faculty members seize the initiative to interact with students when they are in the cafeteria, in study halls, and throughout the residential community. Most faculty members are available seven days a week to meet with students. And students often come to see faculty for tutoring and advice at their homes in the evening as well as on weekends. Doing college-level work becomes a routine part of students' lives, a faculty member told us:

> I find one student always comes to my house almost every day knocking and asking, "Can you explain to me this problem?" A few days ago, twice in a row I had two girls [come] to my house, knock on my door asking questions on the math problem. This was around 9:00 in the night. So it's almost 9:00 and they're still working on their math.

Why is the FYRE program a story of success? To begin with, the program is anchored in a vibrant residential community in which all involved—faculty, staff, and students—embrace the responsibility to cultivate their own learning as well as the growth and development of others. That FYRE is a residential community—one separated from the everyday lives of most students—is a distinguishing hallmark that underpins the success of the program. The first semester is fundamental to the success of the program. Without exception, first-year students need to become disciplined learners. And faculty and staff, with a combination of tough love and a demanding schedule that in many ways echoes the Toolbox program that preceded FYRE, provide students with ongoing tutoring, instruction, workshops, exercise, and out-of-class experiences that prepare them for the rigors of college.

Finally, FYRE embodies a genuine learning community that prepares students for the academic challenges they will face in college. From their course work to the extensive tutoring they receive from faculty and staff and their peers, students who begin the program with very modest capabilities in mathematics and English often have significant gains in their academic preparedness for college. In fall 2011, for example, FYRE students completed all their classes at a rate eleven points higher (97 versus 86 percent) and passed all their classes at a rate nearly thirty points higher (62 versus 35 percent) than their non-FYRE peers. FYRE students finished all of their classes. Their grade point average (GPA) was half a point higher in pre-algebra, Introduction to MS Office, and College Strategies. Not surprisingly, their fall to spring retention rate was also higher (by six points). By providing a sanctuary that is at once demanding and nurturing, the program has helped FYRE graduates go a long way toward becoming self-directed learners who are prepared to flourish in college.

The FYRE program has had impressive outcomes. As reflected in data from its first year, compared with peers on the main CMI campus, FYRE students had (1) higher grades in English, math, and computer courses; (2) higher first-semester completion rates and fewer withdrawals; and (3) improved retention through the first and second years of college. However, as this narrative is being written, the FYRE program on the Arrak campus is being closed. Why? While having a separate program a considerable distance from the main campus has been highly successful, major financial challenges at CMI have made it impossible to continue the program on the Arrak campus. Although the FYRE program is being discontinued, the concept of a residential learning community upon which FYRE was built lives on: a residential learning community is now being established on the main CMI campus.

California State University at Sacramento (Sacramento State): Fostering Activism

Located in one of California's major metropolitan areas and serving more than 28,000 students, Sacramento State offers fifty-eight undergraduate majors, forty-one master's degree programs, and two doctoral degree programs. While the green and lush campus is located not far from such popular destinations as San Francisco, the Napa and Sonoma valleys, and Lake Tahoe, most students are from the Sacramento area. A majority of the undergraduates at this California State University campus are first-generation and minority students, many of whom come to Sacramento State with significant familial responsibilities and modest financial resources. The diverse student body is made up of over one-fifth AAPI students and nearly one-fifth Latino students, along with a sizable African American population. As is the case at most AANAPISIS, the diversity of AAPI students at Sacramento State is nothing short of breathtaking: along with substantial numbers of Hmong and Chinese students, there are significant numbers of Koreans, Filipinos, other Southeast Asian students, and multiracial students. Closely tethered to this ethnic diversity, some AAPI students are immigrants, whereas others have lived in California for generations. There is relatively little language commonality across these groups.

Many AAPI students enter Sacramento State tentatively, often with uncertainty and off-campus commitments. For many students, one of these challenges is a lack of a positive self-identity. Some students are embarrassed by their parents or grandparents and the journey that brought them to the United States. Along with this, as an employee at Sacramento State put it:

> Many of the AAPI students are in survival mode. At a very young age they or their older siblings have to translate for their parents . . . helping them with their income tax. . . . I went through that, too. My father was an immigrant from Asia, and my mother passed away—she was an American-born Chinese—when I was thirteen. And then one of the things I had to do was fulfill some of her roles, because my father did not speak or write English, so I lived that life, too.

Small wonder that many AAPI students enter college with a considerable amount of fear, uncertainty, and shyness.

Several years ago, the then director of the Asian American Studies program began looking at some longitudinal data and found that while AAPIs were coming into Sacramento State academically prepared, they did not graduate at the same rates as similarly prepared students from other racial and ethnic groups. Coupled with this, there were many campus-wide programs for most minority groups—including African Americans and Hispanic/Chicano students—but there was not a single campus-wide program for AAPI students. As one professor put it, many "were not getting a sense of community on our campus. There's a lot of different AAPI groups here. There's a lot of different individual clubs. They're all in little silos. They just didn't feel engaged with other AAPIs and with the university as a whole." This lack of engagement, he reasoned, made it easier for these students to decide not to finish degrees. To better serve the needs of AAPI students, including the challenges that many of them were facing, the ethnic studies faculty took the initiative to develop the Full Circle Project (FCP).

The Full Circle Project is a comprehensive, institution-wide innovation that is anchored in a campus-wide collaboration among programs and units across academic affairs and student affairs. Along with improving retention and graduation rates for AAPIs, the FCP aims at providing students with an education driven by a vision of an "ethnic studies education" that permeates the entire first year of college. As the FCP program director puts it, AAPI students need to understand their own experience and "connect it with the broader Asian American studies, Asian American movement. . . . We easily could just have created a first-year program like everybody else does. That has success. That's very successful. But we wanted to push the envelope a little bit more than that."

Modeled on support programs developed for first-generation students, low-income students, and students of color, the FCP is a cohort of seventy-five AAPI students—with one-third of FCP students also in the federally funded Educational Opportunity Program (EOP). The program provides students with targeted academic support while also requiring that they become involved on campus and in the local community. In addition to enrolling in a three-credit ethnic studies course (Introduction to Ethnic Studies or Introduction to Asian American Studies) each semester of their first year, FCP students take a three-credit ethnic studies first-year seminar (ETHN 21) in the fall and a one-credit ethnic studies cocurricular activities course (ETHN 98) in the spring. In keeping with its ethnic studies roots, the FCP involves students in the campus and local community. Along with their classes—especially the ETHN 21–ETHN 98 sequence—and ongoing interaction with program advisers and peer mentors, FCP students also become involved in the Sacramento State Leadership Initiative (LI). The LI is a certificate program designed to develop students' leadership and professional skills and to serve as a foundation for participation in campus life. Through both the required courses and the LI, students engage in campus and community-based formal and informal service-learning activities; many visit and become involved in the nationally recognized 65th Street Corridor Community Collaboration Project. In ETHN 98 all FCP students work in coalitions to develop and present workshops or other community organizing events that address an issue that emerged in their course work. In what follows we elaborate on what it is about the FCP program that is having a significant impact on student learning and persistence.

An Ethnic Studies Education

The Full Circle Project, the program leader is quick to emphasize, represents a "cultural shift" in higher education: "FCP really is an ethnic studies driven program" that provides AAPI students at Sacramento State with the basic foundation of a college education. From the point of view of a student services administrator who helped design the program, the FCP "reinforces who [students] are from a cultural perspective and as a result . . . they've really taken hold of the campus because . . . they feel like it belongs to them."

True to ethnic studies, the FCP encourages AAPI students to view their learning throughout college as closely linked to activism and community organizing.[6] To begin with, students in the core ethnic studies courses explore, often for the first time, the ways that racialized communities in the United States have established their identities and found voices in the American narrative. As they reflect on issues of social injustice and survival as well as the cultural vibrancy of racial and ethnic groups, FCP students are encouraged to develop critical and reflective interpretations with respect to the places of their respective communities in U.S. history and, in concert with that, to cultivate the dispositions and skills of community activists who are prepared to engage in social change not only within but well beyond the Sacramento State campus. Three features of the ethnic studies program at Sacramento State— exploring racial and ethnic identities, sharing stories of the activism and leadership of racialized individuals and groups, and providing opportunities to think critically—are the major shapers of the FCP. Each is elaborated on here.

Exploring Racial and Ethnic Identities

The widely known "model minority myth" fails to acknowledge the uncertainty that many AAPI students have with respect to their racial and ethnic identity. As an ethnic studies faculty member puts it: "A lot of students, particularly Southeast Asian students, don't know that much about their family coming over here because they just didn't talk about it very much. They just know their parents struggled and it's been hard. They don't know about being a boat person or the refugees and that kind of stuff to a certain extent." Another ethnic studies faculty member emphasizes that because many AAPI students at Sacramento State are unaware of their own stories, they "are not on solid ground." As AAPIs, they are unsure about the roles they can and wish to play in their own education.

To help AAPI students find solid ground, the FCP has them begin their college career as part of a cohort of students who read, reflect on, and talk about the experiences of AAPI students in the United States. This ethnic identity component, a student services person stressed, is a hallmark of the program—and it is "something that we have not seen before." As an ethnic studies faculty member explained it, students "learn a little bit more of their own history . . . [and get an] introduction to racial and ethnic groups into the United States, race relations. . . . What is prejudice? What is discrimination?" in a way that inspires them "to become further involved, either on campus or in their own racial or ethnic communities."

These ethnic studies basics are reinforced across the FCP experience. In their first-year seminar, students not only read about strategies for being successful college students but also read and reflect on an ethnic studies primer developed by the faculty for this course. As part of the seminar and the FCP, they attend the first phase of the Leadership Initiative—a phase that more than 90 percent of students completed in the first year of the FCP—that focuses them on "individual values . . . [such as] consciousness of self and commitment." According to the program director, this identity work is "never just, 'Oh, you're Asian.'" An ethnic studies education is anchored in an activist view of self, which in turn is anchored in cultural history:

> Don't forget about everything else. You are your history, and it's part of the whole Asian American experience. Asian American history is American history; ethnic history of different groups is American history. So they get that in their course work. . . . We focus on really the beginning of ethnic studies in the 1960s: serving the community, working with other groups, empowerment, building coalitions, a number of things. We not only teach that but they actualize it, they engage in it.

An FCP student elaborated: "We didn't just learn about their struggles but we learned about how they overcame them." All of the students we interviewed at Sacramento State emphasized their development of an AAPI identity. One observed with some surprise: "I didn't know what a Hmong person was. I thought that all of them . . . came from China." As he read about Hmong American history and listened to his Hmong peers tell him their stories, his Hmong identity began to "make sense" to him. For another student, a Hmong woman, it was a conversation with the Asian American mayor of Oakland that linked Chinese immigration and the Chinese exclusion laws with her own agency. A brief conversation with an Asian leader convinced her that as a second-generation Hmong American who was getting a college education, she was carrying the Asian American narrative forward. "Full Circle emphasizes that."

Sharing Stories of Activism and Leadership and Learning

Students in the Full Circle Project learn history. Historical narratives, often told by AAPIs for AAPIs, play a central role not only in the core curriculum but in field trips and service-learning experiences as well. Students described the class to us as enriching their sense of their past and their possibilities—and as eye-opening. As one student elaborated:

> Throughout all of my grade school experience I've only been taught the U.S. perspective of history. To get the perspective of history from Asian Americans, Asians, immigrants, Asian Indians and everyone else's perspective—it was really eye-opening to see the different side of things. It helps put into perspective just really the importance of what was going on and what exactly did happen instead of just seeing one side of it like we had for the past twelve years before college.

The narratives at the center of the FCP experience go far beyond course readings and class discussions. Faculty we interviewed listed event after event that showcased AAPIs. For example, FCP students have met Gates Millennium Scholars, the producer/director of the first Asian American film, *The Curse of Quon Gwon,* and many others who talk about growing up as AAPIs and the ways that their history inspired what they do now. To this end, a faculty member emphasized the "absolute home run it was" when they brought in the first AAPI Supreme Court justice in California: "She spoke and it was great. She talked about her growing up as a Filipino American. She talked about her family as Filipino farm workers and that the work she [did] inspires what she does today. It was great."

Relevant and inspiring Asian American history was tethered to these events. When the Ethnic Studies Department screened the first Asian American film, faculty asked FCP students to help make the event happen. Student volunteers— "Half the class volunteered," a faculty member told us—orchestrated a campus-wide event that showcased the work of previous generations of local activists. Faculty saw in the students "commitment and inspiration." Students described realizing that Asian people have made their own history and that they were, almost in spite of themselves, adding to that narrative.

Finally, FCP faculty and students draw on one another as role models and as sources of narratives that help to ground their AAPI identity and testify to their AAPI agency. As an administrator at Sacramento State put it:

> I think one of the things I was going to say about students' involvement in the Full Circle Project is they come in as new students, and they have all of these people in leadership positions, in positions of authority, who do identify as Asian / Asian-Pacific Islander. . . . We have had a number of events where Congressman Matsui and others in the community . . . have been in front of them and have been speaking to them, where all of a sudden . . . they are actually starting that efficacy piece.

As one student put it:

> We see our professors all the time, and our staff . . . come into our classes every . . . chance they get. Just knowing that, wow, our staff members are Asian Americans and here we are. . . . But having our staff be our role model, it was like, wow. You're Asian American, I'm Asian American too, and if I can see someone in this position that is the same color as I am it pushes me. It makes me proud. It's like, dang, I can do that. . . . I can do the same thing you're doing or get there higher.

Providing Opportunities to Think Critically

Students come to recognize that no one is "just" Asian, the FCP program director emphasized to us. Questioning assumptions about ethnicity and narratives of the lived experience of racial and ethnic groups is a founding concept of ethnic studies. FCP staff and faculty members stress that critical thinking and reflection play central roles in FCP classes and the Leadership Initiative. The core classes, a former Ethnic Studies Department chair explains, "give students the tools to do it, to think analytically." These tools are tightly linked with the founding principles of ethnic studies.[7] Ethnic studies emphasizes the idea that one returns again and again to data in order to question assumptions and explanations and to make note of the agency of members of racialized groups. Research in an ethnic studies framework is not the simple gathering of facts, but rather questioning who is gathering and sharing facts and how that work is done. These basic methods are at the center of learning and teaching in the FCP. The capacity to take and reflect on critical perspectives is central. In class discussions and field trips, students learn, one faculty member noted, "to look at [experience] from an insider's perspective, not [only] following a chronology," and they become increasingly aware of their own perspectives while also considering those of others. The Leadership Initiative is designed, a counselor told us, so that students figure out campus resources, engage the campus, and "think critically about . . . 'Okay, what about myself?'" To use the words of a student services staff member, FCP students "learn in the classroom and build leadership out of the classroom, but also go out and be in the culture and in another culture." They learn to develop standpoints and to take responsibility for using those standpoints to contribute to social change.

Another ethnic studies faculty member described this basic tool at length. For him, perspective taking involves a "shift from being the person who sits and takes notes, knows how to take tests, can regurgitate for the professor exactly, or I should say the high school teacher, exactly what they're supposed to for the test." The ethnic studies core guides students in "thinking critically and asking questions and challenging and doing it in a way that is as much as possibl[e] consciously done in conversation with their values." He went on to describe the process. Students begin by identifying issues about which they feel very passionate. After asking lots of questions, they reflect on where their interests come from, how their history—a history that has been steadily enriched by their ethnic studies education—informs what they can do about what they care about.

The interests of students lead them to engage in research. In their ethnic studies courses, students read textbook chapters and journal articles concerning the history and study of race and ethnicity in the United States as well as a series of book chapters and journal articles about higher education in the United States. In completing course assignments, students are guided by ethnic studies faculty and campus librarians in gathering both primary documents—for example, published policies for a local school district or demographic information about human trafficking—and selected research literature. This research informs their conversations in their classes and their engagement in required service learning. While they learn ethnic studies content, the outcome of the courses is to engage students in research that leads to cultivating ideas and, in turn, to disseminating these ideas in ways that contribute to social change on and off campus.

Reflecting on their coalition projects, students described how they felt obligated to look critically at issues that "really shaped me" and "apply that [thinking] in workshops . . . doing whatever I can." And they described using this same tool to think more critically about how they are managing their lives as students and how—in the case of Hmong daughters and sons—they would adapt their new understanding of power relations to their roles in traditional Hmong families. Those students who had completed the final phase of the Leadership Initiative described putting into play what they had learned about U.S. history, organizational theory, interpersonal communications, theories of leadership, and social change. As part of the Leadership Initiative, they set up an electronic portfolio and met with a career counselor, beginning to "translate their involvement in leadership development into a résumé and start preparing for their professional life after college." They described a growing understanding of the sources of their own values and habits as well as those of others, and they added to this knowledge of history, sociology, and culture a set of strategies for communicating and collaborating with others.

An Activist Education

The focus in ethnic studies on identity, stories, and critical thinking not only engages students in their education but at the same time encourages them to put their education in the service of social change. As the director of the FCP puts it, the program helps students develop critical and reflective understandings of their own experiences "but also really connects them with the broader Asian American studies, Asian American movement." At one level, being part of a movement provides a safe and supportive place in which to develop identities and critical awareness. The program, an administrator told us, is patterned on the learning community developed by the Washington Center at Evergreen State University: "FCP is built on relationships and not just the standard way of going into the classroom where you never get to know the names of your peers." An ethnic studies faculty member confirmed her assertion. For him, "relationships count. When you see somebody struggling, you speak to it. Period." As routine practice, he attends to students' engagement and not simply their performance; he described "pulling students aside" to find out why they are disengaging. For one student, this kind of proactive relationship with faculty and peers was critical: "You have your own family, but Full Circle, honestly, it's a family too." Having a family on campus was, for him, the difference between staying and leaving.

> The FCP is not just any family. It is an ethnic studies family committed to community organizing for social change. It has, to use a faculty member's phrase, a strong "activist bent." The program is anchored in a department, two senior faculty members explained, with a vision that includes a commitment both to service to the community and to the completion of a bachelor's degree in students' areas of interest. Reflecting on the program design, these faculty members and others returned to a set of core experiences. FCP students meet early in their fall term with other AAPI leaders at Sacramento State and then again in the spring for a celebration. By the end of the fall semester, students began to move beyond their initial academic or ethnic cohorts and began to feel that the college was theirs. One student recalled an activity in the fall retreat in which AAPI students asked one another about whether they were first-generation college students and whether their family supported them in their college education: That workshop . . . it made us see that these Asian American peers next to me, their story is similar to mine, that we shouldn't be afraid to talk to each other because we're different. We share similar stories, and we are going through this program and college together as a group. Ever since the retreat, I'm not afraid to approach them anymore.

These students were also not afraid to speak to their campus and local community. A faculty member told us that by the end of the first year of the program, more than 90 percent of FCP students completed one or more LI certificates, and more than twenty participated in the 65th Street Corridor Project. They also worked together to put on more than a dozen events on campus and in the local community dealing with issues such as academic success in high school, access to health services, discrimination, environmental degradation, human trafficking, and LGBT rights. These events, he went on to tell us, were impressive: the students "stepped up to the plate, not only off campus but on campus as well." True to the ethnic studies framework, students find their place in their education and communities by doing community service.

While opportunities to become involved in community service are incorporated into the ethnic studies courses, we identified three structured paths to service. The first, the Sacramento State Leadership Initiative, is a path some FCP students start on as early as the EOP Summer Bridge program. Based on the social change model of leadership development, the LI is a natural partner for the ethnic studies–based FCP. The LI consists of a series of workshops and events through which students learn theories of organizational behavior, interpersonal communications, and leadership. Their reflections link this content to their own experience as students and emerging leaders within a set of interlinked organizations—the FCP cohort, student organizations, service-learning sites, and Sacramento State University.

The LI is designed as a hub to engage Sacramento State students with campus resources and organizations. To complete LI certificates, students write reflective papers about each event or activity they attend. They write about the ways in which they are growing in dimensions that resonate with ethnic studies, dimensions that include conception of self, collaboration, citizenship, and change. Students become involved through adviser and mentor encouragement and ETHN 21 assignments and move through a series of levels in which they earn certificates. A student services leader explained the LI structure:

> The Green certificate really focuses on the individual values within that model. The model has individual, group, and then community values, so the certificates are broken up accordingly. The Green certificate is the individual values, which are consciousness of self, congruence, and commitment, and then the group values make up the Gold certificate, which is collaboration, common purpose, and controversy with civility. . . .

Hornet Pride is our third certificate, and that is citizenship, which is one of the community societal values, and then we actually have a workshop in there on change, on social change, which specifically helps them to plan for what the fourth certificate is, which is planning a social change project that they will actually implement in the community or on campus.

The ETHN 21–ETHN 98 sequence shadows this basic structure, requiring students to reflect on their development as community organizers and inviting students to use the LI to build professional and social capital and sometimes extra credit.

Nearly all FCP students complete the first certificate, compared to about a third of all first-year students. Some complete all four certificates their first year of college. Across our interviews, students told us how much the LI had enhanced their college experience. One student, for example, explained that she planned "to commute back and forth. I thought I was going to come to school, go home, hours of studying and midterms and finals." The LI taught her how "to be involved in the school, . . . to get to know the resources and know people, get connections." The LI also has an impact on how students view being in college. For one, LI events—and the continual reflection assignments—"really helped clarify a lot of things and put things into perspective." Another recalled connecting with other students—including graduate students who facilitated LI events—and realizing that college "is not always about class and midterms and finals; it's more than that."

Another student emphasized to us that the LI events linked her to resources on campus—from free movies to workshops on using writing citation styles—but also, to her surprise, turned her into a leader even though she "wasn't really the leader type" and had no intention of being a leader in college. The LI helped her realize that "I am capable of this. I have done this." As she continued to reflect during our conversation about what her participation meant, she realized that through participating in the LI she became a successful college student who was actively building community at Sacramento State. One of her peers, a young Hmong woman, added another layer to this process of development. She described developing as a leader through an ethnic studies framework, analyzing the identity ascribed to her as an Asian woman and coming to the realization through her participation in LI events: "Okay, if I don't want them to think of me like that I'll have to put myself out there . . . have to be loud and not so quiet. That's one thing that they really teach us . . . to do. If we want to change how people think, we have to change the way we do it as well."

A second structured path to service is the coalition project in ETHN 98. For many students, this experience is the capstone of their FCP first year, and we came to see the ETHN 21–ETHN 98 sequence of courses as the heart of the program. In their fall ETHN 21 course, students explore their interests as AAPI college students by reading classics from ethnic studies literature side by side with readings on learning, college-going, and careers. As they read, talk, and write, the course instructor explained, students reflect on "how their interests reflect their development, their experiences" and identify a set of contemporary issues of importance to them. By the end of the fall semester, they are ready to focus in on an issue and align themselves with others to form coalitions that will do something about the issue in a local community. In groups of four to seven self-selected participants, students meet and reflect on their shared values and, in turn, begin their inquiry by identifying a mission or problem statement to guide their project. All of this work is done in the open through forums and profiles on the class website and culminates in community organizing projects.

Early in the term students in each of the coalitions present their mission statement to the entire class. The topics of such projects have included everything from marriage equality and gay rights to access to health services. An instructor of one of the ethnic studies courses was

> blown away about how deeply students thought about the values; how eloquent they were and how well-formed these mission statements were. These were first-year students. I couldn't believe it, and again, these are projects around drug or sex trafficking, or poverty, like really big, heady, meaty topics, and they were so well articulated and thought through, and it was really inspirational to see these students work together in that capacity, toward social change.

In participating in such service-learning experiences, students begin to seize their voice and pursue their identity as activists—as leaders for social change.

Several students spoke passionately about their participation in an anti-discrimination coalition made up of six students. Working from January through May, the group explored the question of discrimination on campus by scheduling an on-campus workshop that included activities that invited Sacramento State students to reflect on discrimination. At one of the activities students were invited to talk about a time when they had been discriminated against on campus and how they overcame it. During another activity, called Examine Yourself, students were asked to write their prejudiced thoughts on a note, post the note, and then read it out loud. According to one of the students in the coalition, when some of these notes were read to the participants at the workshop "there was silence and we read it again out loud. The people that, the students that attended [our] workshop were stunned, and we were stunned, too. . . . In our ethnic studies classes we talk about discrimination and prejudice and all that. So we applied that into our workshop." To illustrate, a member of the coalition said, "Some of them [students in the activity] were like, 'Asians can't drive' or 'I'm scared to walk at night when there's African Americans around' or stuff like that."

What impressed the faculty who observed the activity was the way that these students were able to apply the theories of culture and identity they encountered in their ethnic studies classes. They were able to communicate complex concepts like racism and discrimination to a potentially unsympathetic audience in ways that opened dialogue rather than shut it down. These first-year students seemed to one faculty member to be integrating their learning about culture, communications, and social change in a public performance.

The ETHN 98 coalition is the core FCP service opportunity. A third structured path to service, the 65th Street Corridor Project, leads students to community service beyond the comfort of the FCP. Reflecting on student participation in the 65th Street Corridor Project, an ethnic studies faculty member described it as the goal toward which the FCP is leading: "The hope is that what FCP students have gained in terms of their community engagement is going to be not just with the university but engagement outside of the university as well. We are creating a cohort, a vanguard of leaders." The 65th Street Corridor Community Collaborative Project was created in 2001 when a new ethnic studies chair arrived at Sacramento State. He recalled the reason for starting the project as the new chair of an established ethnic studies program. The vision was a return to

a renewed commitment to service to the community. . . . That was part of a founding principle of ethnic studies, but yet by 2001 I thought it had become diluted across the country, and ethnic studies in many ways had evolved into being service courses to fulfill [a] general education diversity requirement, as opposed to the original mission. I just think you should do both.

The 65th Street Corridor Project is both. The partnership with seventh through twelfth grade schools in a low-income and diverse Sacramento community began with the creation of a ninth-grade ethnic studies course and led to the development of three components: the Student Bridge program, which brings middle and high school students to Sacramento State to gain an understanding of college-going culture; the Parent Bridge program, which gives parents an opportunity to learn about college preparation and access; and "a tutoring and mentoring program that is now the heart of the project." Most Sacramento State students become involved through the ethnic studies program, often through credit-bearing ethnic studies internships or directed studies courses. These students learn the principles of the discipline by engaging in community service, and at the same time contribute to a legacy of community service. Over eleven years, the project's founder observed, 2,500 university students have started a dozen projects in schools serving more than 20,000 elementary and secondary school students, family members, and teachers. During that time the project established a venue for community concerns to be heard and a strong partnership with the Sacramento City Unified School District.

Doing both—learning ethnic studies and serving a community—is having a significant impact on FCP students. As they read ethnic studies literature, spend time in the 65th Street Corridor, and reflect on their experience, FCP students find themselves thinking critically about who they are and what it means to live in a poor, ethnically diverse urban neighborhood. They become, a project evaluator told us, markedly more able to understand "the perspective of other people who are culturally different from them." At the same time, they become activists. Reflecting on her time mentoring middle school students in the 65th Street Corridor, one student described finding out that she was herself a role model, someone whom others could call on when they needed help getting something done. Another project participant, a former Sacramento State graduate student and now a Sacramento State staff member— described the experience as being "a part of something bigger, . . . helping these students, and then the school, and then the community at large all at one time."

The benefit of service, she mused, was not "pay" but both "something down the line" and "an intrinsic reward, in real time."

When asked why the FCP is working, a person closely associated with the project emphasized the connections between faculty and students, between students and a living AAPI history, and among students. These connections, she went on, reinforce cultural identities and students' "understanding of themselves in the world."

> They build confidence and esteem for themselves. And then they're able to go back out and give to their communities through the 65th Street Corridor Project. . . . And when you give back, it reinforces everything that you've done in your life as important. . . . So you're taking the learning and you're making it real when you go out and apply it rather than just learning it and closing the book. I think that when you actually build and foster leadership and then civic and community engagement, it reinforces the learning process, which is the whole theme of the Full Circle Project.

Echoing this perspective, almost everyone we talked with communicated that the ethnic studies program goes a long way in inviting and supporting students to seize their identity and to better understand and appreciate the identities of others.

The program is doing what it was designed to do. FCP students persist from fall to spring at rates ten percentage points higher than non-FCP AAPI students even though a larger proportion of FCP students come from low-income families and are first-generation students. They earned higher grades and were more likely to be in good academic standing than non-FCP AAPI students. As important, the evaluation of the FCP program is shedding light on the educational progress of AAPI college students. Since the program was established, FCP staff members have collaborated with institutional researchers, university faculty, and the Institute for Higher Education Leadership and Policy to complete a longitudinal quasi-experimental evaluation of the program. This mixed-methods study will gather data for FCP participants and similar non-FCP Sacramento State students course-taking patterns and interviews along with a series of measures of students' attitudes and perceptions of service learning, leadership, cultural identity, and empathy. Early results show that

FCP students had grown substantially with respect to ethnic perspective taking in comparison to non-FCP students. As a person who administered the survey put it, "The difference basically is if you're actually in the setting and getting that firsthand experience in FCP, then people are able to basically take the perspectives of other people who are culturally different from them." As a person closely involved in the program put it, "Full Circle Project is like first-year programs on steroids." True to its ethnic studies roots, the FCP is contributing to a critical and productive understanding of the experience of racialized communities in the United States.

North Seattle Community College: Navigating College and Personal Lives

Part of the Seattle Community College District that opened in 1970, North Seattle Community College (NSCC) is an open-door comprehensive community college. Located within easy access to the University of Washington and downtown Seattle, NSCC has been designed to address the needs of its community and provide educational opportunities that lead to college transfer, professional-technical training, adult basic education, and continuing education. Today, the college serves over 11,000 students in degree programs and another 3,000 in continuing education programs. One-third of NSCC's degree-seeking students are people of color, with AAPI students making up just over 10 percent. Roughly one-half of NSCC's students enroll in transfer programs, and about one-quarter pursue professional/technical degrees and basic education or developmental courses. To serve a demographically and educationally diverse student body, NSCC has been actively engaged in establishing relationships with regional institutions of higher education and employers; it balances transfer education with career and technical education as well as opportunities for adults to complete a GED or develop new skills.

When we arrived on campus, before 8:00 a.m., many of the buildings were locked, with lines of students waiting to get in. Along with these students, we funneled into the main building, which looked more like a community center than a building at a community college. The NSCC campus is green and often glistening with raindrops. The students seem happy and busy. Many of them see NSCC as a motivator in their lives, even a savior to some. The institution provides direction and assistance across the board, and students clearly seem pleased to have found both the institution and its helpful staff and faculty.

Although somewhat conventional in design, the campus has bits of character sprinkled throughout. During a break from our interviews, we wandered around the campus center and stumbled upon a cardboard cutout of Xena. For those who aren't familiar with her, Xena was a superhero of sorts in the form of a warrior princess who suffered a difficult past and was attempting to redeem herself through acts of kindness to others. The television series, filmed in New Zealand, has a bit of a cult following, so we were surprised to see the cutout of Xena in the student center. What was most interesting was that Xena was wearing a cap and gown. During our sessions with faculty and staff throughout the day, we asked about Xena and her cap and gown. Interestingly, Xena had meaning to many of the students at NSCC. Each year the cutout of Xena was rolled out and dressed in a cap and gown during graduation, and the idea of being a "warrior" about getting an education was one that many students aspired to.

Eventually, we walked outside the student center and came upon an outdoor carnival. Whereas one might typically see eighteen- to-twenty-year-olds running carnival booths and dunking tanks, there were people of all ages and racial and ethnic backgrounds participating. The carnival looked more like a community event than a traditional college event. Always game for fun, we decided to join in with the students and staff, even entering the pie-eating contest and coming in second. Throughout our visit NSCC students welcomed us, cheered us on, and were excited to have us on their campus. These students were proud of their college and made this clear to visitors.

The 2010–2016 NSCC strategic plan outlines a college that is adapting to a rapidly changing environment in two ways. Foremost, the college is responding to profound changes in the composition of its service area and student body. Between 2000 and 2010, over 70 percent of the new residents in the neighborhoods within a five-mile radius of the campus were persons of color. By 2010, the college qualified as an AANAPISI. Increasingly serving a racially, ethnically, and linguistically diverse student body, the college has been "developing strategies that will yield stronger cross-cultural respect and greater inclusion throughout [NSCC]'s campus and culture." The 2013 NSCC accreditation self-study describes restructuring the college around diversity, community partnerships, and new pathways to transfer and work that both address the developmental education needs of students and include innovative approaches to teaching and learning. At the same time, the college is transforming policies and programs so as to be relevant during a period of rapid change in technologies, modes of communication, labor markets, and public commitments to higher education. More than one-half of NSCC students work while they go to school, and roughly two-thirds attend part-time. Most of NSCC's students need their college education to pay off in local labor markets in the near term. In response, NSCC has reached out to its students and feeder schools to understand students' aspirations and barriers to those aspirations and, at the same time, has reached out to employers to identify the kinds of certificate and degree programs that can lead directly to employment. In turn, the college has updated degree programs and instructional technologies. In making this investment in the educational infrastructure during a period of declining state support, the college has become adept at partnering with workforce development agencies and other social service providers, funders, and the private sector. It became the site of the Washington State Opportunity Center for Employment and Education in 2011.

Faculty and staff at NSCC have come to a simple but profound realization: if a college education is to empower diverse, academically inexperienced students to find a stable place in a competitive and globally networked city, they need to ensure that students are able to navigate their way through college to their goals. To that end, NSCC is appointing and developing "navigators." The students who are part of the Northstar Peer Navigation Program and the staff who serve as OCE&E College Success Navigators meet students in a gatekeeper course or at the beginning of students' academic pathway. Navigators play a three-part role: knowing a group of students well enough to be able guide them to information and resources; supporting and challenging these students academically and personally as they enter and move through college programs that lead to jobs and additional opportunities for personal and professional development; and feeding information back into students' home program of studies that enables the program to make adjustments to better serve these students. As one administrator put it: "We found that [the] navigator model works very well, so we figured why not implement the navigator model for a lot of different programs? . . . A lot of the population here, ... they're here primarily for jobs to get an education to go back to work. [They are] making a stronger connection . . . with the peer navigators who provide that one-on-one support."

Our visit to North Seattle Community College focused on two programs—OCE&E and the Workforce Development Council Nursing Cohort program. In both of these programs, NSCC is applying the navigator model to help students and clients progress toward self-sufficiency.

The Navigators in the OCE&E: Navigating toward Self-Sufficiency

NSCC's experimentation with navigation is closely linked to the OCE&E—which is housed in what is known as the "Big Blue Building" on the NSCC campus. Championed by the Speaker of the Washington State House of Representatives, this policy initiative has established at NSCC "one-stop satellite offices" of public employment, workforce development, and social services agencies. The OCE&E integrates access to employment, counseling, public benefits, and educational programs and services both to improve the situations of people struggling to achieve self-sufficiency for their families and also to make better use of public resources. The building's integration manager sorted the resources in the building into social services, educational services, and employment services and listed nearly thirty different resources provided by more than two dozen different partners—many of whom pay rent to the state rather than to a private landlord.

A stand-alone center within a community college, the OCE&E has, in many ways, recast the college itself as a point of access to resources and services that help people navigate toward stable positions in local communities and labor markets. NSCC Peer Navigators refer students to the community as well as to health and family support resources in the Big Blue Building. In the same place, people who are ready to improve their lives connect with navigators—OCE&E College Success Navigators along with staff from a host of other organizations who play the same basic role—who customize support for them as they struggle to achieve self-sufficiency and prosperity for their families. While we focused on the work of Peer Navigators and the OCE&E College Success Navigators, we came to understand their work as part of the OCE&E initiative and as vitally linked to the diverse staff members in the NSCC Financial Assets Building Program. Navigators at NSCC help many students continue their college education and also help potential students become ready to access educational resources, first in the OCE&E and then often at NSCC.

A Balance between Education and Work

Navigators and OCE&E staff members share a basic assumption about the people they serve: most NSCC students and the clients of the OCE&E are people who work and who, in most cases, need postsecondary education to help them learn how to negotiate the local labor market and to provide them with skills that are valued in those markets. As an administrator put it, whether first-generation college students or the holders of graduate degrees, many NSCC students arrive saying "I need something to get back to work. I'm not transferring. I just need something to get back to work." Most have the characteristics of nontraditional students: they are age twenty-four or above, are financially independent, are parents with dependents, and/or are part-time students if they are students. Balancing education and work and family, often while managing significant financial instability, is, in the words of an NSCC administrator, "one of the biggest challenges" NSCC students and OCE&E clients face. He stressed that Seattle community college students need to finish classes and degrees quickly so that they can make use of their education at work but also to improve their odds of graduating. Most NSCC students do not have the time or academic or financial resources to be successful as full-time students.

For many students, progress depends on balancing conflicting demands. For instance, an English-language learner who went on to become a Peer Navigator described his and his fellow immigrants' need to balance completing academic courses in English with learning the English they need to get better jobs:

> So I have to work. It's really hard to find, specifically at this time in the financial crisis, to find a good job without having good skills or to improve your language and to start your life. I have a family here so I have to support them, so a lot of things going. So it's really hard for immigrant people to study without getting help.

OCE&E clients of the Financial Assets Building Program perform a similar balancing act. As a financial literacy instructor explained, clients who begin the process of learning how to manage their financial lives are often necessarily focused on making ends meet. They often don't see the value in investing energy or scarce resources in saving money or building a credit rating or in an asset like a college education. As much as they need financial resources, they need to become financially literate to be able to manage their financial resources.

Whether the navigators who circulate in the OCE&E are guiding students toward degrees or clients toward the resources that might enable them to pursue an education, they play parallel roles. In physical sites that open access to a range of human resources, navigators play the role of honest brokers who collaborate with clients on a plan for becoming self-sufficient and then support their progress and challenge them to keep going.

Early in our interviews, we found that it was difficult to draw a clear line between NSCC students and OCE&E clients. It was hard to see where the NSCC navigation programs stopped and access to OCE&E resources and services began. For us, understanding the ways in which the Peer Navigators and OCE&E College Success Navigators contribute to student success started with understanding the OCE&E. This one-stop center has been designed to make providing and accessing resources more sustainable. Staff members who work for various social services emphasize the ways in which pooling resources formerly located in different buildings spread across the city in a single state-owned building makes starting the journey toward self-sufficiency far more efficient. Clients seeking to upgrade job skills park in a single lot or pay a single bus fare—at the behest of the legislature, Seattle Metro rerouted buses to drop off at the OCE&E—in order attend a résumé-writing workshop, meet with employment counselors, attend a job fair, or talk one on one with a representative from a community-based organization or a social service agency. An NSCC staff member, a financial educator, said that when she discovers that clients are short on food, she doesn't wonder whether they qualify for food stamps. Instead, she says, "'Let's go out here, and I'll check you in and you can go upstairs and talk to somebody.' It's just really nice to have it all in one spot, instead of saying, 'No, you've got to go across town.'"

The integration of services in the OCE&E and across the college is more than the co-location of resources. The college is being redesigned to promote collaboration. The OCE&E is managed by a neutral party with the title of Integrated Services Manager who, in her words, has nothing to do with how any partners run their business but instead keeps the idea of integration on the table—"service integration, staff integration, cultural integration, IT integration." As she elaborates: "I really understand that the decisions aren't mine.

The decisions are the agencies' and the people who work here and I think ultimately if we keep in mind that we're actually here to serve people, our customers, whoever they are." She and other college administrators stress the need for staff to learn "how to come out of silos" through professional development that builds knowledge of the contributions of others and also cultural competence. In some ways, as a financial educator who contributes to the Financial Assets Building Program—and to college navigation indirectly— explained, the service providers in the OCE&E offer not prepackaged content and processes but the active presence of a collaborative guide: "We started this as a pilot, and it's just really kept going as a pilot. . . . I'm here every Monday. People can come in and talk to me about any kind of financial issues or services that they may need."

Equally important, the site offers multiple resources. Because it provides office space and access to clients, the center has become a site for the Express Advantage Community Teller, a program run by the nonprofit arm of the Express Credit Union that provides clients with access to basic banking services and opportunities to build a credit rating and financial assets. Without leaving the building, clients can establish a bank account and, through resources that Express Advantage raises regionally, qualifying clients can receive seed money to open an account. Because it hosts a financial education program, the OCE&E can provide clients with access to financial educators from American Financial Solutions, a nonprofit credit counseling, financial education, and debt consolidation agency that is part of the NSCC Foundation. With regular office hours in the OCE&E, an American Financial Solutions financial educator provides clients with support in developing budgets and negotiating with creditors, and also connects them with foundation resources that support debt forgiveness and legal advice. Because of the OCE&E's central location, an NSCC career services liaison is able to bring in more employers and even other colleges to the job fairs she organizes there. Each of the College Navigators and OCE&E staff confirmed what the OCE&E integration manager offered: accessing one service puts clients and students in touch with many services that move them toward stability.

Pathways to Self-Sufficiency
The basic design features of the OCE&E inform NSCC navigation initiatives and have expanded NSCC's capacity to help people in its service area—whether they

are primarily students or clients—navigate toward self-sufficiency. The co-location and integration of services and resources shifts the focus of the staff in the building from providing access to a single resource to guiding clients toward their goals. An OCE&E administrator who herself reports to a policy committee tasked with integrating employment services, human services, education, and workforce development described the change in outlook. Staff from different departments learn about the services of all the other partners and increasingly see their jobs as connecting clients to the resources that will help them become stable members of their communities.

The focus on helping people navigate toward self-sufficiency is present even more in the NSCC Peer Navigators and OCE&E College Success Navigators. The idea of providing students with navigators is, one administrator stressed, becoming more popular in the college and the region. A mix of students and staff, NSCC employees and people from community-based organizations, NSCC navigators meet high-barrier, underserved, low-income people as they come in the door, either at the OCE&E or at any other NSCC building. An administrator elaborated: "They will work with you and explain the difference between advising and registration and the difference between advising and counseling, and they will hold your hand and walk with you to registration to help you get registered, and they will go to the bookstore with you."

Across our interviews, staff and students emphasized that navigators work with newcomers rather than working for or doing work for them. They are connected to departments or constituencies where resources are located. One of the navigators we interviewed—a Libyan student who had recently completed the English as a second language sequence at NSCC—explained why connections matter: "That's why I am part of the program. . . . If they have students come from [the] Middle East or come from Africa, maybe I can see [from] their faces, 'Oh, they need help.' So I try to be close to them. Sometimes they are just, 'Oh, it's a professor; they scare me.'" Because this peer navigator shares their experience and their goal, students who are otherwise afraid to ask for help are willing to connect with him. As his supervisor put it, they are willing to "talk to him and say, 'Well, how did *you* do it?'"

Such connections are closely linked to where and how NSCC navigators do their work. Whereas students are introduced to navigators through departments, classes, or other formal programs or by referral from advisers or faculty, navigators interact with students between programs, in the cafeteria, or in a student center or lounge. Interactions with navigators often lead to moving between places, as navigators know available resources, and their clients might "need to talk to American Financial Solutions and might need to talk to Express Credit Union and might need some food benefits and could use some résumé help and might need to see the nurse." They are trained not so much to solve students' problems as to be a person with knowledge on whom students can lean as they develop the strategies they need to move forward. Because of who they are and where they engage students, navigators can check up on students without being intrusive. One student said that after a navigator offered help in applying for financial aid "over and over and over," he thought: "He's really nice, a nice guy. Why don't I ask him?"

Navigation results in more than individualized support. It often leads to creative approaches to charting paths to self-sufficiency. In order to mash up resources and programs to meet students' needs, navigators and OCE&E staff listen and ask the right questions. The building coordinator described a typical interaction this way: "Well, just a second. . . . You signed up for phlebotomy . . . but let's see how are you doing. Where are you at? Maybe you need some food. You got food? You paying the bills? How are you doing with rent? You stable? Home life stable?" Part of working in "this damn blue building" is not losing focus on the progress of the people who come through its doors. This includes initiating conversations not just about academic progress and employment needs but about how to adjust the assumptions of employers and employees so as to include the diverse students and clients moving through the NSCC campus.

The conversations initiated in the navigation process are often transformative. These conversations are often initiated by a person's desire to change his life. By keeping each conversation focused on priorities in people's lives, navigators mediate new paths to repaying debt, or becoming credentialed for a higher-paying job, or escaping a destructive relationship or living situation. In many cases, these paths include resources to which students and clients have never had access and often could not even imagine. These new paths often lead to financial and academic support that students had never considered. For students who tentatively come to a student orientation through an OCE&E referral, the new path is postsecondary education itself. Staff members who collaborate with the Financial Assets Building Program recall interacting with individuals dealing with issues—a father figuring out how to pay child support or a college stop-out dealing with substantial debt—who "in the back of [their] heads . . . want to be students." As an OCE&E administrator told us, many OCE&E clients who gain access to resources that help them become financially stable walk into the Big Blue Building certain that college is beyond their grasp. But they look around them and think, "Hmmm, you look just like me, and you're going to school. Like, why can't I go to school too?"

A Process for Navigating toward Self-Sufficiency

There is a general consensus among students, staff, and faculty about why navigation is such a major contributor to student success: it provides access to diverse resources and higher retention in academic programs. Collaboration with navigators and OCE&E staff leads students and clients to map out new paths—sometimes literally with campus maps, Free Application for Federal Student Aid (FAFSA) forms, a budget, and a degree plan—and, in turn, to convert transformative moments into plans for becoming self-sufficient.

Navigation begins with gathering and sharing information about the individual's progress toward self-sufficiency—the challenges they face as well as their goals and assets. "Working together and sharing information" about resources and client needs, an OCE&E administrator told us, is hardwired into the navigation process. She and other college administrators recruit and develop staff and faculty who "get it"—they understand that client needs are better met when those needs can be viewed by multiple staff members with different areas of expertise—always while respecting client privacy. A student services administrator explained the approach this way:

> If we're a little bit more holistic and we work together and we do, I don't want to say pry into the student, I call it intensive advising, . . . students will stay and they'll be more reciprocal. They will talk with their instructor more, as opposed to just sit at the back of the class and carry their worries within. If they're struggling or they know they're failing, talk to the instructors so you can get some help early on.

The navigators and other OCE&E staff we interviewed get it. They all see themselves, in the words of one staff person, as "a resource person" who is gathering enough information to "plug clients into the system, whatever they need."

In interviews with administrators and frontline staff members, a set of formal information-sharing practices emerged. Standing department and cross-department meetings routinely take up current cases and explore who has resources that match student needs. Student orientations, midquarter check-ins, and in some cases required weekly meetings are designed to identify students' needs and track their progress. These formal practices are matched by a set of informal ones. Staff regularly huddle around new information about the needs of individuals or groups; they linger after presentations about services and resources in NSCC classes and OCE&E workshops in order to follow up with individuals; and they share stories in meetings and hallway conversations about novel solutions to client problems, and walk between departments—often with a client in tow—looking for novel solutions. They also follow up with referring faculty and staff.

Systematic sharing of information supports the frequency and effectiveness of follow-up. OCE&E staff members use departmental intake forms to begin a client profile. As clients work with different navigators that profile deepens. Students and financial literacy navigators sit side by side and review a credit report or fill in an online budget template or a FAFSA or an inventory of personal barriers. The administrator who oversees all of the College Navigators described a common contact sheet that tracks client interactions and outcomes. The OCE&E integration manager has begun integrating information technology between three separate state agencies and is beginning to build a single data warehouse. The process of navigation remains rooted in personal contact, which helps to ensure that clients or students are connected with every resource possible.

Routines for knowing who students are feed the next step in the process: individualizing support. NSCC has taken this approach because of what they know about their students and clients. Navigators and staff have learned that clients have packed schedules and face personal barriers that range from bankruptcy to domestic violence to cancer. As a student services administrator emphasized, many students come to college not to complete a generic degree but instead to move toward very personal goals, often with limited financial stability or prior educational experience. If they are to improve their situation, most will need personalized support.

In response, NSCC has positioned navigators across departments so that they are present when clients voice a need for resources. For example, an administrator with Express Advantage explained to us that clients who seek banking resources through the Community Teller program set up an account with a financial coach who is prepared to help them navigate toward their goals, potentially referring them to American Financial Solutions and help in getting a student loan or Department of Social and Health Services for support in buying food. The coordinator of the College Navigators program described a similar process: students in a developmental math class who are struggling with the same concept may meet after class with a navigator who knows the curriculum and can pass back to their instructor information about what area of the course is tripping students up.

Two basic principles seem to guide the process of individualizing support: "walking them over" and "letting them get to work." This kind of support involves linking each client with exactly what she needs to get started. The College Navigator coordinator explained this principle this way:

> We call it the "handoff." Specifically, because I found and I think a lot of other navigators have found, if we simply just give a business card and say call this person, it doesn't always connect. Sometimes a student may not; they may be a little shy. They may not want to take that initiative, but walking them over and helping them make that first contact really, really makes a big difference.

"Walking them over" is not, however, "you doing the work for them," a financial adviser emphasized: "It's about getting the individual, the client, to set financial goals for themselves . . . whatever they may be. . . . The individual works with the coach. The coach is there to provide support, to provide guidance, and to be a resource." She offered an illustration of a student who came to her with nearly $100,000 in debt. With her at his side setting up the next steps, the student "made the calls . . . to set up payment arrangements." He was in "the driver's seat"; she pointed him to the information he needed. In a year, "he knocked out $35,000 in debt." The interaction worked because "*he* focused."

Getting to work, it is worth noting, happens in spaces—sometimes in an office and other times in front of a computer—from which clients themselves can reach their goals. Our interviews kept circling back to tools and places where clients could access tools. A student described being led to web surveys that helped her understand how she learned and a worksheet that helped her realize she could not work full-time and go to school full-time. Staff talked about the difference a bank account or a loan or a debt management plan could make. The common denominator across these tools is what one navigator called a success plan, another called a budget, and still another called a résumé. As clients express what they are working toward, what resources they have, and what options are available to them, their navigators link clients with the resources that will help them in moving toward their goals.

Individualized support matters for students and clients. An ESL student recalled being walked over to a navigator's office and talking about financial aid, a resource that enabled him to complete his program and prepare to move on to do graduate work at another institution. Another student, a young woman who started college after high school and "was like really excited and . . . failed," described the role of her College Strategies class with a navigator:

> For me, yes. It's a lot to do with confidence as well. That class really prepared you to be confident and navigate your life. This is how you navigate community colleges, and if you have questions we will be able to help you answer them, as opposed to when I got out of high school there was career guidance, but it was like they were trying to guide 1,200 people, 1,200 students, and there wasn't someone that was saying . . . "you can do it."

That confidence, she added, led her to ask her vice president if the national organization for which she works could support her education. It did. "And that's a big part of why I'm still . . . continuing to go to school quarter after quarter."

As we listened to this young woman we were struck by where the process of supporting progress toward self-sufficiency seems to end. The administrators and staff we interacted with often named the end point as financial literacy. As we puzzled over this phrase we came to realize that the presence of the OCE&E at NSCC has forced administrators and staff involved with the center and a growing number of staff, faculty, and students across the campus to blur the lines between what the integration manager labeled educational services, social services, and employment services. At NSCC, all three of these are valuable for people seeking to become more self-sufficient. Students often begin with few educational or financial resources and often with various kinds of debt, such as student loan and credit card debt, but also with a lack of confidence, limited English language ability, or the need to contribute to the immediate financial support of others.

The staff and administrators we interviewed believe that people who start college with limited resources and academic experiences can use educational and social services to become self-sufficient. The students we interviewed are proof positive. As we listened to both groups talk about what it takes to make effective use of educational or social services, many individuals named this capacity "financial literacy." This phrase seems to mean competence in navigating barriers to accessing resources that support achieving goals. By extension, financially literate people know their goals, barriers to reaching those goals, and the resources for overcoming barriers. They know what financially literate people do.

The OCE&E and the NSCC navigators systematically promote financial literacy. As students and clients walk onto the campus, they meet navigators who help them to develop a budget or plan that articulates personal or community goals, assets, resources, and obligations. Budget in hand, they gain access to financial, educational, and relational assets and resources that they need to get started on their plan. As they begin to move forward with their plan, their navigators challenge them to put assets and resources to use with resilience and creativity.

The Workforce Development Council Nursing Cohort: Navigating a Pathway to Employment and Education

Like the OCE&E, the Workforce Development Council (WDC) Nursing Cohort program provides clients with access to comprehensive resources and services in a one-stop setting. The clients are members of a cohort of thirty-two current entry-level health-care employees who are completing the prerequisites for a nursing degree; the one-stop office is the NSCC campus. The program, which is based on a partnership between NSCC and the WDC of King County funded by the U.S. Department of Health and Human Services Healthcare for All Nursing Careers Program, is one of several WDC college cohort programs.

The WDC model provides highly motivated students seeking to enter high-demand professions with an innovative pathway to certifications and skills. The cohort is established through a competitive process facilitated in part by TRAC Associates, a private employment and training agency that has been operating in the Seattle area for about thirty years. Industries are chosen based on their regional contributions; employers in these industries participate based on their willingness to support their employees through the program; and students are selected based on employer recommendations and an interview. The WDC model was developed in response to the gap between existing college program offerings and the needs of students and local labor markets. In the case of the NSCC Nursing Cohort, local nursing programs—including the highly regarded bachelor's degree program in nursing at NSCC—have not been able to keep up with regional demand for nurses and provide only limited access to adults working in entry-level health-care jobs who are seeking to upgrade their skills.

As we listened to the students, staff, and faculty involved in the WDC Nursing Cohort, we became increasingly aware of the distance between the traditional academic pathway to a credential in nursing and the students who are successfully navigating the WDC pathway. The gap has to do with what one student called "knowing what we are getting into" and being ready to "be stretched." First-generation college students—including students of color and low-income students—often enter NSCC motivated but with little understanding about how to make use of the opportunity. Many of these students believe that getting into college is the hard part, and so they struggle when they discover that staying the course is the hard part. Many, as a student at NSCC put it, "don't really know how to be college students." Another student, a first-generation NSCC student herself, said that on her first try at college she had little in her experience that she could draw on when her courses got tough; after a while she just "stopped going."

The way many traditional academic programs are organized and taught puts a premium on knowing what "one is getting into." Traditionally underrepresented students often enter college taking courses that require them to handle difficult and high-volume content at an inflexible pace. Instructions and assignments and even expectations can seem "ambiguous, ambivalent" to students. At least two students in the cohort felt that faculty in traditional courses often seem uninterested in feedback from students about whether they understand what they are getting into or whether the course works for them. Reflecting on what they are learning from WDC students, two staff members described their growing awareness of the extent to which many academic programs are built around competitiveness and students advancing to the next level based on scores. A program staff member said that in such an environment mistakes are a source of fear and an opportunity for judgment rather than an opportunity for "figuring things out when somebody is actually there to help you." A faculty member said that adults who have been away from school—even if they have been working in the profession they are studying—find reentering the academic environment stressful. Pathways to the credentials and skills that working people desire often seem to be designed for other people.

The WDC Nursing Cohort program is designing a pathway for students who are likely to struggle in traditional academic programs—all of these students work, one-half are first-generation college students, and 60 percent are students of color. By applying the NSCC navigator model, the program meets the academic requirements of existing degree programs while turning traditional higher education on its head. At the heart of the program is what the Instructional Lead called a net of relationships that was able to hold up under the weight and complexity of the challenges in getting every member of a cohort of working students through a sequence of rigorous STEM classes.

> So it was not just academic unpreparedness. That was just one issue. It was complex family lives, it was single wage earners, it was financial issues, it was language issues, it was ability to handle stress, poor high school preparation. You just stack that up. The traditional community college model is you have a single instructor, as you know, in a classroom dealing with twenty-five to thirty-five students. If students don't pass, well, you've done your best and you hope they get tutoring and things like that. In this model we knew if we wanted to try and support 100 percent of these thirty-two students to make it through we had to create a net wide enough that met together and held together through the entire grant that could work spontaneously.

This net is held by a professional learning community that is collaboratively designing a student-centered degree program, a program that is navigable for working people as they individually and as a cohort pursue educational and professional goals important to them and to their region.

The metaphor used by the Instructional Lead for the WDC Nursing Cohort is apt. The program is a "net" that ties together college staff, employers, workers, and social service agencies into a set of interlinked learning communities all learning how to move students toward credentials and skills that, in turn, connect students with local communities and economies. This net is foremost a partnership among a college, an industry, public agencies and not-for-profit organizations, and working students. Rather than another traditional academic program at a college, the WDC Nursing Cohort is a collaborative initiative that is aligning the skills of individuals with the skills the region needs. In part because the cohort is established in a competitive process, employers and students see student progress as part of the job. Students are prepared, the Nursing Cohort navigator told us, to talk about and work through inconvenience in return for the development of relevant skills and knowledge. The cohort is formed, the Instructional Lead added, around explicit commitments from each partner—including the students. All partners share a commitment to support all the students in the cohort, to learn how to support all cohort members, and to adapt existing approaches to professional development and postsecondary education in order to support every cohort member. Each partner is also committed to ongoing weekly communication concerning student progress and needs; representatives of employers, the WDC, and NSCC meet monthly to talk through the "big picture."

A Student-Centered Partnership

As staff members and students reflected on why the partnership works, they zeroed in on two key dynamics. First, the partnership is focused almost exclusively on student progress toward agreed-upon goals. The goal is straightforward: students pass classes that roll up efficiently into a degree. The devil is in the details. In order to stay in the cohort, each working student needs to pass two NSCC classes (ten to twelve credits) each quarter with at least a 2.8 GPA. At the end of the first year, each student must pass the Health Education Systems Inc. (HESI) nursing school entrance exam. Employers need to adjust work schedules so that employees can attend classes two days a week and every Saturday. Funders cover expenses from tuition and books to bus passes. NSCC faculty members report course performance at the assignment level to navigators and work with navigators to design interventions for students at risk of not passing. The bottom line is simple: every student passes. In the first year, more than 90 percent of the cohort completed all classes, including all of the math and English courses required for an associate degree as well as traditional weed-out courses like anatomy and physiology. In summer 2013, all but one student passed the HESI entrance exam.

Staff explained that this success is the result of hard work on the part of students and coordinated support from the program. They point to weekly and monthly meetings at which employers, the WDC, and the college talk about student performance. An NSCC administrator described to us the processes and protocols designed to keep students, staff, and faculty focused on student development and support for student development. This focus on student progress is not lost on students. In reflecting on why the program works, they highlight the opportunity to talk openly with college staff and their employers about their progress and their needs. "The program and our navigator take care of all of the background stuff for us," one student said to us. Another student added, "You can just kind of let that go and just focus on the stress of the class and the work, and so that is cool."

The focus on student progress is matched by responsiveness to what the Nursing Navigator called "reasonable requests" from any of the partners. She recounted an instance in which a student came to her with a work scheduling problem; she called the employer, and the student's schedule was adjusted so that she could maintain her health and succeed in her education and in her job. TRAC Associates staff, she added, play a critical role as employer liaison and coordinator of community services such as health care, child care, scholarship and financial aid resources, rent and utility assistance, and transportation and food assistance. Students told us about the ways in which their navigator and their work supervisors advocated for them as students, helping to resolve problems at school and at work. When we sat in on an instructional team meeting, we watched as navigators, instructors, the program Instructional Lead, and the TRAC Associates coordinator reviewed information about student performance across classes and asked each other to adjust the timing of tests, modes of assessment, the order of assignments, and even the deadline for completing classes. Both the Instructional Lead and the navigator emphasize that such exchanges are part of the program and have led to a second chance for students whose life circumstances have kept them from completing their course work successfully. These partners are willing to discover ways to support employee development while limiting stress and attrition.

College as Professional Learning Community

The WDC Nursing Cohort is a kind of professional learning community, providing all participants with shared opportunities to "engage [their] creative and reflective capacities in ways that strengthen their practice."[8] As a community, the WDC cohort cultivates professionals in every stakeholder group. Participation in the grant leads both employers and representatives of the WDC, for example, to learn about how adults develop new skills and what working people have to balance in order to be good students, good employees, and good family members. Both faculty and students marvel at the willingness of the WDC and employees to listen to student challenges and to develop strategies for restructuring the work environment—from adjusting schedules and position descriptions to providing mentors. At the same time, according to the Instructional Lead, staff and faculty who "are not trained to educate and even understand the lives of [WDC] students" are learning how to be a team of educators who see the primary responsibility as the success of "frontline workers who are recent immigrants, . . . students of color, . . . first-generation students." In our visit to a co-instructional team meeting, we observed faculty brainstorming how to make a body of knowledge relevant for working students, how to teach differently, and how to assess students' professional competences.

WDC students are also learning to play the role of professional student. As their navigator observed, students are selected because their employers and nursing educators believe that they are committed to being good nurses. This selection process leads the cohort not only to believe but also to act as though they are already professionals—"the cream of the crop," as one student put it. As another student in the cohort added, members of the cohort share the desire "to advance and make themselves better, and . . . they love and are passionate about what they do." As developing professionals, students are expected to take responsibility for getting and giving help; providing honest and positive feedback to one another; becoming structured and disciplined within and outside of class; and, to use another student's phrase, "putting yourself out there."

The various stakeholders in the program are developing as professionals in two distinct ways. First, they co-construct norms that support the learning of working students, their teachers, and employers. The program is grounded in the belief that the entire cohort can and will succeed. The Instructional Lead, for instance, arranged to host a reception at the end of one term at which students heard the NSCC vice president say, "I'm proud of you." As she elaborated:

> So they were finishing their statistics exam and coming in, and every time a student would come in they'd stop and clap for each other. . . . We need to do more of that. We need to commit to saying, "Okay, if you fail, I'm failing. I'm not going home until you succeed." They need to help each other. You know you have a navigator who is this warrior princess [much like Xena] here just advocating for you and not sleeping at night because she's just thinking about you. But you need to do this for yourself and for each other.

The willingness of participants to "hold the net" is widely shared. Review session coordinators push students to text and e-mail questions right up to exam time and believe that "everyone will rock the face off that exam." Navigators meet weekly with students. Instructors and staff—often joined by funders and employers—"come together as a team . . . to look at how students are doing. We put their grades up on the projector, we go through every single student as a team. From that weekly conversation we realize what pieces are missing."

Second, participants play collaborative roles. The navigator links them all together, but stakeholders are selected in part, both the Instructional Lead and a college administrator emphasized to us, based on their readiness to collaborate. For example, WDC cohort faculty host a small-group instructional diagnostic in which they invite a trained mediator into their class to hold focus groups aimed at finding out what pieces are missing. Faculty members share their grade books and assessments with other program stakeholders and coordinate assignments across classes and even disciplines. Similarly, students are accepted into a cohort that, according to both students and staff, is learning to push people out of their comfort zones.

Curriculum and Instruction for Working Students

Three distinct features of teaching and learning in the program are especially noteworthy, beginning with the way in which the WDC Nursing Cohort curriculum is designed to build buy-in to explicit and challenging standards. Program expectations are grounded in a nonnegotiable standard: patient safety. The students in the cohort and the faculty are committed to ensuring that every student masters the skills and knowledge they need to be competent nurses and, by extension, is prepared to pass the National Council Licensure Examination and, in so doing, become a licensed nurse. As one student put it, "There's a grade point that we just can't go below." Another student put it this way: "You can't be a good nurse and be carried along."

The focus on clearly defined professional standards guides teaching and learning in major ways. Program stakeholders set personal goals and collectively clarify what students and teachers need to do and what support they need to have in order to achieve their goals. The Instructional Lead meets individually with employers, faculty, and funders to talk through what it would take to support a cohort of working adult learners in a nursing degree. The navigator recalled faculty from different disciplines who have never met and "have no idea what one another taught" establishing learning outcomes for the cohort and then, along with the Instructional Lead, using those outcomes to design course syllabi and assignments. The result was a richer mix of learning opportunities, all keyed to formative assessments and support through review sessions and campus tutors. According to students in the cohort, these standards promote what one called "focus." The program standards focused this student on "the learning targets we will build on in nursing school."

The emphasis on explicit professional standards is closely linked to providing students with feedback on their learning. One instructor, for example, uses early intervention with students either objectively through tests or subjectively, telling them, "Here's what's needed from you, here's what will be difficult; let's start now to move you to proficiency." Another described developing multiple methods for identifying mastery, whether through projects or oral explanation or online quizzes. She prepares students to pass the National Council Licensure Examination but pushes them past a "pass the test, pass the class mode" to even higher standards.

The importance of feedback with respect to the development of specific competencies is not lost on other stakeholder groups. For students, this feedback is motivating. One student, for instance, described the grading process as "very interactive . . . it's really nice to know where you stand" and said that the detailed feedback motivates her to "stretch herself" and "put herself out there." Another student said: "I've been doing my pre-recs for a long time trying to get into nursing, and just. . . . While you're working and taking care of kids . . . but you just can't catch up. But this program has been fantastic, and I'm able to keep up while we're in here." The continuous feedback, she said, keeps her engaged and at the same time connects her with "educational support, emotional support." Despite her busy life and a forty-five-minute drive to school, the feedback on how she is developing as a professional has propelled her along. Employers and the WDC seem to be having a similar experience. The Nursing Navigator meets regularly to explain to them what the bar is, whether any of their students are below the bar, and what the partners—including students themselves—can do to help each student move toward competence. This information has led to revisions in program policies and, not infrequently, adjustments in student work schedules.

Teaching and learning in the WDC Nursing Cohort make extensive use of blended learning strategies. While a fixed schedule of required, face-to-face courses in the disciplines makes up the instructional heart of the program, faculty, staff, and students alike believe that the blending of disciplines and learning environments is critically important in advancing student learning. For the Instructional Lead, this blending is the result of focusing on the goals of working students and is "nothing short of miraculous." As she described it: "As faculty members begin to understand the stories and know the students, they will rethink their courses. Not reduce the rigor, but they will pedagogically kind of rethink, 'Well, you know, I could do this differently. I could do that.'" She went on to say that as NSCC faculty "become aware of the depth and breadth of the struggles that the students are going through," they come to understand that fifty minutes of course content is of limited value to a working adult who "didn't get any sleep because her kid is in the hospital." They come to realize that it isn't that their students don't care; rather, it is that their lives require multiple learning opportunities to approach relevant content and show mastery.

The adoption of blended learning strategies has a direct impact on what students learn; the environments in which they learn; and the assignments and assessments that guide their development. The faculty members who teach classes for the WDC Nursing Cohort are NSCC faculty—"great, top-notch instructors," according to one student—from across disciplines, and they teach courses that meet the requirements set up by their home departments. With the support of the navigator and the Instructional Lead, they are redesigning their courses to meet the needs of their working students. In practice, faculty members are blurring fields of study in two ways. Foremost, they are teaching their own areas of expertise as part of the nursing education of employed entry-level health-care workers. Practically, this has meant inviting nursing faculty to review and revise the key topics in prerequisite courses in math, biology, and psychology and to develop course learning outcomes that are realistic for working nursing students and at the same time pass muster in academic departments. The cohort math instructor, the navigator explained, "wanted to know what kinds of things would be useful for them" and designed problems that used math concepts through examples drawn from the field of nursing.

The willingness to adapt what students study is matched by a willingness to adapt where they learn. Opportunities to engage content come at the cohort from multiple directions. Weekly meetings with their navigator connect students with support services that, according to one student, are "kind of built into this program." These meetings can lead to a schedule of tutoring appointments for a student or strategies for rearranging a student's home life to make room for studying—whatever the student needs. Face-to-face classes are augmented through multiple modes of contact. Saturday review sessions are mandatory. The chemistry review class instructor invites students to text her with questions, and she e-mails out links to relevant materials. For the most part, students move across these different learning environments seamlessly. One explained her routine this way: "So I get up in the morning, get online, do the online class, reading, homework, whatever you have to do, and then I drive in. . . . The nine-to-fivers, I think, have it a little differently." On reflection, another student mused: "This design used to be called a hybrid course . . . and I feel like it should be a model for all college classes. . . . It increases the flexibility."

Perhaps most important, though, is the way the program defines prerequisite courses. The instructional team is committed to creating a curriculum for adult learners, one that helps learners "see how their classroom learning and their day-to-day activities are related and relevant . . . through concrete experiences in which they apply the learning in real work." This commitment leads to the cooperative design of assignments. Instructors expect the navigator and the Instructional Lead to be involved in co-instructional meetings at which faculty from different disciplines review all the assignments in which the cohort will engage in a given quarter. They brainstorm approaches to presenting math or statistics or chemistry or physiology that will be relevant for the cohort. They wonder together whether a task—a multiple-choice quiz, or a case study, or an oral review of a model of the circulatory system—gets at what students need to learn in a way that students in the cohort seem to learn. As part of the program design, each of their classes includes a nursing scenario that enables them to document how their students are developing as critical thinkers and problem solvers in nursing.

Participants in a student focus group confirmed the value of putting academic content in a nursing context. These students appreciated that instruction "was tweaked for our course." One explained her surprise in finding that her assignments in psychology and introductory chemistry dealt with "the actual work that you are familiar with and the jobs we currently have now." This "amazing" integration made academic work interesting and, for her, immediately applicable in her work life. Another student mentioned noticing how much psychology and the anatomy and physiology of the brain are tied together. Still another student described how math problems that asked her to apply concepts to settings "that we need to deal with" stimulated her interest and created focus and a willingness to keep trying even when the problem seemed ambiguous and ambitious.

Educational Data That Make a Difference

The WDC cohort and its success are the result of design: NSCC and the WDC set out to build a net that could hold an entire cohort of working students and a curriculum that is relevant to their lives. One of the program's critical features is the ongoing use of multiple assessments to support student success. Education assessment is defined by three purposes:

- Assess to Assist (early assessment to determine math, writing, speaking, study, and reading skill levels)

- Assess to Adjust (small-group instructional diagnostic provided for each class somewhere near midquarter including faculty/student discussion of course elements that can be adjusted)
- Assess to Advance (using summative assessment to support academic rigor and self-mastery)

This commitment to using multiple assessments is more than rhetoric. The program sustains a net that holds onto a cohort that is developing competencies by continually framing problems and success, testing, trying out the next version of the model.

Program assessment was clearly visible in the meeting of the instructional team that we observed during out visit to NSCC. In their collective and weekly brainstorming process, two chemistry faculty members, a psychology faculty member, the Instructional Lead, the navigator, and the TRAC Associates coordinator gathered to discuss how each student is doing in their courses, determine what their needs are, and develop strategies for how those needs can be met, and by whom. Their assessment of student progress was guided by students' current status in their classes; taking turns, faculty projected on a screen the grade book from the course management system. The conversation shifted from talk about classroom performance, grades, the navigator's observations from one-on-one meetings with students, observations from the faculty who teach all of their courses, to observations about communication with the WDC and employers. Data, quantitative and qualitative, were being used to keep the entire cohort moving forward.

This data-driven process involves ongoing assessment of student competencies. The stakeholders we interviewed in our visit and the participants in this meeting share the belief that the cohort is made up of extraordinary people who are ready to become good nurses but whose lives occasionally threaten to disrupt their career and educational progress. This basic assumption led the group to begin their conversation about student progress with a frank discussion of who is currently advancing and who is not: "Who are we worried about?" The aim of the discussion of student competencies is not to identify participants who are not ready for the program—every member of the cohort is considered ready. Rather, this talk supports a back-and-forth among partners about emerging competence, about who—faculty and staff as well as students—needs to "step up," and what level of performance individuals need to achieve on future assessments in order to demonstrate competence. Having the numbers helps faculty members judge the pace of each student's development and whether each student's growth makes mastery likely within the time constraints of the course. Group members engage in substantive discussions of which students are at risk of not showing competence not because they feel that grade point indicates, as the navigator explained, "what kind of nurses they'll make" but because the Nursing Cohort classes are designed so that a passing grade represents the acquisition of the knowledge and skills for becoming a good nurse.

Consensus about which students are and are not passing—that is, not yet meeting what the navigator called professional standards—triggered a new kind of engagement with the student progress data. The group transformed summative information about student competence into formative data that could be used to develop strategies for assisting individuals and adjusting instruction and even program policy. The most immediate interest was in using the data to develop plans for assisting the entire cohort and individual students. The numbers led the group—with help from the Instructional Lead—from sorting students into one group that is "okay" and another that "we are worried about" to a conversation about points of discontinuity in student performances and similarities among students who were thriving or struggling. This shift in focus was matched by a shift in the kind of evidence the group discussed. Faculty members from courses and review sections explained students' recent engagements with past assignments and upcoming learning opportunities, noting specific evidence that indicated what skills and content a student had mastered and what skills and content were still out of reach. The navigator shared information gleaned from weekly meetings with students that shed additional light on roadblocks. The Instructional Lead called attention back to information from the small-group instructional diagnostic about the continued need for advice about how to study anatomy and physiology.

As the group made sense of these stories, it began to identify why individual students were not passing. As members offered hypotheses and an informal model of the current situation, the Instructional Lead asked again and again, "Do students know that?" and in turn invited the group to think about what students needed to know about their performance in order to step up. As participants took notes, the group worked collaboratively to describe cycles of feedback that would help students understand the bar they needed to get over, the content and skills they still needed to acquire, and strategies that might facilitate that learning and help them find space in their lives to do that learning.

Intermittently through the discussion of how they might use student progress data to assist individual students, the group considered how these data might suggest what they needed to adjust with respect to their instructional model and the program itself. During the meeting we observed, the group engaged in a substantive discussion of pace, agreeing that "there's not enough time," and then came up with ways to alter courses to make more time; they added an optional test to one course and an emphasis on a promising online exercise in another. In separate interviews, the Instructional Lead and the navigator noted that these past meetings led to conversations with other partners that resulted in even more significant changes in policy. The navigator, for example, described frequently using information gleaned in conversations with students and the weekly team meetings to encourage employers to adjust student work schedules. The Instructional Lead described using student progress data to convince the WDC to write a new program policy that allowed cohort members who were unable to complete a course to retake it and in another instance to increase math tutoring resources.

The nursing students we interviewed confirmed what we had observed in the instructional team meeting. They described constantly knowing whether they have met the professional standards, knowing "where you stand." While students described their overall standing in terms of passing courses, they also defined progress in the program as success in acquiring the skills and knowledge they need to be good nurses. In turn, they recalled program staff "constantly asking us what we can do to make it better next time" and feeling obliged to offer good positive feedback that could support change. For example, two students in a focus group reflected on their experience in a general education course with a faculty member whose approach to grading was "always [to] leave room to improve" rather than to indicate competence. In collaboration with the navigator, the instructor adjusted his approach in order to help these students move toward their goals. In another interview, the Instructional Lead observed that this incident has helped the instructional team talk to general education faculty about teaching in the program. One student summed up what progress data are used for in the program: "The constant attention to student progress data literally allows us to change the course midway through once we've gotten used to it . . . gotten actually a good idea of what it is. We can actually change things that are not working for us, and I believe that's crucial to our success." He also summed up why this attention to data is so critical for working students: "I've had classes where the instructor was not open to feedback. I dropped the class. If it's not working for me, I can't put up with it." The WDC Nursing Cohort works for these students because the program discovers and "takes care of background stuff" and helps them to focus on becoming good nurses.

At North Seattle Community College, public postsecondary education is one of a suite of social services that contribute to the health and well-being of Seattle and surrounding communities. To make college more accessible and, in turn, to strengthen the social fabric of its neighborhoods, NSCC has set out to make explicit the connection between postsecondary education and thriving in the city by positioning navigators at multiple points of access to the campus. Navigators have a threefold task: they talk with students, staff, and faculty about what college means for students in their care; they walk these students to the resources they need to get started on their education; and they have open, straightforward conversations with them about the resources they need to succeed. The fundamental moving parts in the OCE&E and the Nursing Cohort are relationships and information. In both programs, navigators open access to education through personal relationships in which the navigator is a conduit to information about sources of support, expectations, and possibilities. Navigators, in short, play critical roles in a human network that provides open feedback on student performances and needs.

This network helps to ensure that the right resources are available to each student at the right time in ways that make those resources accessible. And the right resources make a difference. In its first year, over 37,000 customers accessed over twenty social, educational, and employment services in the OCE&E. In their first year, over 90 percent of the students in the Nursing Cohort stayed in the program (the persistence rate from fall to spring for NSCC students in other programs is roughly 40 percent). Members of the cohort completed their math requirements at a rate sixty points above the average NSCC student and earned higher average grades in their core courses. In the summer of their second year, all but three of the students in the cohort passed the HESI, a nursing school entrance examination used by programs across the country; two of the three who did not pass were so close that they will be admitted to the NSCC nursing program. This new AANAPISI is showing new ways that college can serve as a gateway to opportunity in a diverse America.

Stories of Student Success in AANAPISIS

The programs highlighted in this chapter represent ways that three very different kinds of AANAPISIS are experimenting with adapting traditional educational practices to support the academic and personal success of diverse groups of traditionally underrepresented students. At the College of the Marshall Islands, the First-Year Residential Learning Community program is providing a vibrant residential community within an AAPI community in which faculty, staff, and students flourish in a highly collegial and supportive environment where students are far away from the distractions of their everyday lives. The Full Circle Project at Sacramento State University is serving diverse AAPI students inside an American university with an ethnic studies program that is educating a new generation of activists. Finally, at North Seattle Community College, the OCE&E and the WDC Nursing Cohort program are opening for working students new and efficient pathways to resources and skills that lead to better lives. Across these two initiatives, NSCC is rewriting postsecondary education as a social service that is supporting and challenging a neighborhood to navigate toward self-sufficiency.

7 | Practices for Educating a Diverse America

Students now entering and pursuing higher education in the United States are more diverse than ever in our nation's history. A vast majority of undergraduates are a diverse mash-up of adult learners, workers who go to school part-time, low-income students, commuter students, and parents who go to college. These students do not share a common academic experience or set of educational habits, or even a first language, and they are far less likely to complete a degree than their traditional counterparts. As many national reports have shown, our nation's colleges and universities are failing these students.

Drawn from a sample of Minority-Serving Institutions (MSIs), which disproportionately serve as the point of entry for low-income students and students of color, the institutions included in this study are fostering learning and enhancing persistence not only for minority and low-income students but also for first-generation college students and other traditionally underserved populations. To better serve our increasingly diverse America, the nation's colleges and universities can learn much from these institutions about practices for advancing equal educational opportunity for all students. In this chapter, we draw on what we learned from the programs we studied at twelve MSIs, highlighting six major practices that are cultivating student learning and persistence. We close the chapter by suggesting that many of our nation's colleges and universities will need to reimagine institutional cultures if they are to make use of these practices for empowering traditionally underrepresented students.

Walk Each Student into College

Not only are students at MSIs highly diverse in terms of their prior education, socioeconomic status, race, and ethnicity, but many students are underprepared for college with respect to such basic competencies as English and mathematics. With regard to English, for example, many students at Hispanic-Serving Institutions and Asian American and Native American Pacific Islander–Serving Institutions come from immigrant communities in which English is not their first language. Moreover, many students come from families that have had little success in school; many lack the confidence needed to succeed in college because their elementary and secondary school experiences have given them little reason to believe they will be academically successful; and some have been told by teachers, family members, or peers that higher education is not for them. Furthermore, many students begin college not only lacking self-confidence but also fearful of failure. At Chief Dull Knife College (CDKC), for instance, many entering students believe that Indians cannot do mathematics, and they have "math shame." Across the programs we studied, a majority of students we spoke with recalled beginning college uncertain as to whether it was for them, what college would demand of them, and whether they would be able to succeed in college.

To address these challenges, the MSIs in this study are "walking each student" into college through establishing educational pathways into college. They meet students "where they are" and provide them with opportunities to begin doing the work of college students—from filling out financial aid forms, to learning time management strategies, to completing college classes—often before they begin their college education. To begin with, most of the MSIs are partnering with school districts and community organizations to focus and "warm" students' educational aspirations. When students take their first step on campus, they are introduced to college-going habits and skills through such means as formal Summer Bridge programs, campus orientations, college strategies courses, and structured interactions with peers, mentors, and counselors. Step by step, students learn how to apply for aid, register for classes, manage their schedules, read college-level texts, and solve college-level problems. At each step students collaborate with staff who understand their home culture and their high schools and, in many cases, their home language. Through the STEM Scholars program, for example, the College of Menominee Nation (CMN) reaches into high schools on the reservation and encourages high school students who are not fully prepared for college and not likely to pursue STEM careers to enter a yearlong program that will guide them to become ready to pursue a STEM degree.

Along with welcoming students and teaching them college-going skills, the MSIs are working with each student in developing a personal map of their pathway through college. Students learn how to navigate the campus and how to access classrooms, teachers, and support staff and resources. Several of the programs we studied enable students to earn credit for initial math and English courses or to improve their placement in those classes. As students come to know the campus, they engage in required conversations with mentors, advisers, and counselors about their current level of preparation, their educational goals, and the educational requirements they will need to meet. Through these interactions, each student comes to embrace the responsibility for meeting college-level requirements and forging relationships with faculty and peers throughout his or her college experience.

Across all of the programs we studied, program staff and faculty routinely communicate to students a commitment that is shared by everyone: believe and expect each student to succeed. This commitment is based on the understanding that students do not lack the abilities to be successful in college but that they have had a lack of opportunities. In short, faculty, staff, and administrators at these MSIs believe from the outset—and students come to believe over time—that every student not only can succeed but is expected to succeed in college. And faculty, staff, and administrators often communicate to students that they will be leaders in their professions and communities. As a faculty member at Salish Kootenai College (SKC) told us: "We give students validation. We give them a sense of value . . . to have the kind of confidence that they know they can succeed." In a similar vein, faculty and staff in the Nursing Cohort at North Seattle Community College (NSCC) believe that every student in the cohort can be "an extraordinary nurse." That validation is an integral part of "walking every student" into college.

Guide Individual Students through College and Chart a Pathway to Their Futures

The MSIs in this study educate many first-generation students who enter college believing that going to college is something they must do to improve their lives but with little understanding of what it means to be a college student and how to pilot their way through college. As an NSCC student expressed this: "My parents couldn't help me. I didn't know what I was supposed to do."

And many students are apprehensive as to whether they will be able to remain in college in light of personal concerns ranging from financial challenges and inflexible work schedules to fear that they will not be able to meet academic standards.

To help students learn how to navigate college, how to be resilient in the face of challenges, and how to succeed academically, the MSIs in the study have reconfigured how they staff the first years of a college education. Students' initial interactions on campus are facilitated by professionals—often members of a team—who collaborate in college-wide programs in which students work with guides variously described as coaches, counselors, mentors, advisers, and navigators. With expertise that ranges from teaching and learning, to financing college, to developing careers, these guides become "mother ducks" for students. They are trusted and caring contacts who not only guide students to the right course and the right skills but help them feel that they belong in college.

The MSIs in the study are reallocating institutional resources—and pursuing grant funding—to establish and sustain networks of relationships with individuals who link them to resources and model educational success. In Morehouse College's Minority Biomedical Research Support–Research Initiative for Scientific Enhancement (MBRS-RISE) program, for instance, prospective STEM students find themselves interacting with faculty mentors who invite them to join research projects and present their work at research group meetings and even at professional conferences. While completing required classes remains an important part of their college education, these students are being guided into STEM. Peer mentors at San Diego City College (SDCC) and Norfolk State University, navigators at NSCC, and faculty at CMN and the College of the Marshall Islands (CMI) play similar roles.

Notwithstanding the specific roles that individuals play in guiding students through college, one common denominator cuts across these guides: charting an educational pathway with each student to his or her future. Why is this important? Given the widely shared belief in this country that the driving purpose of college is to get a degree, it is hardly surprising that a large proportion of college students focus more on attaining their degree than on charting a path to their future. For example, Sacramento State University has found that many students who are ready for college struggle to do what they need to do to persist in college because they are unclear about why college matters to their lives beyond getting a degree. At NSCC, many citizens using social services don't even think about linking college to their lives.

To help students make a connection between college and their lives after college, guides at the MSIs in the study work with students to develop a formal plan for their education. In many instances, career and educational plans come to play the role of "contracts." In exchange for committing to a course of study and often a sequence of extracurricular activities as well, students gain access to support or early enrollment or even a comprehensive scholarship. A required part of students' plan at CMN and SKC is an internship in their chosen field of study. Ultimately, these plans align majors with their interests and life goals and scaffold a series of interactions between students and guides—students, staff, and faculty who serve as experienced points of contact to provide students with information, wisdom, and motivation—who help students navigate college along with becoming more resilient and more self-sufficient.

Provide Diverse Learning Opportunities Outside of the Traditional Classroom

The people we met at the MSIs in the study were very aware that many of their students are not traditional first-time college students. They come from "all over." Many arrive on campus with sometimes staggering diversity in terms of academic preparation, knowledge about college, and commitments off campus. For example, many of the Hmong students in the Full Circle Program at Sacramento State University juggle commitments such as financially supporting their families, fulfilling their role as a son or daughter, and finding the time and energy to be a college student. Staff and faculty members at all twelve MSIs told us again and again that a majority of their students enter college uncertain and anxious about whether "they can do it." Uncertain that they belong in college or can stay, many are reluctant to ask questions or to commit completely to their own education.

Anchored in their recognition of the diverse and often formidable challenges that students are facing, the MSIs in the study proceed with the shared assumption that the diverse needs of students can be met only if students have multiple opportunities to learn that go far beyond the traditional classroom. Most noteworthy, these institutions invest in customizable learning tools and learning experiences. More specifically, they use course management systems and off-the-shelf computer-based learning systems—such as at El Paso Community College (EPCC), CDKC, and SDCC—that provide students with a semester's worth of assignments and assessments that are often linked to videos, simulations, intelligent tutors, and practice exercises. And in many of the programs we studied, students have opportunities to complete inquiry-based learning modules—such as at CDKC, Morehouse College, NSCC, and SKC—that address locally relevant problems, often using the tools available in state-of-the-art science labs on campus or through internships at major research universities and labs or a service-learning placement. In campus labs, students also have a chance to learn the ins and outs of placement tests, federal financial aid forms, and professional licensure exams.

These learning tools are made available in diverse spaces—emporia, computer labs, tutoring labs, classrooms, group study rooms, campus performances, and workshops—that almost inevitably come with formal or informal networks of support. In fact, the MSIs have reconfigured faculty and staff roles so that their job includes keeping students actively involved in a set of overlapping educational and professional networks. The programs in the study draw students into learning communities and cohort groups or supplement traditional courses with additional instructors, tutors, coaches, peer mentors, and/or advisers who facilitate opportunities for students to revisit everything from course content to their own study habits. Several programs connect students with professional networks from the local to the national level. At CMN and Morehouse College, cohort groups guide students into STEM professions, linking them with national organizations, internships, apprenticeships, graduate schools, and jobs. As part of their education at SKC, NSCC, SDCC, and Sacramento State, students become active participants in networks of scientists or community organizations that are solving local problems.

In enriched and networked spaces, students pick up where they left off, catch up, and work ahead. For example, at EPCC, multicultural, multilingual advisers and tutors greet students and work with them as they move through a placement program. The program blends high-tech resources with high-touch relationships to customize the experiences of students—especially those seeking to enhance their basic college-level skills in mathematics and English. At EPCC and other MSIs in the study, students come to see as routine checking into a computer lab to work at their own pace or meeting up in study groups anchored by a supplemental instructor right after class, or in one-on-one tutoring sessions with tutors and faculty, or in what a CDKC administrator called "organically forming cohorts" of classmates who are wrestling with the same learning objectives. Tutors, peer mentors, counselors, and faculty are a phone call, e-mail, or text away, and in most instances, communicating with them regularly is not optional. Across the programs we studied, finding an approach to learning that "works for you" is simply part of going to college.

Relationships in these networked spaces provide students with support, en couragement, and feedback while also challenging them. As a STEM student at SKC describes this, these relationships are not "really [about] who you know; it is how you know them. You can meet all the people in the world but unless you know them as friends or as colleagues in that kind of respectful fashion it is not going to do any good." At SKC collaboration through networking in vites students to think about ideas and solve problems from multiple points of view without worrying about grades or the pressures of classroom dynamics. Promoting participation in learning communities and networks is an inte gral part of what SKC faculty members do. As we learned during the study, participation in informal and formal networks not only enhances students' learning while they are in college but also develops an appreciation that being collaborative—and contributing what they are learning to enrich the lives of others—should be a lifelong obligation.

Infuse Culturally Relevant Learning Opportunities into the College Experience

Many MSI students arrive at college with a limited sense of how a college edu cation might enhance their everyday lives and the welfare of their commu nities. A longtime administrator at SDCC told us that too many students wander through college without thinking much about where they are coming from and what their education means for them and their communities. To prepare students not only to flourish in the workplace and their personal lives but to contribute to the economic, social, and cultural well-being of communities, the MSIs in our study infuse the history and experience of underrepresented students into traditional curricula.

In some instances, MSIs have restructured the curriculum and co-curriculum. The education of developmental math students at CDKC and CMN includes the study of Native American history and language; STEM students at CMN and SKC have the option of joining active chapters of the American Indian Science and Engineering Society. Ethnic studies and Asian American history are among the required core classes for Asian American and Pacific Islander students in the Full Circle Program at Sacramento State University. Across the programs we studied, students are asked to reflect on how their futures are linked to their past and, in so doing, invited to use college to at once preserve and advance their respective cultures.

The cultural relevance of these educational opportunities extends beyond formal course work in two distinct ways. First, program staff members help underrepresented students see themselves in college. The programs we studied rely heavily on peer or near-peer mentors and tutors as well as staff who come from students' home communities and speak students' home languages. Like MSIs across the country, they hire substantial numbers of faculty from minority communities, and many of these faculty members are involved in research and educational initiatives in students' home communities and high schools and have formal relationships with the careers and educational experiences students move on to. This network of campus professionals affirms that underrepresented students belong in college and testifies to challenges and pathways to success for these students. Especially at the Tribal Colleges and Universities and Historically Black Colleges and Universities in the study, students emphasized the value of learning from faculty and staff who share both their educational experience and their racial and ethnic heritage and also expect them to contribute to improving the situation of other underrepresented students.

Second, the programs in the MSIs we studied provide students with formal opportunities to engage in real-world problem solving. They invite students—whether they are completing their first year or finishing up a degree in electrical engineering—to get involved in basic research, service learning, internships, and apprenticeships that take on issues of concern to them and their communities—from food security and environmental pollution, to the development of local businesses, to the availability of scientists and teachers who are prepared to serve communities of color. By way of illustration, first- and second-year students in the STEM Leaders program at CMN learn with tribal elders and legislators about problems on the reservation and then go off the reservation to meet working scientists in internships and at meetings of national organizations of scholars and, in turn, bring home new approaches to tackling local issues. At Morehouse College, MBRS-RISE program work with faculty on research projects that lead to publication. In the Full Circle Project at Sacramento State University, students become engaged in the 65th Street Corridor Community Collaborative Project, working with administrators, teachers, students, and parents from local schools to build a healthier and more vibrant community.

Through their involvement in the activities of local businesses, community organizations, and labs as well as work sites, we learned that students become more collaborative, more invested in their education, and more committed to framing and solving problems that are important to them and their communities. In so doing, these institutions are helping minority and other underrepresented students maintain and replenish their identities by engaging in culturally relevant learning. And in so doing, they learn to give back to their communities and become better able to move between worlds and thrive wherever they find themselves.

Immerse Students in Collaboration

Many American colleges and universities view college as a place for students to be educated to become independent and self-directed and, in so doing, realize their individual potential—especially with respect to career prospects and social mobility. In most institutions, successful students are people who have learned to compete. Schoolwork is rarely framed as an interdependent activity in which each student draws on the resources of others and serves as a resource for others, an activity that values each student's ability to adjust and respond to the needs of others. And most students entering higher education today have come from educational backgrounds where the primary emphasis was placed on individual achievement, not on collaboration. Many underrepresented students—as faculty and staff at the MSIs emphasized to us—have been alienated by traditional educational settings in which concern for the success of all is trumped by fierce competition.

While the MSIs in this study are educating students to navigate their public and private lives, they are also placing primary emphasis on teaching students to become collaborative. In educating students to be collaborative, MSIs are teaching them to learn *with* and *from* others and to embrace personal responsibility to contribute to their communities and the lives of others in college and beyond. By placing major emphasis on students' learning to be collaborative as well as academically successful, they are providing safe and supportive places in which students are obligated to be active participants in their own education as well as the education of their peers.

The MSIs we studied routinely scaffold situations in which students learn from other students. Learning collaboratively is structured into the educational experience. As students participate in Peer-Led Team Learning (PLTL) and Supplemental Instruction (SI) and required study sessions or work with peer tutors or in a math emporium, they come to expect to learn from other students. They begin to value confirming their progress (explaining how they understand a topic or approach and solve a problem) with their peers and contributing to the progress of others. We observed SDCC students interacting with an SI group on a math problem. The tutor initiated and steered the session, but as students got down to work, they began writing in the margins of one another's notebooks and then on a whiteboard. Soon they were editing one another's work and calling one another's attention to textbook passages, turning back to their tutor only when they hit a snag and then when they had solved the problem. These formal opportunities to collaborate as learners seem to promote a vision of education as a process through which students talk through their current understanding with other learners and then troubleshoot their understanding until they are satisfied with the outcome.

Along with teaching students to be collaborative, an institutional commitment to collaborative learning has two other impacts. First, routine engagement in collaboration often seems to influence the roles students and teachers are willing to play. Simply put, students become ready to teach, and teachers are ready to learn. At Morehouse College, students in PLTL learn to embrace the role of teacher and the role of learner. At NSCC, students teach frontline staff what they need from a college education and how they learn. Students in the Nursing Cohort program at NSCC meet with a navigator every week; program instructors and support staff meet weekly to discuss the progress of every student; and once each quarter the entire cohort provides anonymous feedback to instructors. As staff, faculty, and employers learn how students learn, they change the course of instruction so that every student can meet course outcomes. CMN students hold one another responsible for their learning, and students take on the role of leader/teacher for the community. La Sierra University uses team teaching. As noted earlier, many of the MSIs establish formal and informal networks that include learning communities, cohort groups, and professional networks from the local to the national level.

Second, in learning to be collaborative, students—and teachers—learn to embrace a commitment to give back to their communities and service areas. Paul Quinn College, which is located in a community where many people lack access to fresh food and have little knowledge of good nutrition, opened an organic farm several years ago. At the "We over Me" Farm, students not only work on the farm but learn about good nutrition, hard work, and activism. But perhaps most noteworthy, students tithe food to the local community and, in so doing, many students are developing and reaffirming a commitment to contribute to the broader whole—a commitment that also is anchored in "servant leadership" as an integral part of the extra curriculum. In a similar vein, the STEM Leaders program at CMN obligates students to give back to their communities through addressing real-world problems. At Sacramento State University, the 65th Street Corridor Project has students engaged in community service and activism that go far beyond the everyday comfort of the Full Circle Program. Students participate in diverse off-campus projects such as tutoring and mentoring junior high and high school students who live in low-income areas of Sacramento.

In summary, immersing students in collaboration is a significant component of the programs we studied at MSIs. From learning communities and informal networks to peer-led learning, students are not only enhancing their learning through collaboration but also developing a deeper appreciation of collaboration—along with an obligation to give back to others over the course of their lives.

Gather and Use Information on the Learning and Progress of Students

The MSIs in this study are gathering data on student learning and progress—such as course completion rates, semester-to-semester retention rates, graduation rates, and grade point averages. While they are using these conventional measures, they have found that such data, by themselves, offer too limited a glimpse of their students' progress. They have come to understand that traditional measures of persistence and performance provide little information about what students are "doing" in college and woefully little insight into why students make progress in or stall out of college. Moreover, they have learned that course completion rates and grade point averages do little more than confirm that students whose lives and academic progress changes week to week and even day to day have not progressed. Because the programs in our study serve students who start college with diverse prior educational experiences and hence progress in college along widely diverse paths, program staff augment traditional measures with information about what students are learning and how they are managing their everyday lives. They begin to gather this information before students take their first classes and refresh it often enough to inform interventions.

Measuring student progress in these programs involves real-time assessment of an unfolding educational pathway. Again and again, staff and faculty at the MSIs emphasized to us, "We know our students." The admission process at many of the MSIs launches an ongoing conversation with each student about what it means to be prepared to start college. Through Summer Bridge programs, student placement, and advising programs, these colleges learn about and document students' prior experiences and their college aspirations as well as their engagement in classes. By the middle of their first term, students in most of the programs we studied attend multiple orientation events at which they learn about placement tests, financial aid applications, learning styles, program requirements, and career options—events that are often required and documented in databases. As students settle into their programs, their grades are tracked—midterm grades as well as final grades—as are their interactions with staff, hours logged in learning systems, and attendance at workshops and classes; in several programs staff, faculty, and administrators collect educational plans, scores on quizzes and exams, and surveys of and written reflections on student development and engagement inside and outside classes.

The gathering of this wide range of data is only part of the story. The programs also establish routines for reviewing and using data. In most of the programs we studied, faculty and staff establish regular meetings for reviewing data, and in some cases, policies for responding to benchmarks. Staff meetings, our participants told us, take up "the data." The data are often collected in spreadsheets that track basic activity. But these programs do more than stay on top of descriptive statistics. They harvest data from computer-based learning systems and course management systems to inform instruction. They scaffold discussions among staff and faculty concerning the progress and needs of individuals and cohort groups. Several programs have institutional research projects aimed at understanding the efficacy of specific interventions. At Sacramento State University, for example, the Full Circle Program has brought together institutional researchers, university faculty, and the Institute for Higher Education Leadership and Policy to study the educational progress of Asian American and Pacific Islander students. In an ongoing collaboration, the group routinely reviews institutional student progress data and augments those data with transcripts from interviews and focus groups and the results from a battery of surveys. Full Circle staff members know not only whether their students persist but also what kinds of self-efficacy and identities they are developing in comparison to a control group.

This thicker, real-time description of students' educational pathways produces data for multiple uses. Foremost, these data guide interventions. Weekly reviews of student progress data trigger e-mails, calls, and texts from a network of staff so that students are pushed toward support while there is still time. These data also drive program design and implementation. In the case of the Nursing Cohort program at NSCC, faculty are able—and students feel that they are obligated—to make midquarter readjustments to instruction and curriculum based on feedback that is gathered through weekly meetings of program staff and faculty and through quarterly student focus groups. At SKC, course completion data grounded an argument for restructuring the departments that serve developmental education students.

The assessment of student persistence and learning in these programs begins with the data that each institution needs for accountability purposes. Program staff and faculty know their enrollments and retention rates; they know how many students transfer, to where, and with what success. But these programs are home to staff and faculty who are continually tinkering with them so as to serve underserved students. These programs invite faculty and staff to use existing data and to do research in order to represent accurately the challenges their students face and to invent and test educational activities that empower students to overcome those challenges.

Toward Educating a Diverse America

While our primary focus has been on identifying practices for cultivating student success, we noticed again and again the ways in which the institutional cultures at the MSIs contributed to the successful implementation of all six of the practices. For example, while the First-Year Experience program at SDCC is not unique, it works for the students at SDCC in part because of the organizational culture in which it is embedded. The campus culture at SDCC, like the campus culture at all of the MSIs we studied, is strikingly different from the campus culture at many colleges and universities where the cultures focus on educating traditional middle-class and upper-class students and, in turn, assimilating all students into that dominant culture. These cultures tend to be highly individualistic and steeped in selectivity and competition. If our colleges are to successfully implement the practices we have identified to empower traditionally underserved students, we suggest that the institutional cultures at many colleges and universities—the values, norms, beliefs, and artifacts that shape and guide the behavior of individuals and groups within the institution—may need to be transformed in four major ways.

Call Out and Strike Down the Deficit View of Students

The stakeholders we talked with in this study regularly acknowledge deficit views of their students. They both rejected these views and talked about these views with their students. In distinction, they believe that every student can and will succeed. They recognize that students fit college into their lives—not the reverse—and, in turn, they create diverse opportunities to learn that give students multiple chances to master the necessary knowledge and skills at their own pace and in their own languages. In so doing, they are validating students as learners and active participants in their own education who will use college as they wish. Colleges that are accustomed to selecting students based on traditional indicators of academic success and providing equal access to a common educational experience will struggle to successfully implement the practices identified in this chapter.

Blur Traditional Roles of Faculty, Staff, and Students: Upend Top-Down Hierarchies

The MSIs in the study realize that the traditional division of labor in higher education and the accompanying roles of students, faculty, staff, and leaders do not serve their students well. As a result, students, staff, and faculty at these institutions are prepared to step into the role of teacher, tutor, mentor, and counselor. To be sure, these institutions understand each of the respective contributions of different professional groups. At the same time, they believe each of these groups can and should contribute to the progress and learning of all students. They make use of team teaching, peer teaching, tutoring, and mentoring students as well as collaborative learning and service learning both inside and outside of the classroom. And across all twelve MSIs, leaders often go beyond conventional practices and connect with students on a regular basis through group interactions and one-on-one relationships. Unless colleges and universities are prepared to blur time-honored roles and responsibilities, they may find that they do not have the resources they need to educate a diverse student body.

Expect Everyone to Take Responsibility for the Learning and Progress of Students

Along with establishing campus-wide cultures in which everyone assumes the responsibility to convey this message to students, faculty and administrators as well as staff take the initiative to understand the challenges students are facing and then connect them with the support they need. In the First-Year Residential Education program at CMI and the Peer-Led Team Learning program at Morehouse College, faculty, staff, and administrators routinely ask students, "How are you doing in college?" and, in turn, "How can I help you?" and then follow up with, "I will go with you to find support." A culture that invites and supports such conversations and accompanying support guides many students who would otherwise be on the margins to find the hope, motivation, and self-confidence they need to be successful in college.

Empower Students to Customize Their Educational Pathways

We were struck during our visits to the twelve MSIs in the study that the conventional "one size fits all students" model does *not* fit all students. Largely because these institutions recognize the radical diversity in the prior experience of their students, they seek to customize—rather than standardize—their students' pathways through college. Staff and faculty share the belief that their students arrive at college with varied resources and goals. In turn, they develop individualized approaches to the ways students register for and fund their education, the ways teachers and tutors present and explain course content, and the ways students show what they have learned. They have realized that if the individual needs of these students are to be addressed, institutions must invite and support students in developing an individual plan, first for their lives after college and then through college. We see little hope of retaining more of the diverse students who now come to college in the United States if a college education remains the accumulation of credits that signal the completion of a series of required topical courses.

A Concluding Note

Along with reimagining institutional cultures, the MSIs in our study are adopting and inventing educational practices for advancing student learning and persistence. In so doing, they are providing students with the knowledge, skills, and habits they need to become self-sustaining in college and beyond. Moreover, by incorporating formal and informal networking and culturally relevant learning opportunities into the college experience, they are also guiding students to become collaborative as well as independent learners. In short, students are being educated not only to be self-sufficient but also to be contributors to their communities and to the lives of others.

If our nation's colleges and universities are to better educate students—including minority, first-generation, and low-income students—who are often not well served by higher education, they need to reach beyond traditional practices. We invite stakeholders across higher education to learn from the MSIs in this study about ways to advance equal opportunities for all students now coming to American colleges and universities.

Conclusion

A College Education for a Diverse Nation

From the time they begin to consider college to their graduation, students at Minority-Serving Institutions are prepared to engage and be challenged by faculty and staff members who know them by name. At the same time, relationships with individual students often push staff and faculty members to adapt their practice so as to help these students meet their educational goals. Serving diverse student bodies rests, to a large extent, on an institution-wide commitment to treating every student as an individual.

Students come to college for degrees that lead to jobs. They also come to college as agents in their own right, as people who are seeking to find their own places in their worlds. They need colleges that provide them with opportunities to study the stories of their cultures and their places in them and also to reflect on the ways in which their futures are emerging from their pasts. Colleges that reach out to diverse students validate students' developing identities and offer them routine opportunities to practice being the people they are becoming. And no less important, these colleges plan with each student a pathway to her or his future.

Reaching out to the diverse students who are now coming to American colleges and universities rests in part on transforming the college curriculum. The MSIs in our study are leading this transformation in multiple ways. They are teaching students to be college-ready before they matriculate. These same schools are redesigning instruction around cohorts with embedded peer tutors and mentors, service learning, and apprenticeships. In first-year courses and senior capstone experiences at these colleges, students study the histories and life experiences of their communities and solve real-world problems that their communities are facing. Collectively, these schools are showing us curricula that are relevant and accessible for diverse student bodies.

Students have always arrived at American colleges having learned much and with much to learn. As they have become more diverse, so has what they know and need to learn and also how they learn—from what languages they speak, to what technologies they use, to what motivates them as learners. These students are unlikely to learn enough from faculty who teach them one class at a time. They need teachers who focus on what they need to learn when they are ready to learn it. In order to create more chances for students to learn, colleges that effectively teach diverse learners blur the traditional roles of learner and teacher. They set up multiple opportunities for people with some expertise—from faculty to supplemental instructors and tutors, to academic coaches, to more seasoned students—to collaborate with learners. This is not to say that traditional roles disappear but that all stakeholders are open to valuing what everyone contributes to teaching and learning.

While for some Americans college is still a residential campus with a quad, college for most is a community resource that they can access in their everyday lives. As colleges relevant to students and their communities, the Minority-Serving Institutions in this book are designed to enrich their community, whether that community is a tribe on a reservation or a national association of biologists. Beyond offering classes, these institutions are forums for cultural events, points of access to social services, and business incubators. They see their mission as the production of more than degrees: they are conduits to educational, social, cultural, and economic resources.

Becoming institutions that understand, value, and respect the diverse students now coming to college in the United States will require transformational change for many colleges and universities. We see this formidable challenge as an extraordinary social and moral opportunity. If our colleges and universities are willing to become open to the kinds of change and innovation we found at MSIs, we have the chance to realize the vision of equal educational opportunity for all Americans. At the same time, we have the opportunity to become better able to uplift both individuals and our society by educating a citizenry—from researchers and teachers, to entrepreneurs and leaders, to community activists and community developers—for a diverse democracy. Colleges and universities that seize this opportunity and embrace and educate diverse students will enrich and enlarge the lives of students and their communities and at the same time become twenty-first-century American institutions of higher education.

If we go back to the students' vignettes at the beginning of this book, shouldn't we all want Kareem and Leticia to have equal experiences and opportunities in college and life with Sara? Not only is the success of Kareem and Leticia a genuine good—the type of good that our nation is built upon in theory—but it advances our goals as a nation and makes us stronger. To better serve our nation's increasingly diverse students, colleges and universities must seize the responsibility to reach out to them and become institutions that understand and value where each student comes from and where each student aspires to go as a college-educated person. In so doing, they can provide a college education that teaches the responsibility to contribute to communities and the lives of others as it also prepares individuals to thrive where they live.

Notes

1. The Challenge of Educating a Diverse America

1. Sharon R. Ennis, Merarys Ríos-Vargas, and Nora G. Albert, *The Hispanic Population: 2010* (Washington, DC: U.S. Department of Commerce, Economics and Statistics Administration, U.S. Census Bureau, 2011); Elizabeth M. Hoeffel et al., *The Asian Population: 2010* (Washington, DC: U.S. Department of Commerce, Economics and Statistics Administration, U.S. Census Bureau, 2012).

2. Hispanics include individuals who identify across the various racial groups. Because collection of data is inconsistent between 1980 and 2010, we decided to show the growth of all Hispanics, regardless of race.

3. U.S. Census Bureau, *Population Estimates, 2001,* http://www.census.gov/popest /data/national/totals/1990s/tables/nat-total.txt; U.S. Census Bureau, "Table 1. Intercensal Estimates of the Resident Population by Sex and Age for the United States: April 1, 2000 to July 1, 2010," 2011, http://www.census.gov/popest/data/intercensal /national/nat2010.html; U.S. Census Bureau, "Table 2. Intercensal Estimates of the Resident Population by Sex, Race, and Hispanic Origin for the United States: April 1, 2000 to July 1, 2010," n.d., http://www.census.gov/popest/data/intercensal/national /nat2010.html.

4. William H. Frey, *America's Diverse Future: Initial Glimpses at the U.S. Child Population from the 2010 Census* (Washington, DC: Brookings Institution, 2011), http://www.brookings.edu/papers/2011/0406_census_diversity_frey.aspx; Daniel Potter and Josipa Roksa, "Accumulating Advantages over Time: Family Experiences and Social Class Inequality in Academic Achievement," *Social Science Research* 42, no. 4 (July 2013): 1018–1032.

5. Susan Aud, Mary Ann Fox, and Angelina Kewal Ramani, *Status and Trends in the Education of Racial and Ethnic Groups,* NCES 2010-015 (Washington, DC: National Center for Education Statistics, July 2010).

6. ACT, *ACT High School Profile Report* (Iowa City: ACT, 2008), http://www.act .org/news/data/08/pdf/National2008.pdf; College Board, *The 5th Annual AP Report to the Nation, 2008,* http://www.collegeboard.com/html/aprtn/pdf/ap_report _to_the_nation_data_at_a_glance_app_a.pdf; Aud, Fox, and Kewal Ramani, *Status and Trends in the Education of Racial and Ethnic Groups.*

7. Don Hossler, Jack Schmit, and Nick Vesper, *Going to College: How Social, Economic, and Educational Factors Influence the Decisions Students Make* (Baltimore, MD: Johns Hopkins University Press, 1998); Boualoy Dayton et al., "Hispanic-Serving Institutions through the Eyes of Students and Administrators," *New Directions for Student Services* 105 (2004): 29–40, doi:10.1002/ss.114.

8. U.S. Department of Education, National Center for Education Statistics, "Table 230. Total Fall Enrollment in Degree-Granting Institutions, by Level and Control of Institution and Race/Ethnicity of Student: Selected Years, 1976 through 2011," 2012, http://nces.ed.gov/programs/digest/d12/tables/dt12_230.asp.

9. James E. Rosenbaum, Regina Deil-Amen, and Ann E. Person, *After Admission: From College Access to College Success* (New York: Russell Sage Foundation, 2006).

10. Eric Grodsky and Erika Jackson, "Social Stratification in Higher Education," *Teachers College Record* 111, no. 10 (October 2009): 2352–2355.

11. John W. Meyer et al., "Higher Education as an Institution," in *Sociology of Higher Education: Contributions and Their Contexts,* ed. Patricia J. Gumport (Baltimore, MD: Johns Hopkins University Press, 2007), 187–221.

12. Anthony P. Carnevale, Jeff Strohl, and Nicole Smith, "Help Wanted: Postsecondary Education and Training Required," *New Directions for Community Colleges* 146 (2009): 21–31; Anthony P. Carnevale, "College for All?," *Change* 40, no. 1 (January 2008): 22–31; John H. Pryor et al., *The American Freshman National Norms for Fall 2007* (Los Angeles: Higher Education Research Institute, University of California Los Angeles, 2008), http://www.heri.ucla.edu/PDFs/pubs/TFS/Norms/Monographs/TheAmericanFreshman2007.pdf.

13. Anthony P. Carnevale, Nicole Smith, and Jeff Strohl, *Help Wanted: Projections of Jobs and Education Requirements through 2018* (Washington, DC: Georgetown University Center on Education and the Workforce, June 1, 2010), 2–3.

14. Carnevale, Strohl, and Smith, "Help Wanted."

15. Anthony P. Carnevale, Tamara Jayasundera, and Andrew R. Hanson, *Career and Technical Education: Five Ways That Pay along the Way to the B.A.* (Washington, DC: Georgetown University Center on Education and the Workforce, September 1, 2012), https://georgetown.app.box.com/s/jd4ronwvjtq12g1olx8v.

16. For a recent review see Sandy Baum, Jennifer Ma, and Kathleen Payea, *Education Pays 2013: The Benefits of Higher Education for Individuals and Society* (New York: College Board, 2013), http://trends.collegeboard.org/sites/default/files/education-pays-2013-full-report.pdf.

17. American Indian Higher Education Consortium, *Tribal Colleges: An Introduction* (Alexandria, VA: American Indian Higher Education Consortium, 1999).

18. Amy Fann, *Tribal Colleges: An Overview* (Los Angeles: ERIC Clearinghouse for Community Colleges, 2002), http://eric.ed.gov/?id=ED467847; Alisa Federico Cunningham and Robyn Hiestand, *The Path of Many Journeys: The Benefits of Higher Education for Native People and Communities* (Washington, DC: Institute for Higher Education Policy, 2007); Wayne J. Stein, "Tribal Colleges: 1968–1998,"

in *Next Steps: Research and Practice to Advance Indian Education* (Charleston, WV: ERIC/CRESS, 1999).

19. Aud, Fox, and Kewal Ramani, *Status and Trends in the Education of Racial and Ethnic Groups*.

20. Michael Cole, *Cultural Psychology: A Once and Future Discipline* (Cambridge, MA: Belknap Press of Harvard University Press, 1996); John Bransford, A. L. Brown, and R. R. Cocking, *How People Learn: Brain, Mind, Experience, and School* (Washington, DC: National Academy Press, 2000); James Paul Gee, *Social Linguistics and Literacies: Ideology in Discourses*, 4th ed. (New York: Routledge, 2011).

21. Beverly E. Cross, "Urban School Achievement Gap as a Metaphor to Conceal U.S. Apartheid Education," *Theory into Practice* 46, no. 3 (2007): 247–255; Stella M. Flores and Otoniel Jimenez Morfin, "Another Side of the Percent Plan Story: Latino Enrollment in the Hispanic-Serving Institutions Sector in California and Texas," in *Understanding Minority-Serving Institutions*, ed. Marybeth Gasman, B. Baez, and C. S. V. Turner (Albany: State University of New York Press, 2008), 141–155; Deborah A. Santiago, *Choosing Hispanic-Serving Institutions (HSIS): A Closer Look at Latino Students' College Choices* (Washington, DC: Excelencia in Education, 2007); Dayton et al., "Hispanic-Serving Institutions through the Eyes of Students and Administrators"; Kassie Freeman, *African Americans and College Choice: The Influence of Family and School* (Albany: State University of New York Press, 2005); Berta Vigil Laden, "Serving Emerging Majority Students," *New Directions for Community Colleges* no. 127 (2004): 200, doi:10.1002/cc.160; Linda Serra Hagedorn et al., "An Investigation of Critical Mass: The Role of Latino Representation in the Success of Urban Community College Students," *Research in Higher Education* 48, no. 1 (February 2007): 73–91; Charles Vert Willie, Richard Reddick, and Ronald Brown, *The Black College Mystique* (Lanham, MD: Rowman and Littlefield, 2006), http://www.loc.gov/catdir/toc/ecip0515/2005017225.html.

22. For the experience of minority students at majority institutions, see Walter Recharde Allen, Edgar G. Epps, and Nesha Z. Haniff, *College in Black and White: African American Students in Predominantly White and in Historically Black Public Universities* (Albany: State University of New York Press, 1991); Joe R. Feagin, Hernan Vera, and Nikitah Imani, *The Agony of Education: Black Students at White Colleges and Universities* (New York: Routledge, 1996); Ernest T. Pascarella and Patrick T. Terenzini, *How College Affects Students: A Third Decade of Research* (San Francisco: Jossey-Bass, 2005); Susan R. Rankin and Robert D. Reason, "Differing Perceptions: How Students of Color and White Students Perceive Campus Climate for Underrepresented Groups," *Journal of College Student Development* 46, no. 1 (February 1, 2005): 43–61; Landon D. Reid and Phanikiran Radhakrishnan, "Race Matters: The Relation between Race and General Campus Climate," *Cultural Diversity and Ethnic Minority Psychology* 9, no. 3 (August 2003): 263–275; Vincent Tinto, *Leaving College: Rethinking the Causes and Cures of Student Attrition* (Chicago: University of Chicago Press, 1987). As a national cohort, minority students

are more likely than their White peers to arrive at college from communities de-fined by immigration and, for the most part, with fewer economic resources and lower levels of parental education; see Aud, Fox, and Kewal Ramani, *Status and Trends in the Education of Racial and Ethnic Groups*; Justin P. Guillory and Kelly Ward, "Tribal Colleges and Universities: Identity, Invisibility, and Current Issues," in Gasman, Baez, and Turner, *Understanding Minority-Serving Institutions*, 91–110. Minority students who find themselves at "minority-serving institutions"—colleges or universities with high minority enrollments—are even less "traditional" than minority students who attend majority institutions. They are less academically pre-pared, more sensitive to the cost of college, and more dependent on financial aid than their peers at non-MSIs, and, in the case of Hispanic students, more resistant to going into debt for a college education; see Walter Recharde Allen et al., *Black Undergraduates from Bakke to Grutter: Freshman Status, Trends and Prospects, 1971–2004* (Los Angeles: Higher Education Research Institute, UCLA, 2005); Thomas F. Nelson Laird et al., "African American and Hispanic Student Engagement at Mi-nority Serving and Predominantly White Institutions," *Journal of College Student Development* 48, no. 1 (February 1, 2007): 39–56; Dayton et al., "Hispanic-Serving Institutions through the Eyes of Students and Administrators"; L. Scott Miller and Eugene E. García, "Better Informing Efforts to Increase Latino Student Success in Higher Education," *Education and Urban Society* 36, no. 2 (February 2004): 189–204; Kathryn Hoffman and Charmaine Llagas, "Status and Trends in the Education of Blacks," *Education Statistics Quarterly* 5, no. 4 (August 2004): 20; Deborah A. Santiago, *Reality Check: Hispanic-Serving Institutions on the Texas Border Strate-gizing Financial Aid* (Washington, DC: Excelencia in Education, 2010).

23. Berta Vigil Laden, Linda Serra Hagedorn, and Athena Perrakis, "¿Donde Estan los Hombres? Examining Success of Latino Male Students at Hispanic-Serving Community Colleges," in Gasman, Baez, and Turner, *Understanding Minority-Serving Institutions*, 127–140; Watson Scott Swail, K. E. Redd, and Laura W. Perna, "Retaining Minority Students in Higher Education: A Framework for Success," *ASHE-ERIC Higher Education Report* 30, no. 2 (January 1, 2003): 1–187; Patricia H. Crosson, "Four-Year College and University Environments for Minority Degree Achievement," *Review of Higher Education* 11, no. 4 (June 1, 1988): 365–382; Caroline Sotello Viernes Turner, "Guests in Someone Else's House: Students of Color," *Review of Higher Education* 17, no. 4 (June 1, 1994): 355–370; Brian K. Bridges et al., "Student Engagement and Student Success at Historically Black and Hispanic-Serving Insti-tutions," in Gasman, Baez, and Turner, *Understanding Minority-Serving Institutions*, 217–236.

24. Rosemary B. Closson and Wilma J. Henry, "The Social Adjustment of Un-dergraduate White Students in the Minority on an Historically Black College Campus," *Journal of College Student Development* 49, no. 6 (January 2008): 517–534; Laura I. Rendon, "Validating Culturally Diverse Students: Toward a New Model of Learning and Student Development," *Innovative Higher Education* 19, no. 1 (Sep-

tember 1994): 33–51; Rebekah Nathan, *My Freshman Year: What a Professor Learned by Becoming a Student* (New York: Penguin Books, 2006); Terrell L. Strayhorn, "Undergraduate Research Participation and STEM Graduate Degree Aspirations among Students of Color," *New Directions for Institutional Research,* no. 148 (January 2010): 85–93; Alisa Federico Cunningham and Kenneth E Redd, *Creating Role Models for Change: A Survey of Tribal College Graduates* (Washington, DC: Institute for Higher Education Policy, May 2000), http://ezproxy.library.wisc.edu/login?url=http://search .ebscohost.com/login.aspx?direct=true&db=eric&AN=ED456947&login.asp& site=ehost-live.

25. Estimates are based on the U.S. Department of Education's National Center for Education Statistics, Integrated Postsecondary Education Data System (IPEDS), Fall 2001 and Spring 2002 through Spring 2011, Graduation Rates component.

26. Kevin P. Reilly, "Answering the Call to Serve in Challenging Times" (keynote address presented at the American Council on Education Institute for New Presidents, Chicago, July 2013).

2. Minority-Serving Institutions

1. Estimates based on U.S. Department of Education's Integrated Postsecondary Education Data System (IPEDS) Unduplicated 12-Month Headcount: 2010–2011. All calculations are for undergraduates enrolled in degree-granting institutions in the United States and the District of Columbia.

2. Justin P Guillory and Kelly Ward, "Tribal Colleges and Universities: Identity, Invisibility, and Current Issues," in *Understanding Minority-Serving Institutions,* ed. Marybeth Gasman, B. Baez, and C. S. V. Turner (Albany: State University of New York Press, 2008), 91–110.

3. Debbie Van Camp et al., "Choosing an HBCU: An Opportunity to Pursue Racial Self-Development," *Journal of Negro Education* 78, no. 4 (2009): 457–468; Debbie Van Camp, Jamie Barden, and Lloyd R. Sloan, "Predictors of Black Students' Race-Related Reasons for Choosing an HBCU and Intentions to Engage in Racial Identity-Relevant Behaviors," *Journal of Black Psychology* 36, no. 2 (January 2010): 226–250.

4. Benjamin Baez, Marybeth Gasman, and Caroline Sotello Viernes Turner, "On Minority-Serving Institutions," in Gasman, Baez, and Turner, *Understanding Minority-Serving Institutions,* 3–17.

5. Alisa Federico Cunningham and Christina Redmond, *Building Strong Communities: Tribal Colleges as Engaged Institutions* (Washington, DC: American Indian Higher Education Consortium, 2001).

6. Amy Fisher and Edward St. John, "Economically and Educationally Challenged Students in Higher Education: Access to Outcomes," *Review of Higher Education* 32, no. 1 (2008): 139–140; Jacqueline J. Schmidt and Yemi Akande, "Faculty Perceptions of the First-Generation Student Experience and Programs at Tribal Colleges," *New Directions for Teaching and Learning,* no. 127 (January 2011): 41–54.

7. American Indian Higher Education Consortium, *Tribal Colleges: An Introduction* (Alexandria, VA: American Indian Higher Education Consortium, 1999); Mikyong Minsun Kim and Clifton F. Conrad, "The Impact of Historically Black Colleges and Universities on the Academic Success of African American Students," *Research in Higher Education* 47, no. 4 (June 2006): 399–427; Thomas F. Nelson Laird et al., "African American and Hispanic Student Engagement at Minority Serving and Predominantly White Institutions," *Journal of College Student Development* 48, no. 1 (2007): 39–56, doi:10.1353/csd.2007.0005.

8. Van Camp et al., "Choosing an HBCU"; Alisa Federico Cunningham and Robyn Hiestand, *The Path of Many Journeys: The Benefits of Higher Education for Native People and Communities* (Washington, DC: Institute for Higher Education Policy, 2007); Deborah A. Santiago, *Choosing Hispanic-Serving Institutions (HSIS): A Closer Look at Latino Students' College Choices* (Washington, DC: Excelencia in Education, 2007); Robert T. Teranishi, *Asians in the Ivory Tower: Dilemmas of Racial Inequality in American Higher Education* (New York: Teachers College Press, 2010).

9. Boualoy Dayton et al., "Hispanic-Serving Institutions through the Eyes of Students and Administrators," *New Directions for Student Services* 105 (2004): 29–40, doi:10.1002/ss.114.

10. Berta Vigil Laden, Linda Serra Hagedorn, and Athena Perrakis, "¿Donde Estan los Hombres? Examining Success of Latino Male Students at Hispanic-Serving Community Colleges," in Gasman, Baez, and Turner, *Understanding Minority-Serving Institutions*, 127–140.

11. Dorreen Yellow Bird, "Changing the Face of Research: Tribal Colleges Address Community Well-Being," *Tribal College Journal of American Indian Higher Education* 18, no. 4 (June 2007): 12–16; John L. Phillips, "A Tribal College Land Grant Perspective: Changing the Conversation," *Journal of American Indian Education* 42, no. 1 (January 2003): 22–35; Cunningham and Redmond, *Building Strong Communities*.

12. American Indian Higher Education Consortium, *Tribal Colleges;* Cunningham and Redmond, *Building Strong Communities;* James T. Minor, "Decision Making in Historically Black Colleges and Universities: Defining the Governance Context," *Journal of Negro Education* 73, no. 1 (2004): 40–52; Andrea L. Beach et al., "Faculty Development at Historically Black Colleges and Universities: Current Priorities and Future Directions," in Gasman, Baez, and Turner, *Understanding Minority-Serving Institutions*, 156–168; Robert T. Palmer and Marybeth Gasman, "'It Takes a Village to Raise a Child': The Role of Social Capital in Promoting Academic Success for African American Men at a Black College," *Journal of College Student Development* 49, no. 1 (January 1, 2008): 52–70.

13. Amy Fann, *Tribal Colleges: An Overview* (Los Angeles: ERIC Clearinghouse for Community Colleges, 2002), http://eric.ed.gov/?id=ED467847; Timothy J. Nichols, Phil Baird, and Diane Kayongo-Male, "Partnerships Offer Promise and Perils: A Study of Collaborations with State Universities," *Tribal College*

Journal 13, no. 2 (2001): 20–23; Daniel C. Thompson, *Private Black Colleges at the Crossroads* (Westport, CT: Greenwood Press, 1973).

14. Charles Wilkinson, *Blood Struggle: The Rise of Modern Indian Nations* (Boston: W. W. Norton, 2006).

15. American Indian Higher Education Consortium, "Tribal Colleges: An Introduction" (Washington, DC: American Indian Higher Education Consortium, 1999).

16. Wayne J. Stein, "The Funding of Tribally Controlled Colleges," *Journal of American Indian Education* 30, no. 1 (1990): 1.

17. There are thirty-four regular members, four associate members, and one international member. On the role of TCUs see Jack Barden, "Linking Tribal Colleges and Mainstream Institutions: Fundamental Tensions and Lessons Learned," in *The Renaissance of American Indian Higher Education: Capturing the Dream,* ed. Maenette Kape'ahiokalani Ah Nee-Benham and Wayne J. Stein (Mahwah, NJ: Lawrence Erlbaum, 2003), 99–120; Cunningham and Redmond, *Building Strong Communities;* American Indian Higher Education Consortium, *Tribal College Contributions to Local Economic Development* (Washington, DC: American Indian Higher Education Consortium, 2000).

18. Between 1996 and 2006, Native Americans had sharper gains in the number of degrees earned than Whites, and the share of Native American students enrolled in four-year institutions increased by 10 percent. TCUs enroll almost 10 percent of Native American undergraduates and continue to struggle to have sufficient space to serve all students seeking degrees (Paul Boyer and Ernest L. Boyer, *Native American Colleges: Progress and Prospects* [Princeton, NJ: Carnegie Foundation for the Advancement of Teaching, 1997]).

19. Keweenaw Bay Ojibwa Community College was granted Title IV status in December 2010, and hence this college is not counted in our analysis of fall 2010 degree-granting institutions.

20. TCUs also reflect their communities through the presence of high numbers of tribal administrators and students and a higher proportion of tribal faculty than are typical in colleges and universities in the United States (American Indian Higher Education Consortium, *Tribal Colleges*).

21. American Indian Higher Education Consortium, *Tribal Colleges.*

22. Ann Marie Machamer, "Survey Reflects Student Development at D-Q University," *Tribal College* 10, no. 2 (January 1999): 38–43; Bobby Wright, "Tribally Controlled Community Colleges: An Assessment of Student Satisfaction," *Community/ Junior College Quarterly of Research and Practice* 13, no. 2 (January 1989): 119–128; American Indian Higher Education Consortium, *Tribal Colleges;* Michael O'Donnell et al., "Information Technology and Tribal Colleges and Universities: Moving into the 21st Century," in Ah Nee-Benham and Stein, *The Renaissance of American Indian Higher Education,* 257–272.

23. Paul Boyer, "Defying the Odds: Tribal Colleges Conquer Skepticism but Still Face Persistent Challenges," *Tribal College Journal* 14, no. 2 (2002): 12–19; Yellow

Bird, "Changing the Face of Research: Tribal Colleges Address Community Well-Being"; Cunningham and Hiestand, *The Path of Many Journeys;* Phillips, "A Tribal College Land Grant Perspective"; Guillory and Ward, "Tribal Colleges and Universities."

24. Jennifer Park and Robert Teranishi, "Asian American and Pacific Islander Serving Institutions," in Gasman, Baez, and Turner, *Understanding Minority-Serving Institutions,* 111–126.

25. Berta Vigal Laden, "Hispanic Serving Institutions: Myths and Realities," *Peabody Journal of Education* 76, no. 1 (2001): 73–92.

26. Doug Massey, Jorge Durane, and Nolan Malone, *Beyond Smoke and Mirrors: Mexican Immigration in an Era of Economic Integration* (New York: Russell Sage Foundation, 2003).

27. Ibid.

28. Benjamin Baez, Marybeth Gasman, and Caroline Sotello Turner, "On Minority-Serving Institutions," in Gasman, Baez, and Turner, *Understanding Minority-Serving Institutions,* 10, 11. There are three institutions that were established expressly for the purpose of educating Latinos: Hostos Community College, Boricua College, and National Hispanic University.

29. Hispanic students increased their participation in college sixfold between 1976 and 2008, but the experience with education in the United States for many continues to be affected by poverty, poor quality of elementary and secondary education, limited interaction with college faculty, few college-educated role models, relatively low commitment to their educational goals, and limited information about college, including financial information. Many enroll in institutions where they find a critical mass of Hispanic students, staff, and faculty who can offer validation and support that Hispanic families are often unable to offer due to lack of experience with higher education in the United States. This preference corresponds with above-average enrollment in public institutions and two-year colleges (especially public two-year institutions), though as a group they show increasing enrollment in four-year institutions. See Deborah A. Santiago, *Modeling Hispanic-Serving Institutions* (HSIS): Campus Practices That Work for Latino Students (Washington, DC: Excelencia in Education, 2008).

30. Santiago, *Choosing Hispanic-Serving Institutions;* Laird et al., "African American and Hispanic Student Engagement at Minority Serving and Predominantly White Institutions"; Stella M. Flores and Otoniel Jimenez Morfin, "Another Side of the Percent Plan Story: Latino Enrollment in the Hispanic-Serving Institutions Sector in California and Texas," in Gasman, Baez, and Turner, *Understanding Minority-Serving Institutions,* 141–155.

31. HSIS employ an above-average number of Hispanic faculty, and the faculty and staff at some HSIS have been found to offer Hispanic students support and to raise their expectations and aspirations, serving as advisers and mentors. There is growing evidence that HSIS are beginning to provide Hispanic students with more opportunities to interact with peers and faculty, and thus are more supportive

campus environments. See Dayton et al., "Hispanic-Serving Institutions through the Eyes of Students and Administrators"; Deborah A. Santiago and S. J. Andrade, *Emerging Hispanic-Serving Institutions (HSIs): Serving Latino Students* (Washington, DC: Excelencia in Education, 2010).

32. Flores and Morfin, "Another Side of the Percent Plan Story"; Deborah A. Santiago, *Reality Check: Hispanic-Serving Institutions on the Texas Border Strategizing Financial Aid* (Washington, DC: Excelencia in Education, 2010).

33. James D. Anderson, *The Education of Blacks in the South, 1860–1935* (Chapel Hill: University of North Carolina Press, 1988).

34. Marybeth Gasman, *Envisioning Black Colleges: A History of the United Negro College Fund* (Baltimore, MD: Johns Hopkins University Press, 2007); Thompson, *Private Black Colleges at the Crossroads.*

35. Estimates based on U.S. Department of Education's IPEDS Unduplicated 12-Month Headcount: 2010–2011.

36. Kassie Freeman, "HBCs or PWIs? African American High School Students' Consideration of Higher Education Institution Types," *Review of Higher Education* 23, no. 1 (1999): 91–106.

37. Susan Aud, Mary Ann Fox, and Angelina Kewal Ramani, *Status and Trends in the Education of Racial and Ethnic Groups,* NCES 2010-015 (Washington, DC: National Center for Education Statistics, July 2010).

38. Stephen Provasnik and Linda L. Shafer, "Historically Black Colleges and Universities, 1976 to 2001," *Education Statistics Quarterly* 6, no. 3 (July 2005): 91–99.

39. Walter Recharde Allen, Edgar G. Epps, and Nesha Z. Haniff, *College in Black and White: African American Students in Predominantly White and in Historically Black Public Universities* (Albany: State University of New York Press, 1991); James J. Davis and Paul L. Markham, "Student Attitudes toward Foreign Language Study at Historically and Predominantly Black Institutions," *Foreign Language Annals* 24, no. 3 (May 1991): 227–237; Sharon L. Fries-Britt and Bridget Turner, "Uneven Stories: Successful Black Collegians at a Black and a White Campus," *Review of Higher Education* 25, no. 3 (2002): 315–330.

40. Minor, "Decision Making in Historically Black Colleges and Universities"; Palmer and Gasman, "'It Takes a Village to Raise a Child.'"

41. Robert T. Palmer, Ryan J. Davis, and Dina C. Maramba, "Role of an HBCU in Supporting Academic Success for Underprepared Black Males," *Negro Educational Review* 61, nos. 1–4 (March 2010): 85–106; Aashir Nasim et al., "Non-cognitive Predictors of Academic Achievement for African Americans across Cultural Contexts," *Journal of Negro Education* 74, no. 4 (September 2005): 344–358.

42. Charmaine Jackson Mercer and James B. Stedman, "Minority-Serving Institutions: Selected Institutional and Student Characteristics," in Gasman, Baez, and Turner, *Understanding Minority-Serving Institutions,* 28–42.

43. Park and Teranishi, "Asian American and Pacific Islander Serving Institutions," in Gasman, Baez, and Turner, *Understanding Minority-Serving Institutions,* 122, 123.

44. Ibid.

45. Ibid.

46. Ibid.

47. Robert Teranishi, *CARE Report* (New York: New York University, 2011), 12.

48. Robert T. Teranishi, "Asian American and Native American Pacific Islander–Serving Institutions: Areas of Growth, Innovation, and Collaboration," *AAPI Nexus: Asian Americans and Pacific Islanders Policy, Practice and Community* 9, no. 1 (2011): 151–155.

49. For groups who came as political or economic refugees, this experience often includes poverty: in 2010, 39 percent of Hmong, 20 percent of Samoans, and 6 percent of Filipinos lived below the poverty line.

50. Teranishi, "Asian American and Native American Pacific Islander–Serving Institutions"; Julie J. Park and Robert T. Teranishi, "Asian American and Pacific Islander Serving Institutions: Historical Perspectives and Future Prospects," in Gasman, Baez, and Turner, *Understanding Minority-Serving Institutions,* 111–126.

3. Tribal Colleges and Universities

1. Northern Cheyenne Tribe, "Northern Cheyenne Reservation: Demographic and Economic Information," 2013, http://www.ourfactsyourfuture.org/admin/uploadedPublications/2694_N_Cheyenne_RF08_web.pdf.

2. Bob Madsen, Ted Hodgson, and Carol Ward, "Pathways to Success in Pre-college Mathematics," *Tribal College Journal* 18, no. 2 (2006): 28–30.

3. Stacey Sherwin, "Boosting Underprepared Students: Salish Kootenai College Uses Research to Build Success," *Tribal College Journal of American Indian Higher Education* 22, no. 4 (June 2011): 20–25.

4. U.S. Department of Education, National Center for Education Statistics, "Table 294: Associate's Degrees Conferred by Degree-Granting Institutions, by Sex, Race/Ethnicity, and Field of Study: 2008–09," 2010, http://nces.ed.gov/programs/digest/d10/tables/dt10_294.asp; U.S. Department of Education, National Center for Education Statistics, "Table 297: Bachelor's Degrees Conferred by Degree-Granting Institutions, by Sex, Race/Ethnicity, and Field of Study: 2008–09," 2010, http://nces.ed.gov/programs/digest/d10/tables/dt10_297.asp.

4. Hispanic-Serving Institutions

1. Diana Natalicio, "Collaborating with K–12 for Academic Excellence," *Presidency* (May 2011): 2.

2. At an initial orientation meeting, staff members review with students the placement process and program requirements and the costs. As part of that orientation, prospective students—even if they are juniors in high school—fill out a joint EPCC/UTEP admission application and discuss how they would be placed into their first

classes, what being placed into remedial education costs, and what students can do to be ready to place into college-level courses. Support for students' college readiness does not end with the orientation and a placement test. Instead, the placement test plays a formative role. Advised to be ready for the test, students discuss their placement results with an adviser—at EPCC or their high school—who helps them make sense of what their scores mean for their progress in college. These conversations often guide students to more college readiness resources. High school students who place into college-level courses may begin to enroll in dual credit courses; those who need to refresh specific math, reading, or writing skills may enroll in a Summer Bridge program. Any potential EPCC student can use one of EPCC's PREP labs to build the academic skills needed to be ready for college.

3. Andrea Berger and associates, *Early College, Early Success: Early College High School Initiative Impact Study* (Washington, DC: American Institutes for Research, 2013).

4. As he elaborated: "Since one of our student workers happens to be a media major, right now a group of peer mentors is working to produce a tutorial video for service-learning students about volunteering—about their first steps, how to contact the organization properly, how to dress and conduct themselves at the interview. It's still a project in progress. So they are doing a great job and they have been really efficient in what they are doing."

5. Historically Black Colleges and Universities

1. National Center for Educational Statistics, Postsecondary Data, Washington, D.C., 2010.

2. Marybeth Gasman, *The Changing Face of Historically Black Colleges and Universities* (Philadelphia: Penn Center for Minority Serving Institutions, 2013).

3. Survey of Earned Doctorates, National Science Foundation, Washington, D.C., 2009. See also Valerie Lundy-Wagner, Julie Vultaggio, and Marybeth Gasman, "Preparing Undergraduate Students of Color for Doctoral Success: The Role of Undergraduate Institutions," *Journal of Doctoral Studies* 8 (2013): 251–272. The other two small liberal arts colleges are Spelman College and Hampton University.

4. National Science Foundation, Washington, D.C., 2011. See also Thai Nguyen, Marybeth Gasman, Clif Conrad, Todd Lundberg, and Felecia Commodore, "Morehouse College: Promoting Black Male Success in STEM" (paper presented at the Association for the Study of Higher Education Annual Meeting, St. Louis, MO, November 17, 2013).

5. Ibid.; Marybeth Gasman, "Promoting Attainment for African American Males in STEM: Lessons Learned from Historically Black Colleges and Universities," in *Beyond Stock Stories and Folktales: African American Men and the Pipeline to the Professoriate*, ed. William Tate and Henry Frierson (New York: Emerald Press, 2011); Valerie Lundy-Wagner and Marybeth Gasman, "When Gender Issues Are Not Just

about Women: Reconsidering Male Students at Historically Black Colleges and Universities," *Teachers College Record* 113, no. 5 (2011): 934–968, available online at www .tcrecord.com. For a more general discussion of why students, including African American men, leave the sciences, see Elaine Seymour and Nancy Hewitt, *Talking about Leaving: Why Undergraduates Leave the Sciences* (Boulder, CO: Westview Press, 1997).

6. National Science Foundation, www.nsf.gov, 2011.

7. Carol Colbeck, Alberto Cabrera, and Pat Terenzini, "Learning Professional Confidence: Linking Teaching Practices, Students' Self-Perceptions, and Gender," *Review of Higher Education* 24, no. 2 (2001): 173–191; Sandra Hanson, "African American Women in Science: Experiences from High School through the Post-Secondary Years and Beyond," *NWSA Journal* (National Women in Science Association) 16, no. 1 (2004): 96–115; Laura Perna, Valeria Lundy-Wagner, Noah Drezner, Marybeth Gasman, Susan Yoon, Enika Bose, and Shannon Gary, "The Contribution of HBCUs to the Preparation of African American Women for STEM Careers: A Case Study," *Research in Higher Education* 50, no. 1 (2009): 1–23.

8. National Science Foundation, www.nsf.gov, 2011.

9. Ebony McGee and Danny Martin, "You Would Not Believe What I Have to Go through to Prove My Intellectual Value!": Stereotype Management among Academically Successful Black Mathematics and Engineering Students," *American Educational Research Journal* 48, no. 6 (2011): 1347–1389; Seymour and Hewitt, *Talking about Leaving.*

10. Marybeth Gasman, "Promoting Attainment for African American Males in STEM: Lessons Learned from Historically Black Colleges and Universities," in Tate and Frierson, *Beyond Stock Stories and Folktales*; Lundy-Wagner and Gasman, "When Gender Issues Are Not Just about Women"; Seymour and Hewitt, *Talking about Leaving.*

11. McGee and Martin, "You Would Not Believe What I Have to Go through"; Seymour and Hewitt, *Talking about Leaving.*

12. Morehouse College website, www.morehouse.edu/about.

13. IPEDS, 2003–2013, U.S. Department of Education, Washington, D.C. Institutional data provided by Tafaya Ransom, director of Institutional Research, and Jann Adams, associate professor of psychology, Morehouse College, 2013.

6. Asian American and Native American Pacific Islander–Serving Institutions

1. Timothy P. Fong, *The Contemporary Asian American Experience: Beyond the Model Minority*, 3rd ed. (Upper Saddle River, NJ: Prentice Hall, 2008), 17–40.

2. L. Ling-chi Wang, "Trends in Admissions for Asian Americans in Colleges and Universities: Higher Education Policy," in *The State of Asian Pacific America: A Public Policy Report* (Los Angeles: LEAP Asian Pacific American Public Policy Institute and UCLA Asian American Studies Center, 1993), 49–60.

3. National Commission on aapi Research in Education (CARE) and Asian and Pacific Islander American Scholarship Fund, *Federal Higher Education Policy Priorities and the Asian American and Pacific Islander Community* (New York: CARE, 2010).

4. Robert T. Teranishi, *Asians in the Ivory Tower: Dilemmas of Racial Inequality in American Higher Education* (New York: Teachers College Press, 2010); National Commission on aapi Research in Education (CARE) and Asian and Pacific Islander American Scholarship Fund, *Federal Higher Education Policy Priorities;* Theresa Ling Yeh, "Issues of College Persistence between Asian and Asian Pacific American Students," *Journal of College Student Retention: Research, Theory and Practice* 6, no. 1 (2004/2005): 81–96.

5. Central Intelligence Agency, "Marshall Islands," *The World Factbook,* 2013, https://www.cia.gov/library/publications/the-world-factbook/.

6. Timothy P. Fong, "Introduction," in *Ethnic Studies Research: Approaches and Perspectives,* ed. Timothy P. Fong (Lanham, MD: AltaMira Press, 2008), 1–5, http://forward.library.wisconsin.edu/catalog/ocn174138849; Fong, *The Contemporary Asian American Experience,* 12–14.

7. Fong, "Introduction," 4.

8. Paul V. Bredeson, *Designs for Learning: A New Architecture for Professional Development in Schools* (Thousand Oaks, CA: Corwin Press, 2003), 34.

Index

70–72; online tutoring, 54; peer mentoring, 61–62, 67; poverty, 50; remedial education, 52–53, 55–56, 58–60, 72–73; S&K Electronics, 69; S&K Technologies, 69; STEM education, 62–63, 66; STEM internships, 64–66, 67–72; STEM relevancy, 63–64, 66–68, 73; summer boot camp, 53; Tribally Controlled Community College Assistance Act, 51; writing labs, 54

San Diego City College, 128–150; basic skills education, 129–130, 148; "borderland" college, 128; case management, 139, 142; challenging students, 144; cohort, 135; collaboration, 140, 143, 147–149; college-going culture, 149–150; college map, 138–139; college readiness, 129–131; community, 147–148; culture of inquiry, 133; educational planning, 130, 136–138; enrollment, 131; Extended Opportunity Program, 130, 131; faculty relations, 140–147; First-Year Experience (FYE) counselors, 133, 135–136, 138; FYE data, 133–134, 149; FYE individual programs, 133–134; FYE network, 133–135; FYE outcomes, 150; FYE overview, 131–132; FYE requirements, 136–137; history, 128–129; individualized support, 141–142; information, 132–133; Math Tutoring Center, 145; Mutual Responsibilities Contract, 132, 135, 137; peer mentors, 135–136, 138; persistence, 131; remedial education, 131; scholars, 143, 146; spaces, 130, 145–146; student body, 129–131; Student Support Center, 148; Supplemental Instruction (SI) overview, 140, 142, 144, 146, 148–149

San Diego State University, 130

Sorrell, Michael, 178–183, 192; accessibility, 182–183, 192; background, 178–181; core values, 183

standardized tests, 2, 4, 6, 15–16; ACT, 4, 15; Advanced Placement exams, 15; SAT, 2, 6, 15; test prep, 2, 4, 6

Teranishi, Robert, 33

Texas Success Initiative, 109

Tribal Colleges and Universities (TCUs), 27–28, 35; academic support, 28; access, 35; community impact, 28; culture, 28, 35; curricula, 27; demographics, 28; Diné College (formerly Navajo Community College), 27; economic impact, 28, 35; enrollment, 28; Indian Civil Rights Act of 1968, 27; local practices, 27; mainstream crossovers, 28; mission, 28, 35; Navajo nation, 27; nontraditional faculty, 27; social services, 28; student retention, 28; student sensitivity, 28. *See also* Chief Dull Knife College; College of Menominee Nation; Salish Kootenai College

Underwood, Robert, 32

University of Missouri–Kansas City, 148

University of Montana, 67

University of Texas at El Paso, 105

University of Washington, 65–66, 228

University of Wisconsin–Madison, 20, 89

U.S. News and World Report, 153

White, William Jefferson, Reverend, 153

White Americans, 1, 7–9, 14–16, 18–19, 24

White House, 10, 16

Wu, David, 32